I'll Read That For You:

A bluffer's guide to 101 books you should read before you die

Margie Taylor

Copyright @ 2019

All rights reserved. No part of this publication may be reproduced, stored in a retrieval system, or transmitted in any form by any means electronic, mechanical, photocopying, or otherwise, without prior permission from the author.

Margie Taylor may be contacted at
margietlr4@gmail.com

www.margietaylor.com

This book is dedicated to my friends and family who read these reviews and provided great feedback. And especially to Patsy Pehleman who had the idea of putting my weekly reviews into a book, and gave it a title.

Many thanks to all of you!

Margie

Table of contents

Introduction 7
Week 1: *The Woman in White*, by Wilkie Collins (1860) 10
Week 2: *The Tale of the Bamboo Cutter*, by Anonymous
(10th Century AD) 12
Week 3: *Through the Looking-Glass and What Alice Found
There*, by Lewis Carroll (1871) 13
Week 4: *Alias Grace*, by Margaret Atwood (1996) 17
Week 5: *The Diviners*, by Margaret Laurence (1974) 19
Week 6: *The Tin Flute*, by Gabrielle Roy (1947) 22
Week 7: *A Fine Balance*, by Rohinton Mistry (1995) 25
Week 8: *The Stone Diaries*, by Carol Shields (1993) 28
Week 9: *Lives of Girls and Women*, by Alice Munro (1971) 31
Week 10: *Life of Pi*, by Yann Martel (2001) 34
Week 11: *The Beggar Maid*, by Alice Munro (1978) 37
Week 12: *The English Patient*, by Michael Ondaatje (1992) 41
Week 13: *Fifth Business*, by Robertson Davies (1970) 45
Week 14: *Neuromancer*, by William Gibson (1984) 49
Week 15: *The First Garden*, by Anne Hébert (1997) 53
Week 16: *The Wars*, by Timothy Findley (1977) 58
Week 17: *To Kill a Mockingbird*, by Harper Lee (1960) 62
Week 18: *A Pale View of Hills*, by Kazuo Ishiguro (1982) 66
Week 19: *The Accidental*, by Ali Smith (2005) 70
Week 20: *Quartet in Autumn*, by Barbara Pym (1977) 76
Week 21: *Rebecca*, by Daphne du Maurier (1938) 81
Week 22: *Moll Flanders*, by Daniel Defoe (1722) 86
Week 23: *Fanny Hill*, by John Cleland (1748-1749) 91
Week 24: *Les Liaisons Dangereuses*, by Pierre-Ambroise
Choderlos de Laclos (1782) 95
Week 25: *Wuthering Heights*, by Emily Brontë (1848) 100
Week 26: *The Scarlet Letter*, by Nathaniel Hawthorne (1850) 106
Week 27: *Sense and Sensibility*, by Jane Austen (1811) 111
Week 28: *Little Women*, by Louisa May Alcott (1868,1869) 117
Week 29: *Great Expectations*, by Charles Dickens (1861) 122
Week 30: *Love in a Cold Climate*, by Nancy Mitford (1949) 126
Week 31: *A Confederacy of Dunces*, by John Kennedy Toole
(1980) 131
Week 32: *Lord of the Flies*, by William Golding (1954) 136

Week 33: *The Bell Jar,* by Sylvia Plath (1963) 141
Week 34: *The Postman Always Rings Twice*, by James M. Cain (1934) 146
Week 35: *The Thirty-Nine Steps*, by John Buchan (1915) 150
Week 36: *The Maltese Falcon*, by Dashiell Hammet (1930) 154
Week 37: *A Severed Head*, by Irish Murdoch (1961) 159
Week 38: *A Bend in the River*, by V. S. Naipaul (1979) 164
Week 39: *The Gathering*, by Anne Enright (2007) 169
Week 40: *The Children's Book*, by A S Byatt (2000) 174
Week 41: *Infinite Jest*, by David Foster Wallace (1996) 179
Week 42: *Decline and Fall*, by Evelyn Waugh (1928) 185
Week 43: *Atonement*, by Ian McEwan (2001) 190
Week 44: *Madame Bovary*, by Gustave Flaubert (1856) 195
Week 45: *Howards End*, by E. M. Forster (1910) 200
Week 46: *The Great Gatsby*, by F. Scott Fitzgerald (1925) 205
Week 47: *Fall On Your Knees*, by Ann-Marie Macdonald (1996) ...210
Week 48: *A Farewell to Arms*, by Ernest Hemingway (1929) 214
Week 49: *The Electric Kool-Aid Acid Test*, by Tom Wolfe (1968) ...219
Week 50: *Portnoy's Complaint*, by Philip Roth (1969) 225
Week 51: *The Elegance of the Hedgehog*, by Muriel Barbery (2008) 229
Week 52: *The Fall of the House of Usher; The Pit and the Pendulum*, by Edgar Allan Poe (1839, 1842) 234
Week 53: *Eugene Onegin*, by Alexander Pushkin (1833) 240
Week 54: *Sons and Lovers*, by D. H. Lawrence (1913) 244
Week 55: *The Shining*, by Stephen King (1977) 249
Week 56: *Absalom, Absalom!* by William Faulkner (1936) 255
Week 57: *Keep the Aspidistra Flying*, by George Orwell (1936) 261
Week 58: *The Shipping News*, by E. Annie Proulx (1993) 266
Week 59: *The Vicar of Wakefield*, by Oliver Goldsmith (1776) 272
Week 60: *Veronika Decides to Die,* by Paulo Coelho (1998) 277
Week 61: *The Virgin Suicides*, by Jeffrey Eugenides (1993) 282
Week 62: *American Rust*, by Philipp Meyer (2009) 287
Week 63: *The Master*, by Colm Tóibín (2004) 293
Week 64: *The Portrait of a Lady*, by Henry James (1881) 298
Week 65: *The Namesake*, by Jhumpa, Lahiri (2003) 303
Week 66: *The Line of Beauty*, by Alan Hollinghurst (2004) 309
Week 67: *Franny and Zooey*, by J. D. Salinger (1961) 314
Week 68: *Lolita*, by Vladimir Nabokov (1955) 320
Week 69: *Of Mice and Men*, by John Steinbeck (1937) 325

Week 70: *A Portrait of the Artist as a Young Man*, by James Joyce (1916) 328
Week 71: *The God of Small Things*, by Arundhati Roy (1997) 332
Week 72: *The Hours*, by Michael Cunningham (1998) 339
Week 73: *White Teeth*, by Zadie Smith (2000) 343
Week 74: *Mother's Milk*, by Edward St. Aubyn (2006) 348
Week 75: *Get Shorty*, by Elmore Leonard (1990) 353
Week 76: *The Secret History*, by Donna Tartt (1992) 360
Week 77: *Fear and Loathing in Las Vegas*, by Hunter S. Thompson (1971) 365
Week 78: *The Color Purple*, by Alice Walker (1982) 370
Week 79: *The Reader*, by Bernhard Schlink (1995, 1997) 375
Week 80: *Tess of the D'Urbervilles*, by Thomas Hardy (1892) 380
Week 81: *Ethan Frome*, by Edith Wharton (1911) 385
Week 82: *Tropic of Cancer*, by Henry Miller (1934) 390
Week 83: *The Forsyte Saga, Book One: The Man of Property* (1906) 394
Week 84: *Thank You, Jeeves*, by P. G. Wodehouse (1934) 398
Week 85: *The Little Prince*, by Antoine de Saint-Exupéry (1943) ..404
Week 86: *The Picture of Dorian Gray*, by Oscar Wilde (1890) 411
Week 87: *Slaughterhouse-Five*, by Kurt Vonnegut, Jr. (1969) 416
Week 88: *One Flew Over the Cuckoo's Nest*, by Ken Kesey (1962) 421
Week 89: *Catch-22*, by Joseph Heller (1961) 426
Week 90: *Brave New World*, by Aldous Huxley (1932) 432
Week 91: *The Inheritance of Loss*, by Kiran Desai (2006) 439
Week 92: *The Talented Mr. Ripley*, by Patricia Highsmith (1955) ..444
Week 93: *Kieron Smith, Boy*, by James Kelman (2008) 449
Week 94: *The Unbearable Lightness of Being*, by Milan Kundera (1984) 454
Week 95: *The Poisonwood Bible*, by Barbara Kingsolver (1998) ...458
Week 96: *The Cider House Rules*, by John Irving (1985) 463
Week 97: *Love in the Time of Cholera*, by Gabriel Garcia Márquez (1985) 468
Week 98: *The White Tiger*, by Aravind Adiga (2008) 474
Week 99: *Death in Venice*, by Thomas Mann (1912) 478
Week 100: *Of Human Bondage*, by Somerset Maugham (1915) ...483
Week 101: *Fugitive Pieces*, by Anne Michaels (1996) 488
Title Index 492

Introduction

So many books and so little time.

That was my feeling two years ago when I sat down, finally, to read. I'd spent four years caring for my terminally ill partner, moving from one end of the country to the other to be near to our kids. And near to the ocean: Ken loved the sea.

His death left a hole in my life. There's no other way to put it. I'd always been a busy person; 30 years as a CBC Radio host and commentator meant constant deadlines, a certain amount of travel, and a continuing sense of purpose. The job was over, my children were grown, my husband was gone. I needed a project.

It couldn't be just any project. If I was going to stick to it, it had to be something that spoke to my passion. And my passion has always been reading. It's what I did as a kid when I should have been out learning to skate or building a snow fort. It's what I did all through high school and university, right up to when my children were born and reading books took a back seat to car-pooling, laundry, and stripping wallpaper. Oh, yes – and work. One of these days, I used to think, I'll get back to reading. One of these days, I'll read all those terrific novels that have been written since I left school. One of these days, when I get time, I'll catch up.

Now here I was with nothing but time. No excuses for not catching up. But where to begin? Luckily, the editors of *1001 Books You Must Read Before You Die* (published in 2010) offered me a map through some of the best English-language fiction ever written. A thousand and one novels, beginning with *The Thousand and One Nights*, written around 850 AD, and ending up, almost a thousand pages later, with A. S. Byatt's *The Children's Book*, published in 2009.

I got out the calculator: at the rate of one a week I could have them all read in 19.25 years. Which is a very long time. And life is short. I remember trying to get through *Ulysses* 40 years ago – I got to chapter 3, the one that's called "Proteus", and gave up.

So I decided to aim for 101. It just seemed more realistic. I didn't read them in chronological order; in fact, the first one on my list, *The Woman in White*, by Wilkie Collins, was published in 1860. I had it on my bookshelf so I decided to make it Number 1. After that I went through the books I already owned, borrowed some from friends, and relied on the public library for the rest.

I looked forward to re-reading Dickens, Salinger, and Margaret Laurence. I anticipated discovering wonderful authors I'd never read. And I liked the idea of sharing my thoughts on these books with a few faithful friends and colleagues who followed my posts. So each week I wrote a review and posted it on my website.

One of my friends came up with the idea of putting these reviews into a book.

"I may never get around to reading half these books," she said. "But now, thanks to your reviews, I feel like I've already read them."

So, if you don't get around to reading these books, you can hold your head up in literary circles!

What I really hope, though, is that my reviews of these wonderful books will spur you to read, or reread, these books. And remind yourself, if you need reminding, why humans have always needed stories.

Week 1: *The Woman in White*, by Wilkie Collins (1860)

I'm not sure how I got through four years of university majoring in English lit and missed reading this Wilkie Collins classic. My excuse is that I majored in 20th century American lit, which is not really an excuse. However, better late than never.

The Woman in White, set in 1850 and published 10 years later, is often considered the first modern detective novel. It was a sensation when it first came out as a weekly serial and more than a century and a half later it holds its own. As detective fiction, it lives up to the billing, in that it's constructed around a crime that feels important both to the main protagonist, Walter Hartright, and the reader. I really wanted to know Sir Percival Glyde's secret, I really wanted to know the story behind the woman in white, Anne Catherick. Why had Glyde imprisoned her in an insane asylum? And what about the other evildoer in the book, Count Fosco? Did he have an Achilles' heel? Why was he so determined to help Sir Percival, even though it's obvious they didn't like each other? The author kept me in suspense right up to the end - all 500 pages.

There are some aspects that do feel dated, in particular the female characters. The women are all (with a couple of exceptions) beautiful but passive and victimized, or nasty, unfeeling shrews. Laura Fairlie, the rich heiress who's the love interest of the hero, has been described as vapid; the adjective fits. She's a typical Dickensian heroine, incapable of doing more than fluttering her eyes and fainting in an emergency. The one woman who has the ability to act with agency is Marian Halcombe, Laura's half-sister. She is described several times - and describes herself - as being more like a man in everything except her outward appearance. A feminist novel this isn't.

Having said this, Collins is remarkably sympathetic to the plight of women, especially in their relations with men. Laura's wealth cannot protect her from the designs of an unscrupulous husband, and Anne Catherick is incarcerated against her will in a madhouse simply on the word of a man. Events like these were not uncommon in the 19th century: women were locked up because they were epileptic, anxious, or suffering from postnatal depression. They could be put away because of "moral insanity", a term for infidelity, or simply because they were "non-compliant". In some cases, imprisoning a woman in an asylum was an alternative to divorce.

Taking into account the times in which it was written (early Victorian), *The Woman in White* remains a classic suspense novel and a very good read.

Week 2: *The Tale of the Bamboo Cutter*, by Anonymous (Original title: *Taketori Monogatari*)

This story is the oldest surviving story of Japanese fiction. It's known as the "ancestor of romances" and goes back at least to the 10th century. In terms of antique fiction that still exists in the English language, it's predated only by the tales told by Sheherazade in *The Thousand and One Nights*, written in Arabic and first published circa 850. And while some of those tales are familiar to us ("Sinbad", "Aladdin", "Ali Baba and the Forty Thieves"), *Bamboo Cutter* is less well-known, at least in the Western world.

It tells the story of a poor bamboo cutter who discovers a tiny, beautiful princess in a stick of bamboo. He takes her home and he and his wife raise her. Not to spoil the story for those who haven't read it, I will say that the princess, Kaguya-hime, is no traditional looking-for-a-prince heroine. She sets her suitors impossible tasks, knowing they will fail. She has no wish to marry, and the reason becomes clear near the ending, which I personally found quite moving.

I recommend the 1998 edition published by Kodansha International, which was rewritten by Yasunari Kawabata and translated by Donald Keene. It's simply a beautiful book to read. The illustrations are by Masayuki Miyata who was a master of *kirie* (cut-out illustrations). These alone are worth the price of the book.

Week 3: *Through the Looking-Glass and What Alice Found There*, by Lewis Carroll (1871)

"When *I* use a word," [he] said, in a rather scornful tone, "it means just what I choose it to mean - neither more nor less."

"The question is," said Alice, "whether you *can* make words mean so many different things."

"The question is," said [he], "which is to be master - that's all."

No, it's not an exchange between the Trumpster and a confused member of the press; it's that master of language manipulation, Humpty Dumpty, being his usual pompous, arrogant, and rather ill-informed self. But he *does* sound familiar.

I first read *Through the Looking-Glass, and What Alice Found There* when I was 7. It was a birthday gift from my parents - a real book, with chapters! It was two books in one, really - *Alice's Adventures in Wonderland* took up the first half. Together, these two stories introduced me to children's literature that was beyond Dick, Jane, and Baby Sally. Here were stories that had characters, and plot, and - heaven forbid - humour! I was hooked. I read and re-read it that first year, and memorized the poems. *The Walrus and the Carpenter* was my party piece - in my fourth year of university, sitting for a history exam that I hadn't prepared for, I wrote out all 18 verses, rather than hand in a blank sheet of paper.

Reading it again, I still find it funny and the characters are still engaging, but after months of observing the Trump presidency parts of it don't seem quite as far-fetched as they used to.

Humpty Dumpty, of course, most closely resembles the American president. He has that smirking, ear-to-ear smile, for one thing, which causes Alice some anxiety:

"If he smiled much more the ends of his mouth might meet behind," she thought. "And then I don't know *what* would happen to his head! I'm afraid it would come off!"

Like Trump, the egg is given to exaggeration. "I can explain all the poems that ever were invented," he tells Alice, "and a good many that haven't been invented just yet." He lacks humility, thinks he knows more than anybody else, and doesn't read. He's also inclined to be paranoid. Take this, my favourite section from that chapter:

"*If* I *did* fall," he went on, "*the King has promised me* - ah, you may turn pale, if you like! You didn't think I was going to say that, did you? *The King has promised me - with his very own mouth -* to - to -"

"To send all his horses and all his men," Alice interrupted, rather unwisely.

"Now I declare that's too bad!" Humpty Dumpty cried, breaking into a sudden passion. "You've been listening at doors - and behind trees - and down chimneys - or you couldn't have known it!"

"I haven't indeed," Alice said very gently. "It's in a book."

"Ah, well! They may write such things in a *book*," Humpty Dumpty said in a calmer tone. "That's what you call a History of England."

Alice's journey through the looking-glass takes place on a giant chessboard. The country is divided into squares by a number of brooks and hedges. The goal is to reach the Eighth Square where Alice, the White Queen's pawn, will be crowned a Queen.

Getting there, though, is not for the faint-hearted. Enemies are lurking in the woods we're told, although we never see them. A giant black crow appears out of nowhere and threatens the inhabitants, and somewhere the slithy toves gyre and gimble in the wabe. Anyone in an official capacity is generally incompetent. The White King's soldiers trip over each other, his Knight continually falls off his horse, and state messengers are imprisoned - for what, we never know.

As for the heads of state, they're all too fond of making promises that can't be fulfilled. The White Queen offers to take Alice on as a lady's maid for two pence a week, and jam every other day. When Alice says she doesn't want any jam today, the Queen says she couldn't have it if she *did* want it:

"The rule is, jam tomorrow and jam yesterday - but never jam today."

It must sometimes come to "jam today", Alice says. But the Queen is firm: No, it can't, she says. "It's jam every other day: today isn't any other day, you know."

"I don't understand you," said Alice. "It's dreadfully confusing!"

"That's the effect of living backwards," the Queen said kindly: "it always makes one a little giddy at first -"

Luckily for Alice, she eventually wakes up and realizes it was all a dream. (If this is a spoiler alert, read the book anyway - it's worth it.)

Unfortunately for the rest of us, we're still dreaming. Wake me when it's over.

Week 4: *Alias Grace*, by Margaret Atwood (1996)

I first read Margaret Atwood's *Alias Grace* shortly after it was published. I've always considered it one of my three Atwood favourites, together with *The Handmaid's Tale* and the classic *Surfacing* (both of which, by the way, are included in my edition of 1001 Books You Must Read Before You Die). Reading it again 20 years later, I'm not so sure.

Based on true events, *Alias Grace* imagines a series of meetings between a celebrated murderess and a doctor specializing in the field of mental illness. The year is 1859. Grace Marks, a one-time domestic servant, is 16 years into a life sentence in Kingston Penitentiary for assisting in the murder of her former employer, Thomas Kinnear, and his housekeeper, Nancy Montgomery. Her co-accused, James McDermott, was hanged; Grace's sentence was commuted at the last minute to life in prison.

Grace has always claimed to have no memory of the crime, although she signed a detailed - and rather lurid - confession at the time. Dr. Simon Jordan has come to interview her, hoping to discover if she has any memory of the crime, and hoping that what he learns will enable him to learn more about the treatment of the mentally ill. During these interviews we learn Grace's story - her childhood, her life as a young girl in domestic service, and her relationships with those who were murdered. We also learn a great deal about life in Canada in the mid-19th Century: dressmaking, laundry chores, cooking, the craze for spiritualism and hypnosis - or mesmerism, as it was called. All these details, well-researched, give the story its substance. But they also tend, at times, to overwhelm the narrative.

Having spent a decade or so writing and researching my own work of historical fiction, I'm drawn to the details. I'm interested in which vegetables grew in the kitchen garden - the shirts and shoes and pots and pans sold by Jeremiah the peddler - the variety of buttons available to the dressmaker. Even for me, though, the minutiae of specifics is too much. I find myself begging the author to just get on with the story.

The problem with the interview-as-storytelling device, as with the diary-as-storytelling device, is that it often just doesn't seem plausible. It requires a huge leap of imagination to accept that someone would remember the details of her dreams so many years later . . . or what the weather was like every morning . . . or what her employer ate for breakfast. Really? you find yourself asking. I can't remember what I ate yesterday, let alone 16 years ago.

It often occurs to me that there comes a point in the career of well-known, successful writers when they stop getting edited. I've seen this with writers I love, like Ian McEwan and Anne Tyler, and I'm certain it happens with writers I haven't read, like Nora Roberts and James Patterson. I really feel it's the case with Margaret Atwood. At 460 pages, *Alias Grace* is a lyrical work of fiction, well-deserving of the Giller Prize it won when published. But in my humble opinion it would have benefited from some judicious snipping.

Week 5: *The Diviners*, by Margaret Laurence (1974)

Are some books better reads when you get older?

I ask that question because it's been so long since I first read this, Margaret Laurence's fifth and final novel, that I came to it this week with almost no memory of the narrative. I remembered Morag Gunn, the heroine, and I remembered Pique, her daughter, who at 18 was so much closer to my age at the time. I knew there was tension between them - and I think I sided with Pique. Why wouldn't I? She played the guitar, which I tried to do, she sang, and she was angry at the world.

If asked, I wouldn't have suggested *The Diviners* as the Laurence book to be included in the list of 1001 Books. For me it was, and likely always will be *The Stone Angel*. Or *A Jest of God,* the book that was made into a movie, *Rachel, Rachel.* Joanne Woodward played Rachel and her husband Paul Newman directed it. Besides Woodward's stunning performance as a lonely, repressed schoolteacher, the film was notable (notorious?) for the scene where Rachel masturbates alone in bed. Not the kind of thing that would shock now, but this was 1968 - it was powerful.

But I am not currently the arbiter of literary taste and never will be. So I borrowed a library copy of *The Diviners*, which turned out to be in large print - easier on the eyes but 730 pages. Whew! It tells the tale of a 40-something writer who has raised her daughter on her own, by her own choice. Pique's father is Jules Tonnerre, son of Lazarus Tonnerre, whose ancestors date back to the Metis rebellion of 1885. Morag has her own history, which is Scottish and entwined with the Highland clearances. The book relates these stories of the past concurrently with those of Morag, her daughter, Christie Logan, her nominative father, and the assorted characters who befriend and sustain her.

I loved the ancestral stories but found myself less engaged with Pique the moody teenager who has to "find herself". Still, when you consider that the whole book is about the search for identity, it makes sense that Pique would need to go looking for her roots. As for Morag, she embodies the conflict experienced by those who grow up determined to get away from the suffocating confines of their small towns but are constantly aching to return. I hear you, Morag - you are not alone.

There's a lot of fucking in the story, which isn't a bad thing, but sex is always hard to write. In Laurence's case much of it comes across as purple prose. Sometimes I think the old way of just alluding to it and then moving on to "In the morning they sat drinking coffee" is better. But then, I'm a bit of a coward when it comes to writing about sex. I usually prefer to turn off the lights and leave it to the reader's imagination.

What I didn't grasp, the first time I read the book, was the sorrow embedded in these pages. I'm 20 years older now than Morag ... 20 years older than Laurence herself at the time. The book brought me to tears; I don't remember crying the first time I read it. All those good-byes, all those life changes that shake and rattle us and leave us, ultimately, older but not necessarily wiser. As Laurence puts it so eloquently, "the infinite capacity of humans to wound one another without meaning or wanting to".

Did Laurence know at the time she was writing that this would be her final book? She must have thought she would write other novels - she lived for another 13 years, after all. But I do think she planned this as the last in her series of books about Manawaka, the fictional Manitoba town based on Neepawa, where she was born and raised. She, like Morag, was in her mid-40s when she wrote it ... an age where you sometimes feel older than you are. I think she was done with Neepawa - excuse me, Manawaka. She was wrong, of course, and she knew it. It's not that you can't go home again, as Thomas Wolfe wrote - it's that you can never really leave.

Week 6: *The Tin Flute*, by Gabrielle Roy (1947)

One thing about majoring in English at university, you read a lot of books. You also accumulate a lot of books, some of which you get around to reading at some point. Others end up being those books that sit on your bookshelves and get packed up in boxes and moved to your next apartment, house, or bedsit, depending on where you are in life.

By my reckoning, my copy of Gabrielle Roy's *The Tin Flute* was moved about 18 times. The last time I remember seeing it in my bookcase was three years ago, when we lived in Guelph and were moving to Victoria. At that point I decided I was probably never going to read it and gave it to a friend. A few days ago, continuing with my 101 books reading, I picked it up from the library. It's a fascinating read.

I think what held me back from reading this, Roy's first novel, was the title - I got it into my head that it was a military story, not my first choice when it comes to reading for pleasure. I don't know why I thought that, except for the fact that it's set at the beginning of World War II. (I may have been confusing it with *The Tin Drum*, by Gunter Grass.) The military does play a part, in that several of the young men - and one older one - enlist, but it's really a backdrop to a story of poverty and struggle in the slums of Montreal.

Which makes it sound depressing. Well, it's not a knee-slapper. But it's one of those books whose characters do more than simply come alive; they remain in your head after you've finished the book. You find yourself wondering how things will work out for Florentine, the vain, self-doubting young waitress who falls for the wrong man and finds herself in an all-too-familiar predicament - made worse by the fact that this is 1939 and the sexual revolution is three decades away. Her life, and that of her family and neighbours, is dictated by poverty and the Church, not necessarily in that order. Her tastes are superficial and naive, and her motives not particularly altruistic, except where her mother is concerned. Yet Roy draws her with such tenderness, such insight, that you feel for the girl. You want her to succeed, even though you're pretty sure that, in the end, her life will turn out very much like her mother's - too many children and too few choices.

Her mother, Rose-Anna, was originally intended as a secondary character, but as often happens when creating a narrative, she developed into a complex and fascinating figure in her own right. Pregnant with her 12th child (yes, 12th - this is 1930s Quebec, remember) she juggles the demands of a hungry, needy family. Her reward is to lose one child to the army, another to illness, and another to a marriage based on a lie. Eugene, her oldest son, signs up to fight in order that his mother will receive a monthly cheque from the government. Her husband, Azarius, is weak and a dreamer; in the end he recovers his self-worth by enlisting, the only way he can see to finally provide his wife with a reasonable income.

I've said the war is a backdrop to the story, and it is, but Roy also explores the motives behind all those young men leaping into uniform to sacrifice themselves for their country. They are all driven by need - financial in many cases, as this is the tail end of the Depression and jobs are hard to come by. But money isn't the only reason - Quebec at the time still has strong links to France, the "mother country", even though most of its inhabitants have never set foot in the country. For many, it's the right thing to do - for others, especially the working-class poor living in the Saint-Henri slums of Montreal, it's one way out of a miserable existence.

The Tin Flute is considered Montreal's first urban novel. Written in French and translated into English shortly afterwards, it won both the Governor-General's Award and the Prix Femina of France. Its publication left the old Quebec behind forever - the old seigneurial system of farms and *habitants* dominated by the Roman Catholic Church. As Philip Stratford writes in the afterword to my copy, "It banished forever the folkloric, romanticized image of the province which had changed little in the previous three centuries. It set Montreal squarely in the mainstream of subsequent fiction."

I'm glad I finally got around to reading it. Better late than never.

Week 7: *A Fine Balance*, by Rohinton Mistry (1995)

Forty-eight hours after finishing Rohinton Mistry's sweeping narrative set in India between 1975 and 1984, I remain gripped by the story, unable and unwilling to relinquish this astonishing, transformational odyssey.

The characters are unforgettable: the beggar known as Worm who, lacking legs and hands, scuttles along the pavement on a wheeled platform; Beggarmaster, who protects and controls a stable of beggars, making "adjustments" to their bodies to increase their supplicant appeal; Monkey-man, who makes a living of sorts with his pet monkeys and murders his dog for killing them; Avinash, the college student who pays dearly for his political activism, and Rajaram, who initially makes his living selling hair and eventually is transformed into "the very very saintly" Bal Baba.

These are only minor characters yet Mistry's genius lies in drawing them with such delicacy, such compassion, and such an eye for detail that they live and breathe in every word, every action. As a reader to whom character is everything, I am in awe of his talent. As individual as these characters are, they are also universal - they are Everyman and Everywoman, overcome by circumstances beyond their control.

A Fine Balance takes place in "an unidentified city" during the final years of Indira Ghandi's turbulent reign. (Ghandi is never referred to by name, simply as The Prime Minister.) Two tailors - Ishvar and his nephew, Omprakash - come to the city from their northern village in order to seek employment. They find work with a widow living in a small apartment in the slums. Dina Dalal has refused to remarry after losing her beloved husband and insists on living on her own, much to her brother's chagrin. She supports herself with her sewing but after 20 years her eyesight is failing and she's in danger of losing her apartment. As a way to keep her head above water, she hires the tailors to work for her and also rents out a room to a college student, Maneck.

Over the course of a year, these four strangers become like family. They support and assist each other and give each other hope that, in spite of the tempestuous times, they will abide and prosper. Ishvar dreams of finding a wife for his nephew; Om longs to return to his village; Maneck dreams of his family home in the mountains; Dina clings to her independence.

The odds, however, are stacked against them. The old Yiddish adage comes to mind: "Man plans, and God laughs". The Prime Minister declares a state of emergency which lasts for almost two years. During that time opponents and critics of the government are detained and tortured, the press is censored, and a program of compulsory sterilization is carried out to limit the population. Our four heroes, along with most of the other characters, fall prey to bureaucratic quotas and regulations that make no sense, not even to those who fulfill them. Justice and the rule of law are suspended . . . the inmates have taken over the asylum.

The litany of terrible things experienced by the men, women, and children who inhabit these pages is almost beyond belief. *Believe it*, Mistry is saying. At the beginning of the book, he includes a quote from

Honoré de Balzac which ends with the words: "But rest assured: this tragedy is not fiction. All is true." If that's the case, it makes the book all the more heart-rending. And humbles those of us who lived during those times and knew little or nothing about them.

Even without the human rights abuses committed by government officials and their lackeys, life for India's poor and illiterate population is circumscribed by a rigid caste system. Ishvar and Om, as members of the "untouchables", occupy the lowest rung. Born into lives of poverty, oppression and degradation, they're relegated to the lowest jobs and are humiliated, beaten, and even killed with impunity. Their efforts to raise themselves above their origins are doomed to failure. And yet you read on, hoping they might be the exception to the rule.

A Fine Balance is not, as you might imagine, a particularly upbeat novel. There are amusing moments and there are shining examples of humanity and pure decency in even its darkest parts. Overall, though, this is a wretched story beautifully written. Having invested so heavily in the characters, I kept hoping right to the end for some relatively happy ending for at least one of them. But Mistry doesn't waver. He has set a bleak course, both for himself and the reader, and he succeeds. Magnificently.

Week 8: *The Stone Diaries*, by Carol Shields (1993)

"What is the story of a life? A chronicle of fact or a skillfully wrought impression? The bringing together of what she fears? Or the adding up of what has been offhandedly revealed, those tiny allotted increments of knowledge?"

So asks Daisy Goodwill Flett, 80 years old, brought to her knees - and her bed - by a heart attack. And a kidney operation. And two broken knees. She is not dying, not yet. But it's the beginning of the end. And Daisy, who has spent decades marrying (twice), raising children, cultivating her garden, enjoying a comfortable, easeful retirement, is searching for meaning. What part has she played in her own life? In other words, who is she?

The Stone Diaries, a fictional biography of a seemingly ordinary woman, was Carol Shields' breakthrough novel. It won both the Pulitzer Prize and the Governor General's Award and established her as a member of the authorial elite. It was nominated for the Man Booker Prize and received the National Book Critics Circle Award. Reading it the first time around was a humbling experience. Struggling to find my own voice as a writer, I was in awe of her ability to delve into the lives of her characters - to carve out layers of being with such finesse, like an archaeologist working with a dentist's probe and a toothbrush.

Which is, after all, the point of the story. Stone, whether it is being quarried or used as a personal metaphor, is at the heart of the book. Daisy is the daughter of Cuyler Goodwill, a stonemason. Her mother, Mercy, whose maiden name was Stone, died giving birth to her. Her second husband, Barker Flett, is the son of Magnus Flett, a stonemason. And the essence of Daisy Goodwill remains untouched, an uncut diamond waiting to be quarried.

On the surface she is, at various times, a pretty ordinary person with an extraordinary beginning. Her mother, naive and obese, is unaware she's pregnant. She delivers her daughter on the floor of her home in Tyndall, Manitoba, and dies soon afterwards. Her grief-stricken father hands her into the care of a neighbour who then leaves her husband and heads to Winnipeg, taking the baby with her. Eleven years later Daisy's father resurfaces. Together they move to Bloomington, Indiana, where he becomes a successful businessman and wealthy member of the community.

Not to give away more than the bare bones of the plot, I will say that from this point on Daisy's life is, as I said, pretty ordinary. And it is that very "ordinariness" that Shield captures with such brilliance. Like Alice Munro and Margaret Laurence, she has the ability to depict life at its everyday, unremarkable pace with words that reveal a stunning gift for observation and intuition.

Reading the book this time around, I am no less in awe of the author's talent. But I found much of it sadder than I remembered and I wonder if this is a factor of age. It's been 24 years. I'm as old now as Shields was when she died of breast cancer. In Victoria, of all places...just across the water. You put the book down and Daisy's ghost is fluttering somewhere in a corner of the room, persisting, nagging you to ask the question: Who are you? No, but really - who ARE you?

It's the universal question: who am I? A mother, a wife, a widow, an aunt. But who am I really? The final assessment - whether or not your life was important, whether or not you lived what we might call a "successful" life - is up to others. Those who are left will have the last word. If we're lucky, they will remember us fondly: "She was a good mom." "He had a great sense of humour." "She never had a bad word to say about anybody." "He was my friend." It's not enough - it never is. But for most of us, it's all we get.

Week 9: *Lives of Girls and Women*, by Alice Munro (1971)

Alice Munro has made a career of breaking the rules of short story writing, so perhaps it's not surprising that two of her collections, *The Beggar Maid* and *Lives of Girls and Women*, are included in a list of the *1001 Books You Must Read Before You Die*.

For the most part, the other 999 books recommended here are novels. And Munro, the first Canadian author and the 13th woman ever to win the Nobel Prize in Literature, is not a novelist. She doesn't need to be. She does something that in my mind is more difficult and requires a talent for precise observation, emotional honesty, and a solid command of the language: she writes short stories.

We tend to think of the novel as the pinnacle of fiction writing - the ultimate goal after honing your craft with a handful of short stories. I disagree. To paraphrase Blaise Pascal, "I didn't have time to write a short story, so I wrote a long one instead."

A well-crafted short story is a thing of beauty. I've never managed it, although God knows I've tried. There's a manila file folder somewhere that contains a stack of carbon copies (yes, they go back that far) of attempts to emulate the writers I devoured in my youth: Katherine Mansfield, Carson McCullers, John Cheever, Flannery O'Connor, Raymond Carver, Ann Beattie, Ernest Hemingway, James Thurber, J. D. Salinger ... to name a few. There's an early short story by Mansfield, "Miss Brill", that's one of the most poignant depictions of the dignity and loneliness of old age that I have ever read. These writers are giants. Along with Munro they humble me. And remind me that before I die I will find that file folder and shred it.

Like *The Beggar Maid* (known better to Canadian readers as *Who Do You Think You Are?*), *Lives of Girls and Women* is a collection of interlinked stories about coming of age in semi-rural southwestern Ontario. In this case, the central character is Del Jordan, growing up on the outskirts of Jubilee, living with her father who raises foxes and her intelligent, outspoken mother. Munro's father did raise foxes, her mother was a teacher, and Jubilee is the fictional stand-in for her home town of Wingham, in Huron County.

But Munro is not writing autobiography. Jubilee is not Wingham - or rather, it is partly Wingham, and partly a composite of several small Ontario towns. Just as Del Jordan is not Alice Munro, but bits and pieces of her younger self, observed and reflected by the older woman. Because this is art - seeing and uplifting the ordinary and transforming it into something that is at once marvelous and real.

And the stories here feel almost shockingly real. A school teacher, "past her prime" as they would say, drowns herself in the Wawanash River. A local radio announcer makes inappropriate sexual advances which Del does nothing to discourage. The Flats Road, where she lives, is home to two "idiots" - Frankie Hall, who is "fat and pale [and] sat out in the sun, beside the dirty store window cats slept in", and Irene Pollox, who "would chase children on the road and hang over her gate crowing and flapping like a drunken rooster".

Within her own family there are secrets: her mother, Del learns, was sexually abused by her brother. And her cousin Mary Agnes, born late in her parents' life and deprived of oxygen at birth, was once taken for a walk by a group of local boys and found naked in the fairgrounds, lying in the mud. It is never spelled out what the boys did to Mary Agnes, aside from removing her clothes, but the reader can guess. For Del, when told the story, the degradation lay in being naked like that, out in the open:

"I thought of Mary Agnes' body being exposed on the fairgrounds, her prickly cold buttocks sticking out - that did seem to me the most shameful, helpless-looking part of anybody's body - and I thought that if it had happened to me, to be seen like that, I could not live on afterwards."

Munro has called her home town "the most interesting place in the world". People's lives, she writes, were "dull, simple, amazing, and unfathomable — deep caves paved with kitchen linoleum".

If Wingham is indeed the most interesting place in the world, it's because the author has made it so. And for that, I am deeply grateful.

Week 10: *Life of Pi*, by Yann Martel (2001)

"[W]hat is the purpose of reason, Richard Parker? Is it no more than to shine at practicalities - the getting of food, clothing and shelter? Why can't reason give greater answers? Why can we throw a question further than we can pull in an answer? Why such a vast net if there's so little fish to catch?"

Why, indeed? Who hasn't wondered at some time or another, about the point of it all. Why are we here? What does it mean?

Piscine Molitor Patel, commonly known as Pi, stranded on a lifeboat somewhere in the Pacific Ocean, has time to consider these questions. More than enough time, actually. In the end, he will have 227 days to ponder those questions in between bouts of feeding himself and the 3-year-old Bengal tiger who is his sole companion and his greatest threat. If he cannot keep the tiger fed, he will most likely be eaten. If he is successful, he may still be eaten in the end. Only a regular diet of fish and the tiger's intense spasms of motion sickness keep the boy alive.

How Pi, a teenage boy from Pondicherry, India, and Richard Parker, the tiger, find themselves in this particular situation is a complicated story. In brief, Pi, his mother and father and younger brother, and an assortment of animals belonging to his father's zoo are on a Japanese freighter bound for Canada. Twelve days into the voyage the ship sinks; the boy's family, the ship's crew, and almost all the animals perish. Pi, thrown into a lifeboat just before the ship goes down, survives, along with a zebra, a hyena, and a female gorilla. Oh yes, and the tiger.

It sounds like the beginning of a bad joke: a zebra, a hyena, a gorilla and a tiger walk into a bar . . . What it is - at least, what I think it is - is a meditation on the nature of storytelling. What is it about the human condition that predisposes us to tell stories - more than that, to crave them in the way we crave food, drink, human companionship, love? Why do our most important stories contain an element of spirituality? And why do we believe some stories and not others?

This last question, I think, is the real point of *Life of Pi*. If we can only believe in stories that correspond to our own reality, to the things we know or have been proven to be true, we're in danger of missing so much. As Pi says, "Be excessively reasonable and you risk throwing out the universe with the bathwater." In the end, when Pi is rescued and is recuperating in Mexico, he tells the men from the Japanese Ministry of Transport about the tiger. He tells them about the zebra who fell into the boat and broke its leg. About the hyena who tore off that leg and ate it, and was then eaten by the tiger. About Orange Juice, the sweet, motherly gorilla who also fell victim to the tiger. He tells them about the blind castaway he encountered late in his ordeal. He tells them how he kept Richard Parker at bay by convincing him that he, Pi Patel, was the dominant animal.

Is that what happened? Does it matter? The men from the Japanese ministry find the original story of the tiger and the man-eating tree (no time to go into that here, read the book) impossible to swallow. We have difficulty believing it, they say.

"If you stumble at mere believability," Pi says, "what are you living for?"

Still, they want another story. A more credible story. And so Pi offers up another, less magical narrative. Instead of a zebra, it's a Taiwanese sailor who's ended up in the boat with a broken leg. The hyena who bit off the zebra's leg is transformed to a bad-tempered cook, the gorilla is Pi's mother. And the tiger - well, the tiger is also the cook. I think.

The investigators are satisfied. This, at least, they can believe. But when Pi asks them which is the better story, they are united in agreement: the story with animals is the better story. And that, I feel sure, is what the author, Yann Martel, is asking of the reader. There is a deep, undeniable longing within us for better stories - stories that will, as Martel has said, make us believe in God.

Life of Pi is about survival, it's about resilience under unbearable conditions, it's about human resourcefulness. It's gripping from beginning to end, terrifying in parts, but also, at times, very funny. If it was only for the originality of its concept it would have deserved to win the Man Booker Prize - it's nothing less than a triumph.

Week 11: *The Beggar Maid*, by Alice Munro (1978)

It's a terrible title, really, *The Beggar Maid*. I much prefer the original Canadian title, *Who Do You Think You Are?* with its double sense of the phrase. There's the familiar, small-town accusation put to anyone who dares to show off, parade herself about as they say, and the simple, thoughtful question: Who *are* you? Who do you think you might be, underneath the skin?

The first sense is the one which appears throughout Alice Munro's early work - what do you think you're doing, getting above yourself? You think you're better than us? You think you have some special rights and privileges? You can imagine Munro growing up in Wingham, struggling to keep a lid on things, not wanting to be caught out "showing off".

Which is ironic, given her chosen career path. As Douglas Gibson, her long-time publisher and friend, puts it, writers are indeed in the business of "showing off": "They're all saying, 'Look at me! Here's what I've written, I think you should pay attention to it!'"

This collection of short stories cum novel, like the earlier *Lives of Girls and Women*, follows a young girl growing up in a small town in southwestern Ontario. But whereas *Lives* leaves our heroine, Del Jordan, balancing on the edge of womanhood, *Who Do You Think You Are?* goes further. And what you really notice is the way the sexual tension moves from the background to take a front row seat.

The young woman's name is Rose. She lives with her father and her stepmother, Flo, in the town of Hanratty. *West* Hanratty, actually, which is distinct from the main town and occupies a lower rung on the social ladder. As we're told in the first story, "Royal Beatings", "In Hanratty the social structure ran from doctors and dentists and lawyers down to foundry workers and draymen; in West Hanratty it ran from factory workers and foundry workers down to large improvident families of casual bootleggers and prostitutes and unsuccessful thieves."

So Rose, like Del before her, is something of an outsider. Not just because she has no money, although that is part of it. But more because of her aspirations. In towns like Hanratty, as in all small towns, there are rules - acceptable ways of behaving. You are not above the rules and if you think you are, it pretty much goes without saying that you will be punished. For hubris. "Pride goeth before a fall" might be the motto of every small town in the country - and many of the larger ones as well.

It is this that sets Rose apart. She wants to get away, she wants to go on to other things, she wants to be somebody different. Hearing about a woman Flo once knew who went on holiday and pretended to be an actress, Rose is envious: "She thought it would be an especially fine thing, to manage a transformation like that. To dare it; to get away with it, to enter on preposterous adventures in your own, but newly named, skin."

Managing transformation is not easy and is seldom straightforward. It requires a willingness to allow some invasion of your person. In one of the short stories, "Wild Swans", Rose is on the train heading to Toronto, having previously been warned by Flo to beware of White Slavers who drug you and smuggle you away to someplace where they keep you and use you and then throw you out on the street when you're degraded beyond repair. This, Flo says, generally takes about three years. Flo has worked in Toronto, when she was younger, so she knows these things.

On the train, Rose, who is still in high school, has an encounter with a middle-aged man who takes the seat beside her; after some initial small talk, he pretends to fall asleep while slipping his hand under her skirt. The account of the pressure of that hand, hidden under his newspaper, progressing slowly but surely up her leg, past her stocking, arriving finally at its destination while she sits immobilized, both victim and accomplice - this is Munro at her best: "This was disgrace, this was beggary." But Rose allows it, welcomes the invasion in spite of herself, partly because it is so absolutely disgraceful, so completely not how she would be expected to react. Which is precisely what makes it desirable.

Rose does leave Hanratty. She goes to university on a scholarship, marries young, stays unhappily married for a decade, divorces, and has affairs. She goes to bed with men, as many of us do, who seem to offer something exogenous - something outside ourselves that can be incorporated into who we are...who we want to be. Knowing that most men, especially those who are married or determined to stay single, don't want to commit themselves this way, she tries to avoid the "familiar twinges, tidal promises" that will ultimately let her down: "The most mortifying thing of all was simply hope, which burrows so deceitfully at first, masks itself cunningly, but not for long."

The final story, "Who Do You Think You Are?", takes us back to Rose's childhood. Back to Flo and her half-brother, Brian. Back particularly to a town character called Milton Homer who commits outrageous acts like marching, uninvited, in the Orange Day parade, and hammering on people's doors, demanding admittance. The story seems like an afterthought, at first, coming at the end, out of place in the chronology. But in it we get a summing up of sorts - some resolution on Rose's part to the ongoing conflict within her: "That peculiar shame which she carried around with her seemed to have been eased." Rose has forgiven herself for "showing off". And so should we all.

Week 12: *The English Patient*, by Michael Ondaatje (1992)

"[U]nder the scarred trees in the half-bombed gardens of the Villa San Girolamo..."

Who wouldn't want to be there?

The place is Tuscany, in a hill town north of Florence; the second European war is drawing to a close. A pilot, burned beyond recognition, lies in an upstairs bedroom in an abandoned villa, tended only by a young woman, a French-Canadian nurse named Hana. She is shell-shocked, reverberating from her experiences caring for the wounded and the dead. And he is more ghost than human . . . his face is unrecognizable, he has forgotten his name. He is simply, to all intents and purposes, the English patient.

While he lies in bed, bandaged, unmoving, Hana reads to him from the books she finds in the villa's library - *Kim, The Charterhouse of Parma,* the *Annals* of Tacitus. A modern-day Scheherazade telling stories to the Persian king. Although it is not her own death she's attempting to defer but his.

Yes, yes, you say, I know all this. I saw the movie. A love story, right? Well, yes and no. If I had to summarize *The English Patient* in a word or two, I might call it an extended love poem. "I have spent weeks in the desert, forgetting to look at the moon, he says, as a married man may spend days never looking into the face of his wife." This, to me, is poetry.

So there is love. But the love story is multifarious and fragmented. The man in the upstairs bedroom is not English at all but Hungarian: he is László de Almásy, a Hungarian Count and desert explorer, and he did exist, although his character here is fictional. And his love affair with a young married woman - a liaison that ended tragically in a cave in the Libyan desert - follows the most conventional arc, which is why they made it into a movie.

Hana and Almásy are joined by two others, a young Sikh sapper whose job it is to trek across the war-ravaged country defusing the thousands of land mines planted by the retreating German army, and an Italian-Canadian working as an operative for the Intelligence Corps. The sapper is Kirpal Singh, whose nickname is Kip; the operative is David Caravaggio, who shares his name and temperament with a 16th Century painter who had a reputation for being violent, touchy, and provocative. This, I think, is not a coincidence.

Caravaggio, whose thumbs were severed by the Italians in Florence, was a friend of Hana's father, and knew her as a child. He loved her then, like a father. Or an uncle. Now, seeing her as a young woman, he begins to love her in a different way, but is mindful enough of his own psychological and physical scars to keep this to himself. Instead he focuses on getting the patient, with whom he shares an addiction to morphine, to tell his story. Because he knows, or thinks he knows, who the English patient really is.

Hana and the Sikh fall in love, and conduct their silent affair in a tent overlooking the villa. But Hana is also somewhat in love with Almásy, whom she sees as a kind of saint. She says as much to Caravaggio, who is trying to make her see she's tied herself to a dead man - or one who soon will be:

"Why do you love him so much?"

"I love him."

"You don't love him, you adore him."

"Go away, Carvaggio. Please."

"You've tied yourself to a corpse for some reason."

"He is a saint. I think. A despairing saint. Are there such things? Our desire is to protect them."

This is a book peopled by saints, from the biblical figures on the ceiling of the Sistine Chapel to the frescoes of Piero della Francesca in the church at Arezzo. And like the painted martyrs depicted by those medieval artists, Michael Ondaatje's saints are all too human. The English patient is a spy; Caraveggio is a former thief; Hana is haunted by images of the child she chose to abort. We are all divided creatures - we are saint or sinner depending on time, circumstance, and opportunity.

The climax of the narrative occurs in August of 1945: the atomic bombing of Hiroshima and Nagasaki. Kip, who sees himself as representative of all of Asia, is devastated. He trusted the West, spent the last few years risking his life for the Allied cause, believed the Europeans to be better than they were. All that trust - all that loyalty and respect and yes, love, for his superiors - betrayed not once, but twice. Seeing the West clearly for the first time - the sheer naked colonialism disguised by good manners and a properly knotted tie - he can no longer be part of this group. He will no longer be their sentinel.

His head filled with images of death and destruction, Kip sets off on his motorbike, leaving behind Almásy, Hana, Caravaggio, and the "meadows of civilization he had tended". He travels south, riding deeper into the thick rain, retracing the route he had taken to the Villa San Girolamo, and the words of the prophet Isaiah, spoken to him by the burned man - the sinner-saint he had once loved - come back to haunt him:

"Behold, the Lord will carry thee away with a mighty captivity, and will surely cover thee. He will surely violently turn and toss thee like a ball into a large country".

Week 13: *Fifth Business*, by Robertson Davies (1970)

Why is it so difficult to like Robertson Davies?

I mean *like* him, as opposed to appreciating his writing, which is exceptional, his insights, which are often brilliant, and his ability to sum up a situation or individual in a few well-chosen words. When it comes to original, memorable epigrams, Davies is right up there with Oscar Wilde, Mark Twain and Dorothy Parker. At a dinner party, I imagine he would be witty, even entertaining - unless you got stuck sitting next to him.

All writers are monsters. Somebody said that, I can't remember who, but it's true. Writers are often not lovely people. Readers would do well to remember that writers feed on other people's misfortunes, tragedies, character flaws. I have a plaque on my wall: "Careful," it says, "or you'll end up in my novel." And it's true. There are a handful of career choices where "nice" doesn't come into it: firefighting would be one, plumbing is another. And writing. Nice writers don't usually write great books.

So it's not that I want Davies to be nice, or even particularly kind. I just want to not find him so insufferably *smug*. It may be unfair to say it but you generally can't read more than a page or two without being reminded that this is a writer who was, as his publisher Douglas Gibson has said, aiming at the role of oracle. He doesn't just want to tell a good story - although he does, in fact, achieve that; he wants you to

45

sit up and say to your partner, "Jeez, Sheila, this guy is really smart!"

Fifth Business was Davies' fourth novel and the first in his Deptford trilogy, to be followed by *The Manticore* and *World of Wonders*. Its hero, Dunstan Ramsay, is troubled by a childhood quarrel with his best friend and life-long nemesis, Percy Boyd Staunton. His friend threw a snowball at him, containing a stone; Ramsay ducked and the snowball hit Mary Dempster, who was pregnant at the time. Mrs. Dempster immediately went into labour, giving birth to her son, Paul, nine weeks early.

The incident is central to the development of the plot. Mrs. Dempster, already considered a little "simple" by her neighbours, becomes more so, ending up tied to a rope by her husband so she doesn't go wandering when he's away. Giving us a very visual image of one who is "at the end of her rope". Ramsay is consumed by guilt, knowing that had he not ducked it would have been he and not the pregnant woman who would have been hit by the snowball. As for Staunton, who shortens his name to Boy, he takes Ramsay under his wing, not so much to assuage his own guilt but to ensure that his friend keeps mum about the circumstances surrounding the event.

The novel is full of interesting characters; Dunstan Ramsay, however, is not one of them. Dunstan, as Davies explains, is Fifth Business. In opera, he says, there's always a character who's the odd man out. He has no opposite of the other sex, and appears to play no essential role. But he, or she, is the keeper of the secrets, or the one who comes to the aid of the heroine, or who does something absolutely essential to the denouement of the story. Dunstan Ramsay, professor, hagiographer, hero of the First World War who lost a leg to the cause, he is this story's Fifth Business.

This may be the place to point out that, as erudite as the definition of Fifth Business sounds, it may be a load of codswallop. According Gibson, Davies "was not above inventing scholarly origins for his titles, such as *Fifth Business*, for the pleasure of misdirecting academic researchers". And that's part of the problem with Davies, for me, anyway - he was a writer who enjoyed playing cute academic games in a realm too darn arcane for the average reader.

I'm coming across like a Luddite, I know, but Davies brings it out of me. He typifies what used to be called a "man of letters", a term we abandoned when we began to acknowledge that there were, actually, women who wrote. Davies always claimed to detest the designation but he did everything possible to reinforce it, including adopting a pseudo-English accent and striding the streets of Toronto in an old-fashioned tweed coat, brandishing a cane.

Early on, Dunstan Ramsay decides that Mary Dempster is a saint. She has, in his mind, performed several miracles, although the local Catholic priest suggests she may be a "fool-saint" - someone who is full of holiness and good will but whose virtue is tainted with madness. And poor Mrs. Dempster does spend her final years in a madhouse, supported by Ramsay and, indirectly, Boy Staunton. While Staunton bounces from strength to strength, becoming richer and more successful every year, Ramsay remains an academic, living a quiet, comfortable life with annual forays to Europe in order to further his research. Eventually he becomes an expert in the field of hagiography, writing several books on the history of the lives of Catholic saints.

Davies has deliberately created a protagonist who is pretty unlikeable, when it comes down to it. He teaches history to boys he appears not to care for; he falls in love once but conveniently falls out of it when he needs to; falls in love a second time in late middle age and again gets over it fairly quickly. He admits to not liking most people, preferring his own company and that of the saints he's researching. As one character describes him, Ramsay is "a man full of secrets - grim-mouthed and buttoned-up and hard-eyed and cruel". The same character accuses him of watching life from the sidelines. "Life is a spectator sport to you," she says, hitting the nail on the head. And later: "This is the revenge of the unlived life, Ramsay. Suddenly it makes a fool of you."

It's a little facile to observe (but I'll do it anyway) that *Fifth Business* is all about saints and sinners. The sinners, like Boy Staunton, may eventually come to a bad end, but at least they *live* while they're alive - they have a life. Dunstan Ramsay, preoccupied with saints and enjoying as chaste and cloistered an existence as your average monk, does not.

In the end I'm with Billy Joel on this one: "I'd rather laugh with the sinners than cry with the saints" - the sinners are, quite simply, much more fun.

Week 14: *Neuromancer*, by William Gibson (1984)

It takes a special mind to imagine the future.

George Orwell had it. He gave us Big Brother, and an image of a totalitarian future: "a boot stamping on a human face - forever".

Aldous Huxley envisaged a *Brave New World*, whose pleasure-seeking denizens were programmed to "love their servitude and . . . never dream of revolution".

From Jules Verne to Robert Heinlen to Arthur C. Clarke and beyond, countless science fiction writers have created alternative realities that challenge, excite, and generally disturb us. They are, in the words of Rod Serling, "the improbable made possible". While most of us have difficulty seeing further than next month's paycheque, writers of science fiction visualize hundreds of years into the future. Their projections are often dystopian, darkly prophetic, and seldom reassuring. As a genre, cozy and comforting it ain't.

In 1984 (appropriately, somehow), an American-Canadian writer emerged from relative obscurity with a novel about a data thief who goes up against an unthinkably powerful artificial intelligence. The author was William Gibson; the novel was *Neuromancer*. Its revolutionary plot and elaborate use of futuristic slang - somewhat akin to *A Clockwork Orange* and *A Hitchhiker's Guide to the Galaxy* - made it an underground hit. Thirty years on the book is considered a kind of cyberpunk manifesto. It was the first novel to win three major science fiction awards -

the Nebula, the Philip K. Dick and the Hugo - and appeared on *Time* magazine's list of 100 best English-language novels written since 1923.

It is also, as you will know, included in the list of *1001 Books You Must Read Before You Die*. Which is why I read it.

Briefly - very briefly - the plot of the novel is this: Henry Dorsett Case, a.k.a Cutter, is a lowlife hustler whose skills at jacking into the pathways of the matrix have been crippled by a disgruntled former employer. In debt to a drug lord and reduced to fencing RAM on the black market, Case is living on the edge of Night City: "Biz here was a constant subliminal hum and death the accepted punishment for laziness, carelessness, lack of grace".

Desperate to the point of considering suicide, Case is approached by a mysterious individual called Armitage who offers him a chance to recover his hacking skills in exchange for taking on an unspecified, but dangerous, mission. Armitage, whose real name is Colonel Willis Corto, is the only surviving solider from a botched military operation called Screaming Fist. Corto, in turn, is under the control of an AI called Wintermute who sometimes appears in the persona of Julius Deane, a Night City importer-exporter, or Lonny Zone, a pimp.

Are you with me so far? Good, because this is only the beginning. As any one of the millions of readers who have made this a global bestseller can tell you, there are plots and sub-plots and stories within stories. Every character has a story and there are almost too many characters to count. There's Molly, a leatherclad street samurai who's been surgically and chemically refined into a weapon of the deadliest kind. Peter Riviera, an actor and sociopath who ultimately betrays his comrades. And Lady Jane Marie-France Tessier-Ashpool who, besides having the longest double-barreled name outside of Tolstoy, is the third female clone of the family dynasty that created the Wintermute AI.

The most important character, however, is the matrix, which is a living, breathing thing, more alive in some ways than the "nihilistic technofestishists" in their polycarbon suits or the "meat puppet" prostitutes with neural cut-out chips implanted that allow their actions to be controlled by others. The matrix is unthinkable in its complexity - a "consensual hallucination" that is at times violent and beneficent, interactive and non-human, and, above all, amoral.

Gibson has been quoted as saying he never had any special affinity with computers. Yet he imagined a global communications network years before the World Wide Web became part of our everyday lives. And he single-handedly created the genre known as cyberpunk.

Considering when the book was written, there are bound to be anachronisms. Case relies on cassette tapes and video cameras, telephones are landlines and Wi-Fi doesn't exist. The dialogue reads like bad Raymond Chandler: "I was expecting something maybe a little less gone, you know? I mean, these guys are all batshit in here, like they got luminous messages scrawled across the inside of their foreheads or something. I don't like the way it looks, I don't like the way it smells . . ."

But these are small things when you consider the brilliance of the concept, and the cutting-edge language of description. This is a man who can write, "The sky above the port was the color of television, tuned to a dead channel." And this: "His eyes were eggs of unstable crystal, vibrating with a frequency whose name was rain and the sound of trains, suddenly sprouting a humming forest of hair-fine glass spines." And this: "Night City was like a deranged experiment in social Darwinism, designed by a bored researcher who kept one thumb permanently on the fast-forward button."

So what or who is Neuromancer? We learn, in the end, that Neuromancer is the other half of Wintermute: "Wintermute was hive mind, decision maker, effecting change in the world outside. Neuromancer was personality. Neurmancer was immortality." Which is another way of saying that Neuromancer is the land of the dead.

Would I have read *Neuromancer* if it wasn't on the list? Probably not. It was a hard slog for someone like me, not given to reading science fiction and a rookie when it comes to cyberpunk. Having read it, though, I feel a little like I did after running my first and only marathon: I'm glad I did it, but I wouldn't want to do it again.

Week 15: *The First Garden*, by Anne Hébert (1997)

The First Garden is not a book I would have chosen to appear on a list of essential reading.

There. I've said it. It's not a bad book - it's a very good book, as it happens. It's just that *Kamouraska* is a better book and if you're going to pick just one of Anne Hébert's novels why wouldn't you pick it? It would make sense. That was the novel that earned her France's Prix des Libraires and the Royal Belgian Academy's prize. It was made into a film by Claude Jutra using a screenplay on which she collaborated, and it established her as an international literary star.

It seems almost perverse to choose *The First Garden,* a rather slight (150 pages) novel Hébert wrote later in life about an aging Parisian actress who returns to Quebec to take part in a stage production of Beckett's *Happy Days*. Does this sound as engaging as the story of a beautiful, impulsive woman who conspires with her lover to murder her husband? I thought not. As I said - perverse.

Checking out the contributors' bios at the beginning of the book of lists, I found this: AB is "a former economist . . . and is completing a DPhil on Samuel Beckett . . . at the University of Sussex". Aha! Well, that explains it. If the professor had been pursuing his doctorate in something else - violence against women, perhaps, or dangerous passions in 19th century Quebec - *Kamouraska* might have indeed made the list.

But it didn't. So, back to *The First Garden*. Flora Fontanges, the actress, abandoned Quebec 20 years ago for a larger stage. She has been successful, achieving fame and financial security in France, as well as giving birth to a daughter, Maude. Things have not gone well between her and her daughter; the young girl has run away several times and now it appears she's gone missing from a commune in Quebec City. An offer to return to Canada to play Winnie in *Happy Days* is an opportunity as well to try to find her daughter. And, perhaps, mend fences.

While waiting for rehearsals to begin, Flora forms a platonic attachment to the young man who's been living with her daughter. Together, she and Raphaël explore the city, searching for Maude, and summoning women from the past and giving them new life, if only momentarily. They begin with Barbe Abbadie, a woman who must have done something important as she has a street named after her. A 17th century merchant's wife, they decide, "gripped by fear and respect", who dies giving birth at the age of thirty. Then there's Marie Rollet, the first European woman to settle in New France - "the mother of the country". And little Renée Chauvreux, found dead in the snow on the fourth of January, 1670.

Renée was one of the King's daughters, the young women who were transported to New France under the sponsorship of Louis XIV. Determined to honour them, Flora and Raphaël stand on the pier at Anse-au-Foulon and recite their names, like saying the rosary. Unfortunately, while doing so, Hébert perpetuates an old rumour about the *filles du roi*. New France had a bad reputation among French peasant women, she writes. And so the king turned to the Salpêtrière, a hospice for the poor of Paris and a prison for prostitutes:

"In the absence of peasant women, they must now be content with these persons of no account who have come from Paris, with a dowry from the King of fifty *livres* per head . . . these *filles du roi*, fresh and young and without a past, purified by the sea during a long rough crossing on a sailing ship."

In fact, there's never been any proof that any of the King's daughters were prostitutes. They were poor, for the most part, and many had been abandoned and had no future in France. They married and produced children and only one, according to the record, turned to prostitution in her new homeland, after being abandoned by her husband.

Increasingly, Flora is haunted by dreams and daydreams, a blend of real and imagined events. Old images of her childhood assail her. Against her will she finds herself back in the apartment on rue Bourlamaque, the home of her adoptive parents. M. and Mme Eventurel take her in after a fire at the Hospice Saint-Louis burned 36 other young girls. Rosa Gaudrault, a young maid - the only one to show love for the child - dies in that fire, risking her life to go back into the burning building and rescue as many children as she could. The Eventurels rename the child and raise her to conform to their idea of a model daughter, suited to their highly stratified society. But she rebels. Her vocation, she believes, is to be an actress. There is salvation in words - she can recreate herself with her gift of speech, of drama:

"Her deepest desire was to live in some other place than within herself, for just a minute, one brief minute, to see what it is like in a head other than her own, another body, to be incarnated anew, to know what it is like in some other place, to know new sorrows, new joys, to try on a different skin from her own, the way one tries on gloves in a store, to stop gnawing on the one bone of her actual life and feed on strange, disorienting substances. To shatter into ten, a hundred, a thousand indestructible fragments; to be ten, a hundred, a thousand new and indestructible persons. To go from one to the other, not lightly as one changes dresses, but to inhabit profoundly another being with all the knowledge, the compassion, the sense of rootedness, the efforts to adapt, and the strange and fearsome mystery that would entail."

Over the years Flora has lived in many different skins: Ophelia, Miss Julie, Hedda Gabbler, Mary Tudor, Phaedra. And now she'll inhabit Winnie, who's determined to remain hopeful while buried first to her waist, and then her neck, in the detritus of her life. Preparing for this role, Flora is haunted by her own past and that of all those women who tried to conform and were so often punished if they did not:

"And thus has Flora Fontanges in the past approached Ophelia, downstream among the drifting flowers, asking the same tormenting question of Ophelia as of Renée Chauvreux, about the bitter destiny of girls. Why?"

Why, indeed? There are no answers to be found. We never find out why Maude is always running away. We never learn why Flora was abandoned as a child, although we can guess. And we never get more than a brief, one-dimensional outline of any of those women summoned from the past.

As for Flora, she, like Winnie, goes back to doing what she knows best. She goes back into exile, returning to Paris with a letter in her bag offering her the part of Mme Frola in the Pirandello drama, *Right You Are*.

It's a good read, as I said, but if you're only going to read one book by Anne Hébert make it *Kamouraska*. I promise not to tell the professor.

Week 16: *The Wars*, by Timothy Findley (1977)

"Only the dead have seen the end to war."

George Santayana wrote this in 1922. He was responding to the idea, popular at the time, that the First World War was the war to end all wars. It was the Great War for Civilization. The war that would be over by Christmas.

It wasn't any of those things, of course. In the end it dragged on for four years, three months, 11 days. It took the lives of nine million soldiers, seven million civilians, eight million horses and countless mules and donkeys. And 21 years later we did it all over again.

There've been many books dealing with this, the first great European war. *A Farewell to Arms* comes to mind . . . *All Quiet on the Western Front* . . . *Goodbye to All That* . . . the four novels by Ford Madox Ford collectively known as *Parade's End*. More recently, we have *Birdsong* . . . *War Horse* . . . Pat Barker's *Regeneration Trilogy*.

And *The Wars*, by Timothy Findley. When it was published in 1977 it was immediately hailed as one of the best stories about that ghastly war. It won the Governor General's Award for English-language fiction and quickly became a literary classic. It's been called the finest historical novel ever written by a Canadian and has been required reading for high school students for years. This is in spite of the efforts of an Ontario mother to get it removed from the curriculum. Fortunately, she was unsuccessful.

The hero of the story is Robert Ross, a sensitive 19-year-old Canadian officer who joins up to fight out of guilt. His beloved older sister has died and Robert, who believes he should have been there to save her, blames himself for her death. Like so many of his countrymen, he has an idealized vision of war. It will be the fire that will purify his soul, the crucible that will forge his manhood. What he is not expecting is that it will destroy him - that his experiences on the Western Front will drive him to the verge of madness and beyond.

The "wars" within the novel are internal as well as external: guilt, shame, sexual tension, the struggle to adapt to a way of life that increasingly makes no sense. And the conflict between the way things should be, in a rational world, and the way they happen in war. In the maelstrom of war there is no right or wrong. There is only the imperative to follow orders. One's moral code means nothing.

Findley has chosen to tell Ross's story from the viewpoint of a historian or biographer who has access to photographs, letters, and documents from the soldier's past. He - or she - is also able to interview some of the people who knew him. And so we have a narrative told from various perspectives - the anonymous researcher, the nurse who cared for Ross in his final days, the woman who fell in love with him when she was twelve.

But it is this fragmented approach that prevents us, I think, from seeing Ross himself. Or rather, seeing *into* him, as opposed to observing his reactions to the chaos of his surroundings. Before leaving

England for France, Ross is taken to a brothel where he ejaculates prematurely. The woman is kind; she assures him that "there's lots of fellows do what you done. Specially the first time." We are told Robert is ashamed, staring at the floor, but the narrative voice is distant. It simply doesn't feel personal.

Later, in a bath-house in northern France, he's locked in a dark, airless room and raped by his fellow officers. He thinks there are three of them but has no idea who they are. It's a horrific scene but the reader is detached, watching from the sidelines.

It's in the descriptions - and there are many - of the war itself that we come to experience real, raw, even violent sensations. Findley thrusts us into the trenches along with the soldiers - drowns us in mud and blood and dead horses, cracks our eardrums with the blasts of exploding shells, blinds us with clouds of chlorine gas. In unforgettable prose, he describes the effects of the *flammenwerfer*, or flamethrowers, introduced by the Germans at the Battle of Verdun - a battle in which the French army suffered 380,000 casualties:

"Fire storms raged along the front. Men were exploded where they stood - blown apart by the combustion. Winds with the velocity of cyclones tore the guns from their emplacements and flung them about like toys. Horses fell with their bones on fire. Men went blind in the heat. Blood ran out of noses, ears, and mouths."

The greatest terror, for some, is that the officers in charge, the men who are sending thousands of soldiers to slaughter, may not actually know what they're doing: "What if they were mad - or stupid? What if their fear was greater than yours? Or what if they were brave and crazy - wanting and demanding bravery from you?"

Their fears are well grounded. Commanding officers are far removed from the front lines. They make "strategic" decisions guaranteed to put their men in harm's way . . . mistakes that cost hundreds of thousands of lives.

On the 16 of June, 1916, Ross commits a final desperate act. Under siege from the Germans, with shells bursting all around him, he breaks rank and releases a barn full of horses and mules who are in danger of being burned alive. His captain, calling him a traitor, closes the gates and tries to kill him. Ross, in turn, shoots the captain between the eyes. For this act of treason - a violent gesture declaring "his commitment to life in the midst of death" - Ross is eventually captured and tried *in absentia*. By this time he's burned beyond recovery; his nose is disfigured and bent, his face is a mass of scar tissue. He will never walk or see or be capable of judgement again. He dies in 1922, at the age of 25.

I cannot think of a better introduction to the horror, brutality, and near insanity of trench warfare than this particular story. If I never read another tale of that terrible war, I will consider myself educated.

Week 17: *To Kill a Mockingbird*, by Harper Lee (1960)

I first read *To Kill a Mockingbird* when I was in my early 20s. It had been out for 10 years or so, and Harper Lee's description of superstition, ignorance and institutional prejudice seemed remote - almost quaint. In the wake of the white supremacist rallies in Viriginia and videos of police officers singling out African Americans for harsh, sometimes deadly, treatment, this story of small-town Alabama during the Depression era seems uncomfortably, even scarily, familiar.

Published in 1960, *To Kill a Mockingbird* is loosely based on the author's family and childhood friends, one of whom was Truman Capote, as well as an event that took place near her hometown of Monroeville, Alabama, when she was 10 years old. It's set in the fictional town of Maycomb and its main protagonist is a six-year-old tomboy who closely resembles the young Harper Lee.

Jean Louise Finch, nicknamed Scout, and her older brother, Jem, live with their middle-aged, widowed father, Atticus, and their black cook, Calpurnia. Atticus is a thoughtful, compassionate man, and encourages his children to look at the world through a humanitarian lens. When they ask why he's taken on an unpopular case, defending a black man accused of rape, he explains that before he can live with other people he has to be able to live with himself: "The one thing that doesn't abide by majority rule is a person's conscience."

Early in the story Scout and Jem befriend an odd young boy named Dill who comes to stay in Maycomb with his aunt every summer. The three of them embark on a campaign to "out" their neighbor, the reclusive Arthur "Boo" Radley, whom nobody has seen outside his house in years. Boo is one of the "mockingbirds" in the novel, a good person injured by the evil of others. The other is Tom Robinson, a black field hand being held on charges of raping a young white woman. It's his word against hers, a situation that pretty well condemns him to the hangman's noose.

The book is in many ways a study in courage. Most notably, of course, the courage of a small-town Southern lawyer to take on an unpopular cause - to defend a black man against the spurious charges laid by a white girl and her father. His attitude towards his client, along with his dignified comportment throughout the novel, has caused the name Atticus Finch to become a byword for moral integrity. But smaller acts of courage appear throughout the story, as when Scout is prepared to fight her classmates to defend her father's name and an elderly neighbour sets herself to break a morphine addiction before she dies. A final courageous blow carried out by the reclusive Boo Radley saves the lives of the children and forces even Atticus to rethink the nature of justice.

Lee draws her characters with the sure touch that comes from long association with the type. Scout's aunt, for instance, appears midway through the book, determined to "take charge" of the wayward tomboy and mold her into her version of a proper Southern lady:

"Aunt Alexandra was one of the last of her kind: she had river-boat, boarding-school manners; let any moral come along and she would uphold it; she was born in the objective case; she was an incurable gossip. When Aunt Alexandra went to school, self-doubt could not be found in any textbook, so she knew not its meaning. She was never bored, and given the slightest chance she would exercise her royal prerogative: she would arrange, advise, caution, and warn."

While this attention to type creates some colourful writing, it can also make for uncomfortable reading, half a century later. Bob Ewell, for instance, the father of the girl who is claiming to be raped, is a personification of "white trash". A drunken no-good who seldom works, he represents the dark side of the American south: ignorance, poverty, squalor, and hate-filled racial prejudice. His lonely, abused daughter, Mayella, who is obviously the victim of some crime, we know, is portrayed as being as bitter and racist as her father. One of the saddest passages in the book is her humiliation on the witness stand as Atticus slowly, even gently destroys her testimony. We are left feeling pity for her. We may not forgive her for what she does to Tom, but we wonder about her choices at a time and in a place where her options are hardly better than those of the black man she hates.

The point is that all these acts of courage - from the defense of Tom Robinson to the shooting of a rabid dog in the streets of Maycomb - have their flip side. Nothing is black and white, as much as the characters would wish it to be. The defense of a black man requires the degradation of a young woman; saving the life of two children involves covering up a crime. This kind of ambiguity permeates the novel. To my mind, it's what lifts *Mockingbird* from what might have been simply a good coming-of-age story to the classic it undoubtedly is. If ever there was a moral story, this is it.

Lee herself was ambivalent about the success of her book. She was quoted as saying that, when it was published, she hoped for "a quick and merciful death" at the hands of the reviewers. What she got, of course, was immediate critical acclaim and the Pulitzer Prize for fiction. Not bad for a first novel, don't you think?

Week 18: *A Pale View of Hills*, by Kazuo Ishiguro (1982)

Memory can be an unreliable thing.

So says the narrator of Kazuo Ishiguro's debut novel, *A Pale View of Hills*. Published in 1982, the novel was praised for its "uncanny mix of surface calm with menace and deep tension", a mix that would be repeated seven years later in his best-known work, *The Remains of the Day*.

In announcing that Ishiguro had won the Nobel Prize in Literature 2017, the secretary of the Swedish Academy described him as a writer "who, in novels of great emotional force, has uncovered the abyss beneath our illusory sense of connection with the world." It is that false sense of connection that confronts not only the characters in his novels but the reader as well, when we realize that the story as written is not necessarily in alignment with the facts.

A Pale View of Hills is set in England and in postwar Japan at the time of the rebuilding of Nagasaki. Etsuko is a middle-aged Japanese woman now living alone in the English countryside. Six years ago her oldest daughter, Keiko, hanged herself. During a visit from her younger daughter, Etsuko begins dreaming about a young girl, Mariko, the child of a woman she knew one summer in Japan.

The way it's told, Etsuko is pregnant that summer and the woman, Sachiko, intrigues her, partly because she's further down the road of motherhood. But Sachiko is an indifferent mother at best. Although given to lecturing Etsuko on the things she'll find out when she, too, is a mother, she raises Mariko with a carelessness that verges on abuse. Even when it becomes apparent there's a child murderer in the area, Sachiko remains indifferent, letting her daughter wander at will.

Mariko is not a happy child. She and her mother have a troubled relationship, and she professes to hate her mother's boyfriend. In spite of announcing several times that her daughter's welfare is of utmost importance, Sachiko continues to make plans for her own happiness, at the expense of that of her child.

Etsuko, who is pregnant, has her own unhappiness to contend with. She spends her days alone in her apartment, from where she can look out past the trees on the opposite side of the river. Beyond the trees she can see "a pale outline of hills visible against the clouds. It was not an unpleasant view and on occasions it brought me a rare sense of relief from the emptiness of those long afternoons I spent in that apartment."

There are numerous similarities between Etsuko and her friend. Sachiko schemes to marry an American and leave Japan; Etsuko will eventually marry a foreigner and move to England. Like Sachiko, she will have a difficult relationship with the child she is carrying - so much so that she will bear some guilt for her daughter's eventual suicide.

At the risk of giving away the plot, for those who haven't read it, the twist comes near the end of the book. Etsuko, who has gone looking for Mariko, finds the child crouching on the bank of the river. The girl says once more that she doesn't want to go away - she doesn't like her mother's boyfriend, she thinks he's a pig. Etsuko replies angrily that she's not to talk like this, adding, "In any case, if you don't like it there, we can always come back."

It's this sudden change in voice - the use of the word "we" - that startles the reader. Are Etsuko and Sachiko one and the same person? Is Mariko actually Keiko, the daughter who hanged herself? A paragraph a few lines on leads us to wonder: did Etsuko kill the child that night on the river-bank? Is it possible her daughter's death was not a suicide at all?

Ishiguro has said he was trying something a little "odd" when he wrote this book. He wanted to show how people use language to deceive and protect themselves. "So the whole narrative strategy of the book," he said, "was about how someone ends up talking about things they cannot face directly through other people's stories."

What can be said for sure is that nothing can be said for sure about this story. The author is intentionally ambivalent; the ending is purposefully ambiguous. And the narrator, Etsuko, is unreliable. Is the story she relates really that of her friend, Sachiko? Or is she remembering a painful event in her own life - one connected with leaving Japan and the subsequent death of her daughter?

Kazuo Ishiguro has been compared to Jane Austen both for his "carefully restrained mode of expression" and for the important things he leaves unsaid. Because we so frequently equate that restraint with something inherently English, it came as a bit of a shock for many readers to learn that the author of *Remains of the Day* was born in Japan, moving to England when he was five.

But Ishiguro, of course, is a hybrid - which so many of the very best English writers are and have always been. Joseph Conrad was born in Ukraine; Henry James was from New York; Salman Rushdie and Vikram Seth were born in India. In my own mind what foreign-born writers bring to the scene is a certain detachment - an ability to stand apart from one's fellow citizens and regard them with a more objective, even jaundiced eye. Ishiguro alluded to this several years ago in an interview with *The Telegraph*:

"There is that slightly chilly aspect to writing fiction," he said. "You do have to be slightly detached to say: how would human beings respond in this situation?"

I love that word - "chilly". Not cold, but cool . . . deceptively muted. Take, for instance, Etsuko's description of how she is haunted by her daughter's suicide and the fact that it was several days before her body was discovered hanging in her room:

"The horror of that image has never diminished, but it has long ceased to be a morbid matter; as with a wound on one's own body, it is possible to develop an intimacy with the most disturbing of things."

That, I would say, pretty neatly sums up Ishiguro's oeuvre to this point: intimate, restrained, and disturbing.

Week 19: *The Accidental*, by Ali Smith (2005)

George Saunders was the bookies' favourite but Ali Smith led the pack as far as sales of her book. I'm talking about two of the authors shortlisted for the 2017 Man Booker Prize, whose winner was, indeed, Saunders for *Lincoln in the Bardo*.

If I had the money, which I don't, being a penniless scribe, I would have bet on Smith, partly because she's Scottish - I like the Scots - and partly because she's been shortlisted so many times (and won so many prizes) she really does seem due for a Booker.

If they gave awards just for being shortlisted (which they do, actually), Smith would have a fistful. *Hotel World* (2001) was shortlisted for the Orange Prize for Fiction and the Man Booker Prize. Four years later *The Accidental* was shortlisted for the Orange, the Booker, and the Whitbread Novel of the Year (which it won). In 2007, *Girl Meets Boy* won the Scottish Arts Council Novel of the Year (as did *Hotel World*) and in 2012, *Artful* was shortlisted for the inaugural Goldsmiths Prize. Two years later *How to Be Both* was shortlisted for the Man Booker, the Folio Prize, the Bailey's Women's Prize for Fiction and, again, the Goldsmiths. It won the Bailey's and the Goldsmiths. And now, with *Autumn*, she's once again on the shortlist for the Booker.

As I said, she's due.

Out of all these books, the one that's made it into my copy of *1001 Books You Must Read Before You Die* is *The Accidental*, a postmodern tale likely based on *Teorema*, a 1968 Italian art-house film written and directed by Pier Paolo Pasolini. No - please - come back! Words like "postmodern" scare the bejeezus out of me, too, and I think the last time I saw an art-house film I was wearing platform shoes and a headband.

In the film, a typical bourgeois Italian family is visited by a mysterious stranger, played by Terence Stamp. The stranger proceeds to seduce every member of the family, including the maid, and then leaves as suddenly and mysteriously as he arrived. In the void created by his departure, the others are forced to confront the uncomfortable reality of their lives. The maid becomes a saint; the mother seeks out affairs with younger men; the son abandons the family to become an artist; the daughter sinks into a catatonic state. And the father, after giving away all his worldly possessions, walks naked into the desert.

Smith's tale is less dramatic but the basic premise is similar. Four members of the Smart family have rented a run-down holiday cottage in a run-down village in Norfolk: "They had driven, on their way here, past repetitions of repetitions of brown-brick Victorian semis and terraces, houses and shops like extras from a post-war kitchen-sink drama, houses brown as decrepit dogs and so on their last legs that someone should take them in hand and have them humanely put to sleep."

Eve, the mother, is upset at the state of the house - it wasn't that way in the brochure. She's come hoping to spend the summer working on a book but has found herself with writer's block, unable to work. And so she spends her days lying on the floor of her studio, leaving strict orders that she's not to be disturbed.

Astrid, her 12-year-old daughter, thinks the house is disgusting, but, being 12, she thinks just about everything and everybody is disgusting. She goes about each day with her brand new camera, filming every detail, as if to prove she exists. Everything is "typical" and "ironic". The village is a dump. The house is substandard. Nothing, Astrid believes, is going to happen the entire substandard summer.

The other occupants of the house are Michael, Astrid's stepfather; Magnus, her older brother, and Katrina, the woman from the village who comes in to clean. Michael is a smug, lecherous university professor who makes a habit of bedding his female students. He has a routine: "He liked to give the little speech about Agape and Eros. He liked to tell the story, how he had admired her in class . . ." etc., etc. When his latest conquest plunges into the act with no preamble, he feels vaguely cheated.

Magnus, the 17-year-old brother, is a math and computer whiz who, on a lark, took part in a prank that resulted in the suicide of a fellow student. He feels deeply guilty; in his depression he refuses to eat with the others . . . refuses to bathe . . . refuses to come out of his room. Having broken someone, he sees himself and his entire family as broken. Over and over again he recites the details of the prank: "They took her head. They put it on a different body. They sent it to people. Then she killed herself."

The stranger who intrudes into this conventionally unhappy family is an attractive 30-something transient who claims her car has broken down. She calls herself Amber; she may also (though we don't know for sure) be someone named Alhambra who makes an appearance at the beginning of the book and whose voice is heard from time to time. Eve assumes Amber is one of Michael's student girlfriends - he thinks she's come to interview his wife. They invite her to stay for dinner. She stays - and stays. She eats with them, engages them in conversation, and challenges the way they look at the world. Bit by bit she proceeds to unravel their lives.

Michael, being Michael, falls in love with her. Commuting back from London, he realizes he's completely besotted with her: "Epiphany! dear God it was an epiphany! the empty seat filled with nothing but goodness was a holy moment! and on a filthy train crossing the filthy fens!" His feelings are not reciprocated; Amber has nothing but contempt for Michael, as does the reader - which isn't to say he's not well-drawn. Reading Michael, you feel sure Smith has run into more than one Michael Smart in her lifetime. They are legion, after all.

Astrid adores Amber. They go on long walks together, and do daring things like facing down the village bullies and pretending to shoplift. At one point, Amber takes Astrid's camera and drops it from the top of a bridge, providing a forceful if rather mean lesson on the nature of "seeing".

As for Magnus, Amber first saves him from hanging himself and then takes it upon herself to heal him by initiating him into the mysteries of sex. They have sex in the loft, sex in the garden, and eventually sex in the village church. Taking communion, so to speak. Everyone, he feels, is still broken, but Amber is possibly less broken than others: "If Amber is a piece of broken-up jigsaw, too, Magnus thinks, then she is several pieces of blue sky still joined up. Maybe she is a whole surviving connected sky."

When Amber isn't physically seducing family members, she's charming them by saying exactly what she thinks. This, we gather, is never done in conventional middle-class families. When Eve relates a rather innocuous tale of how she met her first husband, Amber lashes out in frustration:

"Is that it? Amber said. Is that the highpoint, the true-blue, the secret-can't-be-told everything-must-go ultimate all-singing all-dancing story-of-you? Jesus God you're going to have to tell me something more interesting than that or I'm going to fucking fall asleep right here at the wheel."

Smith is at her best in these moments - when she's giving us these quirky, sharply observed portraits of characters so real, so believeable, you'd know them in the street. I'm sure I went to school with Astrid - I may possibly have *been* Astrid at some point when I was young.

I'm not so sure about the rest of the story. As much as I believe Smith is incapable of writing a poorly crafted sentence, I can't help feeling she's having a little fun at our expense. It's like going out for drinks with the smartest girl in the office, laughing at the jokes she makes, and realizing afterwards that the joke was on you.

Week 20: *Quartet in Autumn*, by Barbara Pym (1977)

"There was something to be said for tea and a comfortable chat about cremation."

It's lines like this that cause Barbara Pym to be referred to as the Jane Austen of the 20th Century. I mean, how perfect is that? Doesn't it just conjure up a certain type of middle-aged woman at a certain time living in a certain place? It does for me, anyway. I love it.

The poet Philip Larkin called her "the most underrated writer of the century". While I wouldn't go quite so far, there's no doubt she was dismissed by the critics in the 1960s for being out-of-date. In spite of her early success and the popularity of six previous novels, she was turned down by her publishers and retreated into obscurity. It wasn't until 1977, with the publication of *Quartet in Autumn*, that Pym regained her public following. *Quartet* was highly praised and nominated for the Booker Prize; as a comeback it was an enormous success.

The book was somewhat of a departure for Pym. Previously, she'd been known for comic novels, somewhat in the style of E. F. Benson's *Mapp and Lucia*. There *is* a lightness about *Quartet*, and the characters are certainly "types". But its underlying sadness is, I think, likely due to her own years spent floundering in the literary wilderness. There's nothing like a decade of rejection slips to foster a writer's sense of isolation and despair.

Letty, Marcia, Edwin and Norman work side by side in an office somewhere in London. They all live alone and they are all approaching retirement. The nature of their work is unspecified, but we're given to understand it's pretty boring, and not all that important: when they retire, they're told, they will not be replaced.

You might think four people who've worked together in close quarters for years would become friends. You might assume they would socialize, at least occasionally, outside working hours. You would be wrong. This is a story about a certain type of Londoner who lives alone in a bed-sitting room, fiercely guarding his - or her - privacy. Edwin is the only one who owns his own home, but none of the others have ever been inside. They wouldn't expect to be invited and would be shocked if they were.

In the meantime, retirement is looming. Aside from Letty, none of them have any definite plans for how they'll spend their leisure years. Letty has a long-standing agreement with her widowed friend Marjorie that she'll move to the countryside when the time comes and share Marjorie's cottage. When Marjorie unexpectedly makes plans to marry the local vicar, Letty is left out in the cold. To compound her misfortune, the landlady of the house where she boards sells the place to a priest of an African religious sect, as Edwin describes him. Loud, exuberant worshipping now takes place the basement of the house on a nightly basis.

"How had it come about," Letty wonders, "that she, an Englishwoman born in Malvern in 1914 of middle-class

English parents, should find herself in this room in London surrounded by enthusiastic, shouting, hymn-singing Nigerians?"

These are not people, I have to confess, that you'd care to dine with. Or spend more than five minutes talking to at a party. Norman in particular is an argumentative, "angry little man whose teeth hurt", and whose spirits are lifted by the sight of a wrecked car on the motorway. Edwin, large, bald, and pink, is obsessed with the rituals of the church; outside of work he attends services throughout the city, craving liturgy and incense like an addict in search of a fix.

The women are better drawn than the men. Pym has an eye - and ear - for the eccentricities of a certain type of semi-genteel, middle-class English woman. Marcia, already rather dotty, declines into near-madness upon retirement. She hoards tins of food but doesn't eat - she keeps a shed full of milk bottles in her back garden - she fills her kitchen drawers with dozens of plastic bags, neatly classified and sorted. Marcia, more than any of the others, is a cautionary tale for those about to retire, or already there.

The secondary individuals in *Quartet* are depicted with just as sharp an eye for character. Letty's next landlady, the formidable Mrs. Pope, does "exactly those things that she wanted to do which made Letty realize that perhaps getting older had some advantages, few though these might be."

And Edwin's friend, the parish priest, is perhaps not as benevolent and all-caring as he might be, given his calling: "Father G. was often obliged to enter houses where people were on the point of death or had already died; indeed he preferred this type of situation to normal parish visiting, with its awkward conversation and the inevitable cups of tea and sweet biscuits."

The autumn of the title refers, of course, to that period of life when we think about mortality - our own and that of our family and friends. Retirement, as much as it might be anticipated, is one of those milestones that looms in the distance, signalling the approach of the end.

But the four characters portrayed here have lived their whole lives in a kind of autumn. They were born into a certain class at a certain time when expectations were low. "Don't get above yourself" would one of their ruling mottos - as much as "Don't drink sherry before 5:00" and, apparently, "Never read a novel in the morning". These are people who wither in the heat of summer, who never really believe in the promise of spring. They're made for the weak light of fall, with its grey, moody skies and the promise of a nice cup of tea at the end of the day.

I read *Quartet in Autumn* with a certain nostalgia. This is the London I remember when I lived there in the seventies. A city of shabby bed-sits and luncheon vouchers . . . shillings in the meter to run your bath and no central heating. Black and white tellies given to breaking down on a regular basis. The England of *Quartet* was swept away by Margaret Thatcher and the European Union, and that's probably not a bad thing.

But Pym deserves to be read. She has a talent for telling a dark story with a light touch, and it is this that gives the book its poignancy. In spite of its themes of loneliness and isolation it's actually very funny in parts and the ending, in particular, is hopeful. Letty, finding herself contemplating an outing with Edwin, Norman, and Marjorie - something that would have been unthinkable a year ago - realizes that life still holds "infinite possibilities for change".

Something we'd all do well to remember.

Week 21: *Rebecca*, by Daphne du Maurier (1938)

There are times when you'd like to get hold of the unnamed heroine of *Rebecca* and give her a good sharp slap upside the head. Yes, she's young. Yes, she hasn't been around much. And yes, she has married a man much older than she - old enough to be her father, in fact.

But good grief, girl, show some spunk! Stand up to Mrs. Danvers. She is, after all, your employee. She may be one of the creepiest housekeepers ever to wield a dust mop but you're never going to get anywhere letting her push you around. Quite being so *nice* - you're getting on my nerves.

The problem for the new Mrs. de Winter is that she's in competition with the old one. When Rebecca, the first wife, was alive, she was everything the new wife is not: confident, creative, strong-willed, beautiful. The villagers adored her. The household staff worshiped her. And Mrs. Danvers, the housekeeper, was very likely in love with her. The way she's written, it's hard to blame them. She was perfect, apparently. She was an accomplished hunter, a good sailor, an excellent horsewoman. She threw fabulous parties. She was fearlessly independent.

Eventually we learn that while Rebecca was all these things, she was also heartless, cruel, and a bit of a slut. Bring it on, I say. When it comes to fictional heroines, give me a bad girl any day. After all, who are you more likely to remember - the saintly good girls who serve and submit or the plotters and schemers who make life more interesting? Consider *Fatal Attraction* - does anyone remember Anne Archer? She played Michael Douglas' wife. She got a best supporting actress nomination for it but does anybody remember her? Of course not. We remember Glenn Close, who played the obsessive, neurotic and ultimately deadly Other Woman. Men, I'm told, had nightmares about her.

Fiction has a long history of memorable bad girls. Moll Flanders was a thief and a prostitute. Becky Sharp was a calculating adventuress. Emma Bovary committed adultery, several times. Lady Macbeth was, well, Lady Macbeth. And the outrageously eccentric Miss Havisham and her beautiful but cold young ward, Estella, are the only really interesting female characters Dickens ever wrote. (I'll be exploring these and other interesting female characters later in these pages. Stay tuned.)

More recently we have *Misery*'s Annie Wilkes, who claims to be Paul Sheldon's "number one fan" and just happens to be a serial killer. Amy Dunne, the missing wife of *Gone Girl*, is willing to lie, blackmail, and even commit murder in order to get what she wants. And who could forget Big Nurse Ratched in *One Flew Over the Cuckoo's Nest*? Nasty, controlling, sociopathic women - I love them all.

My guess is that Daphne du Maurier did, too. Which is why the title of her classic tale of a house haunted by its former occupant is named after the first Mrs. de Winter, not the second. The new wife, in fact, doesn't even get named. Du Maurier claimed not naming the narrator was an interesting technical device but I think she was making a point: the beautiful Rebecca, dead though she may be, is still the novel's protagonist.

The story is told in flashbacks. The second Mrs. de Winter, shy, self-conscious and insecure, is working as a paid companion to a vulgar and arrogant American woman when she meets and falls in love with the wealthy widower Maxim de Winter. Within a few weeks he proposes marriage and whisks her off to Manderley, his country estate on the south coast of England. On the surface, it's a dream come true, but right from the beginning she has a nagging feeling that all is not well. For one thing, all she knows about her husband-to-be is that his wife died in a tragic boating accident. He's reluctant to tell her anything more, and he never actually says he loves her.

"I was to marry the man I loved. I was to be Mrs. de Winter. It was foolish to go on having that pain in the pit of my stomach when I was so happy. Nerves of course."

Upon arrival at Manderley, she's overwhelmed by the grandeur of the place. Every decoration and every stick of furniture has been chosen by her predecessor. The flowers are placed as Rebecca chose to place them, the meals are prepared according to Rebecca's desires. The housekeeper, Mrs. Danvers, resents the young woman's presence; she would resent anyone who would dare to replace her beloved employer, but it doesn't help that Maxim's new wife is simply not up to the job. Over and over again we are reminded of Rebecca's presence - in death she continues to dominate the household:

"She was in the house still, as Mrs. Danvers had said; she was in that room in the west wing, she was in the library, in the morning-room, in the gallery above the hall. Even in the little flower-room, where her mackintosh still hung. And in the garden, and in the woods, and in the stone cottage on the beach. Her footsteps sounded in the corridors, her scent lingered on the stairs. The servants obeyed her orders still, the food we ate was the food she liked. Her favourite flowers filled the rooms . . . Rebecca was still mistress of Manderley. Rebecca was still Mrs. de Winter."

Rebecca was du Maurier's fifth novel and it remains her best known. It also remains consistently underappreciated by those who write it off as "women's fiction" or just a Gothic romance. It may indeed deserve those labels. But in the hands of a writer as adept as du Maurier it becomes much more than a romantic ghost story. What she's created is a disturbing narrative of suppressed sexuality and psychological control. In essence, it's a very modern tale . . . a study of the duality of human nature.

Rebecca, the first Mrs. de Winter, represents the dark side - the libido, forbidden feelings of lust, rage and vengeance. Carl Jung gave the dark side a name: he called it the shadow. And while the shadow can be destructive, even evil, it has the potential to be creative and powerful. It is the door to our individuality. It demands to be recognized.

In the end the narrator makes a choice: forced to recognize Rebecca for what she was, and her husband for what he is, she embraces her own dark side. It comes with a sacrifice - she will never again be innocent - she will never again be treated as a child. It's the painful price we pay for self-knowledge. The price, I think, is worth it.

Week 22: *Moll Flanders*, by Daniel Defoe (1722)

Having decided to spend the next few weeks revisiting some of my favourite "bad girls" I've started with the author who literally wrote the book on virtue succumbing to vanity and vice: Daniel Defoe and his eponymous heroine, Moll Flanders. (Spoiler alert: while virtue wins out in the end, it doesn't so much triumph over vanity and vice as outlast them.)

Hailed as the precursor to the modern novel, the book's full title provides a fair synopsis of the story: *The Fortunes and Misfortunes of the Famous Moll Flanders Who was born in Newgate, and during a life of continu'd Variety for Threescore Years, besides her Childhood, was Twelve Years a Whore, five times a Wife (whereof once to her brother) Twelve Years a Thief, Eight Years a Transported Felon in Virginia, at last grew Rich, liv'd Honest and died a Penitent.*

Published in 1722, the book purports to be the autobiography of a woman whose real name we never learn but who eventually calls herself Moll Flanders. (At the time it was written, "moll" was a common term for a prostitute, so the name is no accident.) She's a colourful character - a gold-digger, a thief, an adulteress, and an occasional whore. She marries her own brother - albeit unknowingly - and so commits incest. And, except for a reunion with one of her sons in her latter years, she's at best an indifferent parent.

Even by present-day standards, these are not qualities we want to instill in our daughters. Or our sons, for that matter. Earlier readers were properly scandalized. In an introduction to an anthology of his work, the late Victorian critic, Charles Frederick Johnson, expressed more than a little antipathy towards both the Defoe and his heroine:

"'Moll Flanders' and 'Roxana' are very coarse books, but it can hardly be said that they are harmful or corrupting. They are simply vulgar. Vice has preserved all its evil by preserving all its grossness. Passion is reduced to mere animalism, and is depicted with the brutal directness of Hogarth. This may be good morals, but it is unpleasant art."

Digs at the author were common. In spite of - or perhaps because of - being an extremely prolific journalist, pamphleteer and successful novelist, he was regarded as something of a hack. There was also the matter of his schooling. As the son of a Nonconformist, or Dissenter, he couldn't attend Oxford or Cambridge; instead he was sent to an excellent academy at Newington Green. It's said he received a better education there than he would have at any English university but his peers never forgave him for not being the true gentleman he wanted to be.

But back to Moll. While the Victorians were working themselves into a lather about morality, the fact is the heart of the book is about money: *Moll Flanders* is a story of economics. Poverty, that "frightful spectre", is the driving theme. At a time when to be female and poor almost certainly meant a short, hungry, brutal existence, Moll was a master of survival. It's her conniving - her refusal to accept her lot in life - that has won the hearts of readers for the past 300 years.

And it's this as well that helps us overlook Defoe's heavy-handed moralizing and the sense, more often than not, that he doesn't really have a firm grip on the plot.

Which is this: Born in Newgate prison where her mother is being held on charges of theft, Moll is taken in by a band of gypsies. She runs away from them at the age of three (!), is given into the care of a poor but kind older woman, is seduced by the oldest brother of a wealthy family, and is eventually persuaded to marry the younger brother. When her husband dies a few years later, she's relieved more than anything. "I confess I was not suitably affected with the loss of my husband," she says, "nor can I say that I ever loved him as I ought to have done".

Still, a woman without a fortune needs a husband. A born entrepreneur, Moll leverages her considerable assets - her beauty, her good manners, and her brains - to keep the wolf from the door. There's plenty of sex, both inside and outside of marriage, some paid for and some not, but Defoe is coy with the details. When it comes to money, however - how much she has, has much she needs, what men give her - he's not only forthright, he's downright meticulous. After their first sexual encounter, the elder brother gives her five guineas. It's the money, not the sex, that stands out:

"I was more confounded with the money than I was before with the love, and began to be so elevated that I scarce knew the ground I stood on."

Moll has good reason to be "confounded" with the money. It's all very well to be in love, and to have someone love you back, but love won't keep a roof over your head or feed you when you're starving. Defoe knew this and so did his readers. He was a businessman long before he began to write novels, and his sense of commerce threads its way throughout the book. After every adventure, we're given an accounting of Moll's finances. After parting with her second husband, she begins to "cast up" her accounts:

"I found my strength to amount, put all together, to about £400, so that with that I had above £450. I had saved £100 more, but I met with a disaster with that, which was this - that a goldsmith in whose hands I had trusted it broke, so I lost £70 of my money, the man's composition not making above £30 out of his £100. I had a little plate [silver], but not much, and was well enough stocked with clothes and linen".

Here's where we really see a difference between then and now. As a society we'll reveal the most intimate details of our sex life to anyone who'll listen, or watch, or buy the sex tape, but heaven forbid you ask us how much money we make. Or what we owe on our mortgage. As a species, we can still be coy; only the details have changed.

I referred earlier to Defoe's moralizing - the constant reminders that Moll is living a wicked life and is sure to come to a bad end:

"I had a most unbounded stock of vanity and pride, and but a very little stock of virtue . . . Thus I gave up myself to ruin without the least concern, and am a fair memento to all young women whose vanity prevails over their virtue . . . indeed I think I rather wished for that ruin than studied to avoid it."

It's the frequent sermonizing that made the story palatable to earlier readers, but it would be a better story without it. What I personally found fascinating was the wealth of information about life in the 17th century: women prisoners "pleading their belly" to keep the hangman at bay; the "liberty of the Mint" which allowed bankrupts to escape from their creditors; how the pickpockets plied their trade at the annual Bartholomew Fair. These are the details, rather than Moll's bank account or even her sex life, that appeal to the modern reader.

In spite of her continual warnings to young women to avoid the path she's taken, there is no doubt that in the end her vice, if we agree to call it that, is rewarded. Moll ends up a wealthy plantation owner living in happy retirement with the man she loves, embracing a good Christian life now that the need for "wickedness" is past. It's hard to believe Defoe wasn't writing with at least the tip of his tongue in his cheek.

Week 23: *Fanny Hill*, by John Cleland (1748-1749)

Forget what you've been told. Disregard the scenes of degradation, despair and early death depicted by Hogarth. The fact is, there was no greater bliss than working the sex trade in 18th Century London. The women in charge of the brothels were kind and caring, the clients were gallant and rich, and the prostitutes themselves were fresh-faced, beautiful and extremely compliant.

This is the picture painted by John Cleland in his elegantly written but tedious erotic novel, *Fanny Hill: Or Memoirs of a Woman of Pleasure.* Published in two volumes in 1748-1749, the novel is part satire, part a critique of social and sexual convention. It was condemned as pornography and banned in England shortly after publication; in the US it was only taken off the banned list in 1966. As far as we know it was the first original pornography written in English - most erotica until then came from France - and it remains one of the most banned and prosecuted books in history.

The story is uncomplicated: Fanny Hill, a naive, uneducated young woman - she's 14 when the story opens - arrives friendless and alone in London after the death of her parents. She's immediately taken in by the madam of a brothel, Mrs. Jones, who pretends to hire her as a maid. The plan, of course, is to train Fanny as a prostitute, after first selling her virginity to the highest bidder. The client is so old and ugly the terrified young girl fights him off and then falls ill for several days. When she recovers, Mrs. Jones sells her instead to a better-looking customer who successfully seduces her. Having lost her innocence, Fanny quickly becomes an eager and lusty working member of the household.

Her first client after the seducer is a wealthy young nobleman named Charles. They fall in love and he sets her up as his mistress in a private apartment. They spend the next few months in blissful cohabitation until Charles disappears, having been sent away by his father to claim his fortune in the South Seas. Fanny, who is three months' pregnant, miscarries, becomes ill, and is nursed back to health by her landlady. Seeing no better way to support herself, Fanny goes back to her former way of living, enjoying a succession of "sprightly gallants", some old, some young, and gradually builds up a nest egg. In the end, an elderly lover conveniently dies, leaving her a small fortune.

Being "not yet nineteen" and a lady of leisure, Fanny takes a trip up north to revisit the scenes of her youth. Along the way - oh happy coincidence! she meets up with her long lost love, Charles, back from his tropical adventures, and on his way to find her. Her story ends with a confession of her indiscretions; Charles forgives her, begs her to marry him, and they wind up married, prosperous, and respectable.

Like *Moll Flanders*, this is a first-person account told in the form of a letter. Also like *Moll,* it's the story of a young woman's successful rise to wealth and independence using her God-given talents.
Unlike *Moll*, however, there's not much to admire about Fanny. She has little or no agency of her own, being nothing but a (male) writer's wet dream. Cleland,

unlike Defoe, seems unwilling to allow his heroine any consideration of male privilege or the oppressed state of women. Sweet, compliant little Fanny gives herself to be used however and whenever her clients desire - gleefully enjoying every carnal moment: "what floods of bliss!" she exclaims at one point, "what melting transports!" In terms of character, she's about as interesting as a blow-up doll.

Fanny Hill was condemned not so much for its descriptions of sex but because Cleland was so brazenly, and obscenely, graphic. There's not an inch of Fanny's body that escapes description ... not a moment of amorous adventure that isn't outlined in exquisite detail. Still, a modern reader seeking titillation might be frustrated by the author's use of euphemisms. They are wildly imaginative, and at times they're very funny. The following scene, describing Fanny and Charles in the act, is typical:

". . . presently the sting of pleasure spurred them up to fiercer action: then began the storm of heaves, which, from the undermost combatant, were thrusts at the same time, he crossing his hands over her and drawing her home to him with a sweet violence. The inverted strokes of anvil over hammer soon brought on the critical period, to which all the signs of a close conspiring ecstasy informed us of the *point* they were at."

Without ever using the word, his descriptions of the penis are positively homoerotic: "that terrible spitfire machine"; "this pride of nature"; "stiff staring truncheon"; "this furious fescue"; "that superb piece of furniture"; "that favourite piece of manhood". Reading this, you can't help thinking, Oh, if only!

I came to the book wanting to like Fanny. Very few heroines, before or since, have been portrayed as openly enjoying sex; the book's defenders hail it as an important piece of political satire, an expression of the libertine movement of the Enlightenment. It certainly deserves its place in the literary and historical canon, and I'm firmly against banning books. Period.

But it's been a bad few months. I find it increasingly difficult to read about young girls being "seduced" - i.e. raped - by men old enough to be their fathers when every day we're confronted by similar stories in the real world.

Plus ça change, plus c'est la même chose.

Week 24: *Les Liaisons Dangereuses*, by Pierre-Ambroise Choderlos de Laclos (1782)

When is the last time you wrote a letter? Or received one?

I'm not talking about messaging someone on Facebook, having a chat on Whatsapp, or even exchanging emails - which, by the way, are going the way of the dodo. Teens have pretty much abandoned email in favour of texting while the rest of us pretend we're too busy to read them.

But no. I'm talking about putting pen to paper and writing an actual letter. Or getting one in the mail that's not from your bank, your landlord, or Canada Revenue. My grandmother set aside time every day to write letters to friends and family. It's something I used to do every week. Now I don't.

And I miss it. I miss actually looking forward to checking my mailbox. I even miss getting those Christmas circulars I used to deplore, telling me all the brave and wonderful things my friends have been up to all year. Now, there's no point: I can read about it every day on Facebook.

I bring this up because *Les Liaisons Dangereuses,* the tale of seduction and revenge by Pierre-Ambroise Choderlos de Laclos, is written as a series of letters - 175 in all. If Laclos is to be believed, the French aristocracy did little else but write letters when they weren't attending the theatre, the opera, or the ballet. And if they were as morally bankrupt and politically corrupt as depicted in this novel - well, heads deserved to roll.

The plot of *Liaisons* revolves around the machinations of the Marchioness de Merteuil and her former lover and partner in crime, the wealthy and dissipated Viscount de Valmont. Accustomed to relieving their boredom by plotting and scheming against others, they form an alliance aimed at violating two respectable young women - one, a virginal young girl fresh out of the convent, the other the chaste and religious wife of a member of Parliament.

Fifteen-year-old Cécile Volanges is due to marry the Count de Gercourt when he returns from Corsica. The Marchioness, having at one time been cast aside by Gercourt, wants Valmont to deflower the girl and make the seduction public knowledge, thereby creating a scandal and humiliating the husband-to-be.

But Valmont has set his sights on other prey: Madame de Tourvel, a married woman with a spotless reputation for faithfulness and piety. She is virtuous and inaccessible - and it's that inaccessibility that makes her irresistible. Valmont decides he must have her. He persuades Merteuil to agree to a bargain: if he can provide written proof that he has slept with Tourvel, the Marchioness must favour him with a night in bed.

In order to win Tourvel, Valmont must first convince her that he's a reformed character . . . that the once decadent playboy is now upright, honest, and penitent. He embarks on an intense letter-writing campaign, to which she eventually, cautiously, responds. Supremely confident, he never doubts that, in the end, love will win out over virtue. She will give in to him, and once she does he'll have no further use for her. As he confides to Merteuil, ". . . the time will come too soon when, degraded by her fall, I shall view her with as much indifference as another."

While everyone knows Valmont is an unscrupulous cad who delights in seducing women and then dropping them, the Marchioness has a very different reputation. Beautiful, intelligent, and rich, Merteuil is the toast of Paris. Everyone, even her closest friends, believe her to be chaste, respectable, and wise. Only Valmont knows her for the shrewd, scheming, and sexually active woman she is. "Conquer or perish" is the motto she lives by. As she admits to Valmont, she learned early on to desire only those things that would be useful to her. Love, passion, and sentimentality are not, apparently, useful.

But this is the 18th century, a time when women - even women as intelligent as the Marchioness - were treated like children. There were many obligations and few choices; for women of noble birth like Merteuil it was marriage or the convent. She did marry, once, but when her husband died she chose the liberty of widowhood over the tyranny of marriage:

"You do not know, Viscount, the reasons I never married again. It was not, I assure you, for want of several advantageous matches being offered to me; it was solely that no one should have a right to control me."

If this were just a story about a nasty, scheming woman and her equally nasty friend, it would not have

maintained its classical reputation for more than two centuries. But the Marchioness de Merteuil is a rich, complicated and essentially modern character.
A woman who has found a way to live life on her own terms. If she wasn't so completely heartless, so utterly devoid of any but utilitarian scruples, we might admire her.

As you can imagine, things don't go entirely as planned. When, after much letter-writing and several months, Valmont wins the heart of Tourvel, he is mocked by Merteuil for breaking the rules of the game: he was supposed to degrade the woman, not fall in love with her. Valmont denies it, but it's true: he loves Madame de Tourvel. Still, his pride is hurt. He drops Tourvel cold, plummeting her into a state of despair from which she will not recover.

By the end of the book, nobody - innocent or otherwise - has won. Reputations are in tatters, hearts are broken, and the Marchioness pays a catastrophic price for her audacity. Society is particularly unforgiving when women break the rules. Merteuil's crime is not that she's lived a morally ambiguous existence - most of her contemporaries have done the same - but that she's been found out. She loses her money, her reputation, and her looks, thanks to an attack of smallpox. The woman who would not submit to the dictates of the age has been completely and irretrievably humiliated.

Readers have long been divided over *Les Liaisons Dangereuses*. It's been seen as a paean to corruption - an expression of the libertine philosophy promulgated by writers like John Wilmot and the Marquis de Sade.

Others, considering the time it was written - seven years before the beginning of the French Revolution - view it as a political critique of a decadent and dying régime.

For me, the book is a window into another era - different rules, different expectations. And a reminder that we ignore the demands of our heart at our peril.

Week 25: *Wuthering Heights*, by Emily Brontë (1848)

"It is a compound of vulgar depravity and unnatural horrors."

So wrote an American critic upon publication of *Wuthering Heights*, Emily Brontë's first and only novel. He was not alone. Shock, disgust and bewilderment were the most common reactions, with one reviewer even suggesting the book should be burnt. Published under the pseudonym Ellis Bell, this dark, imaginative tale of the power of love to transcend the grave challenged almost every Victorian ideal of morality, justice, and heroic behaviour.

Had readers known the author was a woman, the reaction would have been stronger. But by the time the truth was revealed, thanks to a second edition published in 1850, Emily Brontë was dead of tuberculosis at the age of 30. Two sisters and a brother had died before her, and another was quick to follow. Her older sister Charlotte, the author of *Jane Eyre*, was left to mourn her sisters, and retrieve their public reputations.

While Charlotte believed her sister was a genius, she felt compelled to explain the book and its characters to outsiders - those readers who knew nothing of the author or the people who inhabited her part of the world. In a preface to the second edition she writes, "To all such people . . . 'Wuthering Heights' must appear a rude and strange production."

But her sister, she says, was not "rude and strange"; she was unworldly, reclusive, and shy:

"My sister Emily was not a person of demonstrative character . . . [her] disposition was not naturally gregarious; circumstances favoured and fostered her tendency to seclusion; except to go to church or take a walk on the hills, she rarely crossed the threshold of home. Though her feeling for the people round was benevolent, intercourse with them she never sought; nor, with very few exceptions, ever experienced."

It was this very isolation that nurtured Emily's romantic nature and gave birth to the wild, romantic and otherworldly tale set in the place she knew well - the bleak and beautiful Yorkshire moors.

The story begins in November 1801 when Mr. Lockwood, a rather vain and pretentious gentleman, rents Thrushcross Grange, a large house situated on the edge of the remote moors of West Yorkshire. On arrival, he decides to pay a visit to his landlord, who lives four miles away in the ancient manor house known as Wuthering Heights. The visit is not a success; the landlord, known only as Heathcliff, is dark, surly and unfriendly, with a temper that verges on violence. He does not welcome visitors and only reluctantly calls his dogs off when they attack. In spite of this cool reception, Lockwood pays a second visit a few days later. This time he meets the other occupants of the house: Hareton Earnshaw, a good-looking but coarse, quick-tempered, and illiterate young man; Catherine Linton, a beautiful but deeply unhappy young widow, and Joseph, an old servant who speaks with an almost indecipherable Yorkshire accent.

A blizzard prevents Lockwood from making the trek back to the Grange - reluctantly, Heathcliff agrees to let him stay for the night, and he's locked into a room that is never normally used. During the night he discovers a diary written years ago by Catherine Earnshaw, a young girl who seems to have a special relationship with the young Heathcliff. He falls into a troubled sleep and wakes to the sound of a tree branch brushing against the window. Still half asleep, he forces his hand through the glass, determined to remove the branch, and finds himself grasped by the cold, icy hand of a young woman, begging to be let in. In an effort to free himself, he rubs the ghostly hand against the broken glass till the blood runs onto the sheets. His terrified shouts finally alert his landlord, who enters the room, cursing him for the disturbance. But when Lockwood tells him the room is haunted, Heathcliff rushes to the window, calling out to Catherine, begging her to return. Lockwood decides that, storm or no storm, he's had enough of Wuthering Heights for one night. Heathcliff escorts him back to the Grange, where the servants are delighted to see that Lockwood is alive, having assumed he was lost in the storm.

Back in the safety of the Grange, Lockwood learns that his housekeeper, Nelly Dean, knows Wuthering Heights very well. She lived there as a child and grew up with the children of the house. He prevails on her to tell him the history of the manor and its strange inhabitants; she agrees to do so, and Lockwood writes the story from her recollections.

As she tells it, Heathcliff - whose origins are unknown - is found abandoned on the streets of Liverpool and brought back to the Heights by the kindly Mr.

Earnshaw. His own children, Hindley and Catherine, don't take to the "gypsy" child but gradually Heathcliff and Cathy form an attachment - an attachment that grows to the point where they become inseparable. They spend their days playing out on the moors; the greatest punishment for either of them is to keep them apart. Mr. Earnshaw, too, loves the boy - more so than his own son, which fosters even greater resentment on Hindley's part and strengthens the bond between Catherine and Heathcliff.

The break between them comes when Catherine chooses respectability over passion. She marries Edgar Linton, whose father owns Thrushcross Grange and who, although weak and tiresome, loves her and will make a "good" husband. The marriage doesn't last long: Catherine dies giving birth to a daughter - the Catherine Linton mentioned earlier - and Heathcliff is plunged into a dark well of despair verging on madness. Near the end of the book, he confesses to Lockwood that he is haunted by his lost love every minute of the day:

"[H]er features are shaped on the flags! In every cloud, in every tree - filling the air at night, and caught by glimpses in every object, by day I am surrounded with her image!"

In Catherine, Brontë created a heroine who was the embodiment of nature itself - tempestuous and pleasing by turns, afraid of nothing, living by her own rules. As Nelly describes her, "A wild, wick slip she was - but she had the bonniest eye, and sweetest smile, and lightest foot in the parish". You could not help but love her.

How different is this from the quiet, painfully shy author of the book - who lived within the bounds of a strictly religious household, the dutiful daughter of a parish curate? In her innermost heart I believe she nurtured a free-spirited creature - a child of nature unfettered by convention. Catherine was that creature.

It's telling, I think, that Brontë, the daughter of a curate, saves her most contemptuous descriptions for the character of Joseph, the old servant who sermonizes and preachifies at every turn. At one point she has Nelly Dean describe him thus: "He was, and is yet, most likely, the wearisomest, self-righteous pharisee that ever ransacked a Bible to rake the promises to himself, and fling the curses on his neighbours." As curates and other men of the church were their only suitable male companions, Brontë and her sisters likely knew them well. We can hope they were not all as "wearisome" as Joseph!

But it's the character of Heathcliff that fueled the moral and critical outrage over the book, and continued to do so for half a century. While he's as handsome and tormented as befits a romantic hero in the Gothic tradition, he's unremittingly cruel, sadistic and, quite frankly, evil. His behaviour is particularly hateful towards his son, Hareton, whom he's raising as an illiterate farm hand in revenge for past wrongs. Right to the end Heathcliff is dark and unrepentant; there is something almost ghoulish - vampirish - in the way he looks forward to the time when he will be dead and buried, reunited with his love, Catherine. Strong stuff, this, even for modern readers.

In her preface, Charlotte assures us that if Emily had lived longer "her mind would of itself have grown like a strong tree, loftier, straighter, wider-spreading". In other words, she would have matured to become a better writer. Still, she concedes the "very real powers" of the novel:

"Whether it is right or advisable to create beings like Heathcliff, I do not know; I scarcely think it is. But this I know; the writer who possesses the creative gift owns something of which he is not always master - something that at times strangely wills and works for itself."

It's regrettable that Emily Brontë didn't live to write other novels but I don't believe she could have written anything better. *Wuthering Heights* contains within it that unnatural beauty of expression few writers ever achieve. I hold it dear to my heart.

Week 26: *The Scarlet Letter*, by Nathaniel Hawthorne (1850)

I confess to having a link - an extremely tenuous one, I admit - to the author of *The Scarlet Letter*. Sarah Averill Wildes, my eighth great-aunt, was hanged on Gallows Hill in Salem, Massachusetts, on the 19th of July, 1692. Her crime, they said, was witchcraft. One of the men who sent her there was Nathaniel Hawthorne's ancestor, Justice Hathorne, the only judge who never repented of his actions. Hawthorne, the writer, is said to have changed the spelling of his name to distance himself from his notorious relative; I have long wanted to write about mine.

In his introduction, Hawthorne jokes that his Puritan ancestors would have found little to commend regarding his choice of occupation:

"No aim that I have ever cherished, would they recognize as laudable; no success of mine . . . would they deem otherwise than worthless, if not positively disgraceful. 'What is he?' murmurs one grey shadow of my forefathers to the other. 'A writer of story-books! What kind of a business in life, - what mode of glorifying God, or being serviceable to mankind in his day and generation, - may that be? Why, the degenerate fellow might as well have been a fiddler!'"

All joking aside, there's no doubt that Hawthorne was haunted by the shadow of his Puritan forebearers. You could say, in fact, that *The Scarlet Letter* was his rejoinder to the rigid, joyless conformity his ancestors preached, and frequently practiced.

The story is set in Boston in the 1640s, during the time when the colony was a Puritan settlement. Hester Prynne is a young married woman who has had an affair with a man she refuses to name, and has given birth to a child - a daughter whom she calls Pearl. In a patriarchal society such as this, adultery is a sin - more than that, it's a crime, and is punishable, in some cases, by death. In Hester's case, the judges have shown leniency: after spending some time in jail, she's taken out to the scaffold in the market square, along with her baby daughter, to be publicly humiliated. But the punishment doesn't end there: for the rest of her life, she will wear the letter "A", woven in scarlet and embroidered on her chest.

While she stands there, the object of censure of every man, woman, and child, she recognizes a figure in the crowd - an elderly stranger, standing near the back, small, slightly deformed, with one shoulder higher than the other. This, she realizes, is her missing husband, who sent her on ahead to America a few years back and was thought to be lost at sea. Now he has turned up, just in time to witness her mortification. He signals to her to show no sign of recognition - he does not want to be known as the cuckolded husband of an adulteress.

It becomes apparent, early on, that the man Hester will not name is the popular young minister, Arthur Dimmesdale, saintly and scholarly and wracked with guilt. Without admitting his part in the crime, he as much as begs Hester to reveal his name to the people. She refuses to do so and he lacks the courage to do it himself. While Hester bears her outward mark of punishment on her breast, Dimmesdale carries his inside - his growing guilt and agony takes its toll on his health, to the point where his followers fear for his life.

One man has guessed his secret, and spends years plotting his revenge. Hester's estranged husband, who now calls himself Roger Chillingworth - a cold name if ever there was one - sets himself up as a physician and works his way into Dimmesdale's confidence. While appearing to be trying to cure him, Chllingworth is actually bent on prying the truth out of the younger man. What he will do with that confession, if he receives it, is unclear. What is clear, however, is that his obsession with Dimmesdale has turned him into something of a monster; by the end of the book, Roger Chillingworth is a fiend, carrying out the work of the devil.

Hester is a strong and resilient character, but somewhat flat, I think. She's simply too good to be very interesting. Instead of leaving the community, which she certainly could do, she chooses to stay, living in a small cottage on the outskirts with her daughter and supporting them with her needlework. She becomes something of a saint, making clothing for the poor, turning the other cheek when she's reviled and rebuffed. While she's to be commended for the stoicism with which she accepts her punishment, it's hard to believe that such a saintly woman would have had illicit sex in the first place.

Her one retort to her critics is little Pearl, a lively and energetic spark who embodies everything the Puritans are not. Hester clothes her in scarlet dresses which she has elegantly embroidered with the same gold thread she used to outline the letter she wears. In her outspoken, and sometimes outlandish behaviour, Pearl is the embodiment of Hester's crime - and a living rebuke to those who judge her for it.

But it's the young minister, Arthur Dimmesdale, who takes up most of the story. Over a period of seven years we observe his struggle to come to terms with what he has done - to expiate himself in the eyes of his Lord. He believes himself to be a hypocrite, walking among his congregation as a kind of saint while harbouring an untold sin within his heart. His inability to reveal his secret is, quite literally, killing him. He grows weaker and more and more frail, in both mind and body.

We don't talk much about sin these days. We prefer to speak in terms of "human failings", "character flaws" and the like. Which may or may not be a good thing. The notion of sin has become rather outdated except by evangelical fundamentalists predicting the end of the world. Whether you believe in it or not, its nature, as demonstrated in the novel, is complex - who, in the end, are the sinners? Hawthorne suggests that the real sinners are the ones who point fingers - those who sit in judgment and cast the first stone. It is not, as the Puritans believed, the sin itself that destroys the individual, but the condemnation and censure that we bring to it.

Eventually, Dimmesdale, almost annihilated by his secret, chooses to make it public. Standing on the scaffold in the market square, Hester on one side and Pearl on the other, he confesses that he, too, is a sinner. He bares his chest to reveal - what? We're never sure. A stigma of some kind, similar to Hester's scarlet letter. Was it self-inflicted? Did Chillingworth, devil that he is, concoct some kind of poison to create it? Or is it merely the outward, visible manifestation of the man's inner torment?

Having - finally - proclaimed himself a sinner, the minister falls to his knees and dies. His archenemy and fellow victim, Roger Chillingworth, having no reason to live now that Dimmesdale is gone, dies shortly afterwards, leaving a large sum of money to Pearl. Hester and her daughter leave the colony, but Hester returns, years later, when Pearl is grown and married:

"Here had been her sin; here, her sorrow; and here was yet to be her penitence."

It may be outdated to say it, but I think there's a kind of beauty in that.

Week 27: *Sense and Sensibility*, by Jane Austen (1811)

There are those who are born to Austen, and those who come to her over time; I'm one of the latter. I managed to gain an Honours degree in English without reading a single Austen novel. I know - shocking! I had to be told that *Clueless* was a modern-day updating of *Emma*, more or less. I saw the movie *Becoming Jane* and enjoyed it (mostly because I adore James McAvoy) but was puzzled by *The Jane Austen Book Club*, which came out the same year. A book club devoted just to Austen? Really? Did this happen in real life?

The answer is yes, you idiot, of course. There are Jane Austen book clubs and Jane Austen wine clubs. There are Jane Austen societies all around the world. There are Jane Austen meetups where Janeites can trade Austen witticisms, drink tea from bone china and organize pilgrimages to Chawton, the Hampshire village where Austen spent the last eight years of her life. Two hundred years after her death, Jane Austen is one of the best known and most widely read novelists in the English language.

Austen lived and wrote during the Regency period, a time of huge upheaval both in England and abroad. The Luddites were smashing machinery, the Glasgow weavers were rioting, and England was at war with France. Very little of this, if any, is reflected in her novels. Instead they are preoccupied with manners - the social hierarchy - and, most of all, marriage. In particular, the marriage of respectable but impoverished young women to equally respectable but wealthier men.

Marrying well was essential to ensuring economic security as well as providing a proper place in the social pecking order. One must not simply marry, but marry well. Yet the heroines of Austen's novels tend to put their hearts above their purses. They are intelligent, sympathetic women who marry for love and are valued for those qualities by the husbands they choose. This may have happened more often than we think, or it may have been wishful thinking on the part of the writer. Austen herself never married, which probably tells us more about her actual thoughts on marriage than anything she wrote.

Sense and Sensibility, her first published novel, is the story of the Dashwood sisters - Elinor, Marianne and, to a lesser extent, Margaret, the youngest. The sisters are well-bred, well-read, and attractive. However, they have no fortune, which lowers their marital currency. They live in Norland Park, a large estate in the county of Sussex. Their great-uncle lived there with his sister; when she died, he invited her son, Henry, to bring his family to live there with him. While Henry has little money, the family lives in relative comfort thanks to his uncle's largesse. When the old man dies, however, he leaves Norland Park to John, Henry's son by a previous marriage. Henry, who now has no way of supporting his wife and daughters, dies a year later, after extracting a death-bed promise from John to look after his stepmother and three half-sisters.

Immediately after the funeral, John, his very unpleasant wife Fanny, and their four-year-old son establish themselves as the new owners of Norland Park. While John initially intends to keep his promise to his father, Fanny talks him out of giving them any money at all. She is, as Austen writes, "a strong caricature of [her husband]; more narrow-minded and selfish". Demoted to the status of guests in what was their former home, Mrs. Dashwood and her daughters would like to move out. But as they have nowhere to go and can't afford much, they stay put for the time being.

During that time, Elinor meets and falls in love with Fanny's brother, Edward Farrars. Edward is shy and not particularly handsome, but he has a good heart and none of his sister's snobbish aspirations. Although he doesn't come directly out with it, it becomes apparent that he's attracted to Elinor and she begins to nurture hopes of some kind of future proposal. Her sister Marianne upbraids her for not being more passionate but Elinor, always the more cautious of the two, hesitates to admit to more than "liking" and "esteeming" Edward, as she's unsure if the affection is mutual.

Six months after their father's death, a distant cousin, Sir John Middleton, invites the girls and their mother to come to Devonshire and stay with him and his wife at Barton Park until they find a home of their own. Elinor is sad to be leaving Edward but they all agree the move is essential, given their situation. They will miss Norland, but for Mrs. Dashwood there are simply too many memories there; they need a new start.

Sir John is a brash, jovial fellow, while his wife, Lady Middleton, is as cold and distant as Fanny Dashwood. (When the two eventually meet, it's a case of like meets like: "There was a kind of cold-hearted selfishness on both sides, which mutually attracted them; and they sympathised with each other in an insipid propriety of demeanour, and a general want of understanding.") Lady Middleton's mother, Mrs. Jennings, is more like her son-in-law in temperament: she's cheerful, friendly and kind, but inclined to be overly intrusive. Marianne finds her unspeakably coarse and vulgar, and makes little effort to be amenable; Elinor, on the other hand, while having no illusions about her hosts, manages to treat them with courtesy and, in the case of Sir John and Mrs. Jennings, even affection.

While at Barton Park the Dashwoods make several new acquaintances, one of whom, the retired Colonel Brandon, falls in love with Marianne. Brandon is a quiet bachelor in his late 30s; 17-year-old Marianne quite naturally dismisses him as old and uninteresting. When Elinor suggests that an older woman might find him attractive, Marianne agrees this could be a possibility. After all, she says, a woman of 27 "can never hope to feel or inspire affection again".

Instead, Marianne falls desperately in love with John Willoughby, a handsome young man who is visiting his aunt on a nearby property. Willoughby is - or at least appears to be - everything Marianne has ever wished for in a beau. He's handsome, gallant, and romantic; they share similar tastes in art, music and poetry; they go for long walks in the countryside and play duets on the pianoforte. Her mother entertains hope of an early marriage, but Elinor isn't convinced. As far as she knows, Willoughby has not actually proposed. And, like Austen, she's not dazzled by appearances.

After two weeks of an intense, whirlwind courtship, Willoughby suddenly and unexpectedly announces that he is leaving. He gives no reason for his departure and refuses to elaborate. Marianne is devastated. She falls into a state of mourning deeper, it seems, than was occasioned by the death of her father.

Meanwhile, two recently discovered relations turn up as guests of Mrs. Jennings. They are Nancy and Lucy Steele and it's obvious from the outset that they're what you might call opportunists. Lucy, the younger sister, confides a secret to Elinor: she has been secretly engaged to Edward Farrars for a year. Elinor is shocked and hurt, but manages to hide her feelings from Lucy. Sworn to secrecy, she tells no one, not even Marianne.

So there you have two sisters, both heartbroken and somewhat betrayed, dealing with their pain in very different ways. Elinor, the "sensible" one, keeps her feelings to herself, maintaining - as far as possible - a calm, composed demeanour. Marianne, on the other hand, is all passion. She shrieks her agony to the rooftops, cries piteously for days, and even, occasionally, succumbs to fits. It's not that her pain is greater than her sister's; it's simply that Austen is illustrating two sides of a coin. And while it's easy to conclude that Austen is making a case for sense over sensibility, her compassion for Marianne shows that she knew and understood the nature of grief all too well.

What you really need to know about Austen is that she's simply great fun to read. She was a shrewd observer of character and a brilliant critic of conventional norms. Her satiric take on social situations seems as relevant today as it did 200 years ago:

"Conversation [was not lacking], for Sir John was very chatty, and Lady Middleton had taken the wise precaution of bringing with her their eldest child, a fine little boy about six years old; by which means there was one subject always to be recurred to by the ladies in case of extremity, for they had to enquire his name and age, admire his beauty, and ask him questions which his mother answered for him... On every formal visit a child ought to be of the party, by way of provision for discourse. In the present case it took up ten minutes to determine whether the boy were most like his father or mother, and in what particular he resembled either, for of course every body differed, and every body was astonished at the opinion of the others."

Brilliant.

Week 28: *Little Women*, by Louisa May Alcott (1868 and 1869)

Concord, Massachusetts in the mid-19th century was an exciting place to be, if you were of a thoughtful bent. For a small town, it was home to a substantial collection of philosophers and writers, the most prominent being Ralph Waldo Emerson, one of the leading lights of the Transcendentalist movement. Emerson's neighbours included Henry David Thoreau, Nathaniel Hawthorne, and the philosopher, reformer, and teacher, Amos Bronson Alcott, whose daughter, Louisa May, wrote the classic *Little Women*.

If you, like me, were an adolescent girl in the early 1960s, you no doubt read *Little Women* and enjoyed it. I certainly did. I identified strongly with Jo, the bookworm, although I wasn't a tomboy like her. For a long time I could recite whole passages of the book, and I remember being very affected by the death of one of the sisters, shy little Beth. I would say that Jo's journey into the world of writing and publishing was at least one of several early incentives I experienced to become a writer.

Which is why it grieves me to say I *really* wish I hadn't re-read it for the purposes of this blog.

First, the summary. Published in two volumes, *Little Women* is the story of a family of girls - Meg, Jo, Beth, and Amy March - who live in genteel poverty with their mother, their servant, and their father, who is away serving as a chaplain to the Union forces during the American civil war. Meg, the oldest, is the pretty one - she's modest and conventional, and most like her mother in temperament. Jo is the "man of the house" - she wishes she was a boy and hates all things "girly". Beth is a shy little homebody, with a gift for music. In a foreshadowing of her early death, Alcott writes:

"There are many Beths in the world, shy and quiet, sitting in corners till needed, and living for others so cheerfully that no one sees the sacrifices till the little cricket on the hearth stops chirping, and the sweet, sunshiny presence vanishes, leaving silence and shadow behind."

Amy, the youngest, is a budding artist. She's pretty, graceful, and ambitious: "Her little airs and graces were much admired, so were her accomplishments, for besides her drawing, she could play twelve tunes, crochet, and read French without mispronouncing more than two-thirds of the words."

The two older girls work outside the home to earn money: Meg teaches the children of a neighbouring family, and Jo acts as a companion and helper to her crotchety Aunt March. Beth stays home and helps with the housework, and Amy attends school. Although all four girls revere their father and regard him as the fount of all wisdom, their mother, Marmee, is the mainstay of the family. Her advice, frequently but kindly offered, guides all their actions.

When the story opens, the girls are bemoaning the approach of a very frugal Christmas - as Jo says, "Christmas won't be Christmas without any presents." The family has recently moved into a poorer neighbourhood, their father having lost all his money, and their circumstances are much reduced. Each of the girls struggles with a particular challenge: Meg longs for past luxuries, Jo is impulsive and quick to anger, Beth is far too shy, and Amy is selfish. Their mother reminds them that when they were young they used to play *Pilgrim's Progress*, working their way from the cellar, which was the City of Destruction, to the rooftop, which was the Celestial City. She suggests they play the game now for real, bearing their burdens cheerfully as Christian did, and this becomes the theme of the narrative.

While the book is not strictly autobiographical, it's clear that Alcott based much of it on her own family and her experiences growing up in Concord. Like Jo, she had three sisters, one of whom, Elizabeth, died young after a lengthy illness. The oldest sister, Meg, is based on Anna, who was dutiful, self-sacrificing, and conformed to the model of Victorian womanhood. Her youngest sister, Abigail May, provided the model for Amy. Like Amy, she moved to Europe and studied sculpture, sketching and painting and eventually came into her own as a copyist and a painter of still life.

As for Louisa May, she, like Jo, was a tomboy who preferred running wildly through the countryside to sitting nicely and being a "lady". She once confided to an interviewer, "I am more than half-persuaded that I am a man's soul put by some freak of nature into a woman's body ... because I have fallen in love with so many pretty girls and never once the least bit with any man." She was an abolitionist and a feminist; having read and admired the "Declaration of Sentiments" published by the Seneca Falls Convention on women's rights, she became the first woman to register to vote in a Concord school board election. She never married and various scholars have speculated about her sexuality. At the very least I think it's fair to say Alcott was a more complex and compelling character than any of the women in her book.

It's interesting to me that she didn't particularly like *Little Women*. She was encouraged to write it by her publisher who wanted her to come up with a girls' book that would have widespread appeal. She agreed but loathed the process: "I plod away," she wrote in her diary, "although I don't enjoy this sort of thing."

Nor do I. If I didn't admire the woman herself, which I do, and hadn't loved the book so much, which I did, I'd be tempted to conclude that *Little Women* is a compilation of sentimental homilies written to convince little girls that the point of growing up is to be submissive, subservient and meek - none of which the author believed for a moment. If the little girls of 1868 accepted that - and many, many didn't - I can guarantee you it won't resonate with a child of today.

Yes, Alcott gave us Jo, the rebel, the female anti-hero. But Jo marries in the end and Marmee gets the last word: surrounded by her children, her grandchildren, and her husband, she reaches out her arms and cries, "Oh, my girls, however long you may live, I never can wish you a greater happiness than this!"

Coda:

Ten *Little Women* homilies, taken entirely out of context, offered here for your edification, without editorial comment:

Work is a blessed solace.

Rich people have about as many worries as poor ones.

It's nice to have accomplishments and be elegant, but not to show off or get perked up.

Women should learn to be agreeable, particularly poor ones, for they have no other way of repaying the kindnesses they receive.

A kiss for a blow is always best, though it's not very easy to give it sometimes.

Don't neglect husband for children, don't shut him out of the nursery, but teach him how to help in it.

Rich people's children often need care and comfort, as well as poor.

Wrongdoing always brings its own punishment.

A woman's happiest kingdom is home, her highest honor the art of ruling it not as a queen, but as a wise wife and mother.

Christmas won't be Christmas without any presents.

Week 29: *Great Expectations*, by Charles Dickens (1861)

What is it about coming to the end of one calendar year and beginning a new one that leads us to think our lives are going to improve? We go to bed shortly after midnight brimming with great expectations and too much eggnog, and wake up the next morning the same person, in the same body, feeling perhaps a little rough around the edges. By the end of January the resolution to transform ourselves has faded, and we've mostly accepted that we are who we are, for better or worse. Which is probably a good thing.

Speaking for myself, I'm contemplating the new year with rather diminished expectations. This is partly the result of my own personal losses and partly due to a year of "fake news", bizarre presidential tweets, and egregious missteps by men wielding power. If we can get to the end of 2018 without it all being smashed to smithereens - well, that at least will be something.

At any rate, it seems appropriate to begin the new year with Charles Dickens' penultimate completed novel, *Great Expectations*. I first made my way through my grandmother's collection of Dickens when I was 12. Like her, I still go back to Dickens when I'm short of things to read. And they're just as satisfying. The story of young Pip and his misguided aspirations is one of my favourites. The image of Miss Havisham in her faded, decrepit wedding gown stands out for most people, but there are so many strong characters: cruel but beautiful Estella, trained to toy with Pip and break his heart; the terrifying man in the marshes, trapped in a leg iron, who secretly plays such a vital role in Pip's life; the gentlemanly Herbert Pocket, passionate and inept, but always hopeful of making his fortune, and the mild, sweet-natured Joe Gargery, Pip's brother-in-law and surrogate father. They are the kind of characters who become friends as you read them, and linger on afterwards. In my case, for a lifetime.

The story opens on Christmas Eve in the early years of the 19th century. Young Pip, an orphan, lives with his fierce sister and her kindly husband, Joe, who is the local blacksmith. While visiting his parents' graves in the churchyard Pip is set upon by an escaped convict who frightens him into returning the next morning with some food and a file. Terrified to disobey, Pip does as he's told, keeping it a secret from everyone, even Joe, who's his closest friend and ally. The convict is later recaptured while fighting with a fellow escapee who claims the first one is trying to murder him.

A year or two later, Pip is invited to Satis House, a dilapidated mansion owned by the wealthy and eccentric Miss Havisham, an elderly spinster, and her adopted daughter, Estella. Miss Havisham has decided she wants a boy come to the house to play and asks Mr. Pumblechook to find someone suitable. When Pip arrives he sees that everything in Satis House, including Miss Havisham, is decayed and crumbling. She wears the wedding dress she wore on the morning of her wedding day, when she received word that her husband-to-be had broken the engagement. The clocks are stopped at twenty to nine; the wedding cake is home to spiders and mice; beetles and other vermin have ravaged the wedding feast. All is in tatters and ruins, including Miss Havisham. She orders Pip to play cards with Estella. He does so, becoming aware for the first time that his speech is coarse, his manners are rough, and that he is "a common labouring-boy . . . [and] was in a low-lived bad way".

These visits continue until Pip is old enough to be apprenticed to Joe in the forge. Once he looked forward eagerly to this; now, however, he finds it a demeaning occupation and dreams of finding a way to somehow improve his circumstances. In the meantime, Pip's sister is attacked by an unknown assailant who delivers a blow to her head, injuring her to the point where she can no longer speak properly or do more than sit and smile by the fireplace. For Pip, this is not entirely a bad thing, as she was given to taking out her rages by beating him with a stick. Joe, however, is devastated, and simple, kind-hearted Biddy moves in with them to help. Biddy is everything Estella is not - sweet, caring, and down-to-earth. Bright and energetic, she cares for Pip and teaches him to read and write. Until he leaves home she's his friend, his confidant, and his tutor.

Four years into his apprenticeship, a lawyer, the inscrutable Mr. Jaggers, arrives with the news that an unnamed person has provided money so that Pip can become a gentleman. Pip assumes his benefactor is Miss Havisham; he also assumes it is Miss Havisham's intention that he and Estella should marry one day.

Pip then leaves the forge and settles into life in London with the amiable Herbert Pocket, who happens to be Miss Havisham's nephew. Together they fall into bad habits, spending more than they have and acquiring a great deal of debt. While this occasionally bothers them, Herbert feels sure he will soon rise in business, and Pip clings to his expectations of wealth.

In his biography of Dickens, Peter Ackroyd calls *Great Expectations* a novel of "the folly of spendthrift youth": "Dickens was a man of infinite nostalgia about himself; what is real, and what remained real for him, is the ambitious boy moving through adolescence to maturity." He had enormous expectations of himself, and his energy, which was surely greater than most people's, was at least partly driven by the spectre of poverty and debt which haunted his childhood. It's no stretch of the imagination to argue that Dickens worked all his life to distance himself, not altogether successfully, from his feckless, improvident father who "all but ruined his family through his own negligence and incompetence".

And so we have Pip, ashamed of his working-class roots, striving to "better" himself by adopting the clothes, manners and paraphernalia of a gentleman. In his new life there is a certain hatred of his past, as there was with Dickens. The author knew, however, that we never escape our pasts, and it is fitting that Magwitch, the convict in the marshes, eventually returns to confront Pip with the shocking, shameful truth: it is he, and not Miss Havisham, who is the benefactor of his good fortune. He has abandoned Joe and Biddy, and given up most of what is good and honest and true, for a chimera.

In the end, the lesson of the story may be that while expectations are all well and good, the greater they are the more likely they are to lead us astray.

Week 30: *Love in a Cold Climate*, by Nancy Mitford (1949)

Are you old enough to remember the Wayback machine? I mean, before it became the name for an archive of web pages on the internet? The original Wayback machine was a plot device on *The Rocky and Bullwinkle* cartoon show; Mr. Peabody, the world's smartest beagle, and his pet boy, Sherman, would set the machine to a particular time and place in history, walk in, and before you could say "Snidely Whiplash" they were back in time.

I was 10 when I first saw the show, and, like most of my friends, I assumed it was just a matter of time before the Wayback machine, or something like it, would become a reality. In the near future we would all be getting three-course meals out of pill jars and letting robots do the ironing. I was *really* happy about the ironing.

I mention this because if they ever do get a handle on time travel, I know exactly where I want to go: back to Oxfordshire, England, in the early 20th century, and hang out with the Mitfords. I've been fascinated with the six Mitford sisters since I bought or was given a copy of Selina Shirley Hastings' biography of Nancy Mitford in the mid 1980s. At about the same time I read Jonathan Guiness' *The House of Mitford* and, quite a bit later, *The Letters of Nancy Mitford and Evelyn Waugh*, compiled by Charlotte Mosley. By the time I got around to reading the books they wrote themselves, I felt I knew Nancy, Jessica and Deborah quite well. (I'm not sure that Pamela ever wrote anything, and I wasn't terribly interested in getting to

126

know Diana and Unity, both of whom were ardent fascists. Diana married Sir Oswald Mosely, the leader of the British Union of Fascists, and Unity was so in love with Hitler she tried to kill herself when England declared war on Germany.)

Quite a lot has been written about the Mitfords, both by themselves and others - they must be the most written-about siblings since the Brontës - and most of it can be found on Wikipedia. There's no point in taking up a lot of space here with details about the family except to say they've been described as outrageous, appalling and overprivileged. They were all that. They were also funny, stylish, daring and smart - well, except for poor Unity, who got the wrong end of the stick about just about everything.

My favourite has always been Nancy, the oldest sister, who. like Jessica, made her living as a writer and journalist. And my favourite books of hers are the three novels she wrote inspired by her own unconventional childhood: *The Pursuit of Love* (1945), *Love in a Cold Climate* (1949), and *Don't Tell Alfred* (1960). She wrote other books before and since, but it's this trilogy that captures a time and place that seems fragile and distant and it's these three books that continue to resonate with modern readers.

The fictional narrator of all three books is Fanny Logan, whose mother, the Bolter (they call her that because she's been married so often) has left her in the care of her Aunt Emily and Uncle David. Fanny divides her time between them and another set of cousins, the Radletts, at their stately home in Oxfordshire. Like the Mitfords, the Radletts have an extensive pedigree, going back to the Norman Conquest. Their mother, Aunt Sadie, is affectionate but ineffectual, and their father, Uncle Matthew, is an eccentric and rather terrifying blowhard who generally notices his children only to bellow at them.

The children have the run of the house. None of the girls go to school, leaving them plenty of time to form secret societies and plot new ways to tease their mother. Not much is expected of them until they're at an age to "come out", at which point they'll attend a series of debutante balls, be presented at Court, and officially enter Society. Again, this seems to be pretty much as things were in the Mitford household. And while the Radlett children are not well educated in a formal way, they have lively, curious minds and grow into lively, curious women. As did Nancy and her sisters.

In *Love in a Cold Climate* we meet another, more distant cousin: Polly Hampton, the only daughter of Lord and Lady Montdore. Polly is a beautiful girl - as Fanny tells us, her beauty is her outstanding characteristic:

"She was one of those people you cannot think of except in regard to their looks, which in her case were unvarying, independent of clothes, of age, of circumstances, and even of health. When ill or tired she merely looked fragile, but never yellow, withered or diminished; she was born beautiful and never, at any time when I knew her, went off or became less beautiful, but on the contrary her looks always steadily improved."

The Montdores are one of the wealthiest families in England. When Fanny is invited to come and stay with them she's torn between her affection for Polly and her dread of doing or saying the wrong thing. Lady Montdore is a formidable creature - ambitious, vain, pompous and outspoken. A list of the food served in the household reminds one that there was a time when people with money regularly ate a seven-course meal. The fact that they weren't all immensely obese can only be attributed to the fact that much of it was left on their plates. And, of course, this was before fast food turned us into gluttons.

But back to Polly. Given their wealth and her daughter's beauty, Lady Montdore has high hopes for an important marriage in the future, preferably to someone with a title. Even the new King of England is not beyond reach, she feels. But Polly won't play along. She shows no interest in any of the eligible men she meets and her coming-out season is a flop. When her father's sister, Lady Patricia, dies, the truth comes out - Polly has, for most of her life, been pining for her lecherous, much older uncle - her aunt's husband. With Patricia gone, Polly sees a way to make her dream come true, and, against the advice of every single person she knows, she goes for it. With predictably disastrous consequences.

Fanny, I believe, speaks with Nancy Mitford's voice. She may not be intended to *be* Nancy, exactly, but the tone is so what you'd expect of a "bright young thing" of the 1920s. Witty, a little cynical, willing to be amused, but also, as my father used to say, calling a spade a spade. Mitford might not dig deep into the psychological motivations of her characters - thank goodness! - but she is unafraid to show us the shadows behind the laughter. When Polly's baby dies shortly after birth, Fanny is prepared to offer heartfelt sympathy, being, by this time, a mother herself. But Polly seems unmoved; the baby's death is more of a relief, apparently, than anything. We can hear Nancy's voice in the background, lamenting the coldness of a woman who would give more thought to ordering a new outfit than the death of a child.

Love in a Cold Climate is all about love - pursuing it, discussing it, and, eventually, finding it. In the end, though, love proves unsatisfying. As it was, I believe, for Mitford. She had a long, unrequited love affair with Hamish St. Clair Erskine, who was gay and eventually married someone else. She married Peter Rodd on the rebound, who was irresponsible and unfaithful, frequently with women she knew. And Gaston Palewski, the French general she considered the love of her life, kept her mostly at arms' length for decades.

At one point Alfred, Fanny's husband, offers this criticism: "General subjects do not amuse you, only personalities." I'd stake my life on that being a direct quote by some man Mitford knew - hopefully not someone she loved.

Week 31: *A Confederacy of Dunces*, by John Kennedy Toole (1980)

Right off the bat I have to tell you that *A Confederacy of Dunces* is not - I repeat, *not* - about the American presidency. How could it be? Its author died in 1969, when Donald Trump was 23, long before anyone could have predicted that this draft-dodging ladies' man would one day be the 45th President of the United States.

No, for an inside look at the chaos and confusion of Trump's presidency you'll have to read *Fire and Fury: Inside the Trump White House*, by Michael Wolff. It's mesmerizing. As is John Kennedy Toole's posthumous bestseller, published in 1980, 11 years after his suicide, thanks to the unrelenting efforts of his mother and the writer she successfully badgered to read the manuscript. Since then, *Dunces* has won the Pulitzer Prize for Fiction, sold 1.5 million copies, and been translated into 18 languages. This for a book that was considered, by almost every publisher, editor and literary agent, to be unpublishable. (Take heart, all writers striving to get your books in print - and be kind to your mothers!)

In *Dunces*, Toole created a handful of intensely memorable characters, all of them failures in one way or another. There is Darlene, the B-girl who dreams of being an exotic dancer; Mancuso, the patrolman in danger of being kicked off the force for incompetence; Gus Levy, who inherited his father's clothing business and allowed it to fall into ruin; and Mr. Clyde, the owner of Paradise Vendors, who sells hot dogs consisting of "rubber, cereal, tripe. Who knows? I wouldn't touch one of them myself." Burma Jones, the floor sweeper at the Night of Joy bar, compares himself to a plantation slave - working for less than minimum wage, he risks being jailed for vagrancy if he quits.

At the centre of this circle of misfits we have the failed genius - Ignatius J. Reilly, "a man of huge appetites and extraordinary erudition". Conceited, opinionated, delusional, and flatulent, Ignatius is an obese slob who lives with his widowed mother. He has a master's degree in medieval culture and a history of academic excellence. He also has a problem with his digestive system, due to his gargantuan appetite for junk food. His hero is Boethius, the Roman senator and philosopher - yes, I had to look him up - who wrote the seminal influence on medieval thought, *The Consolation of Philosophy*. Although he did some teaching in the past, at the time the book opens Ignatius hasn't worked for several years. Most days he lies in bed eating, belching, and filling page after notebook page with deep thoughts on how the world has deteriorated since Fortuna, the goddess of luck, turned on humanity: "Having once been so high," he writes, "humanity fell so low. What was once dedicated to the soul was now dedicated to the sale."

When Ignatius does venture out - to the movies, generally, in order to bark scathing remarks at the screen - his appearance is, well, eccentric. He favours a green hunting cap with ear flaps (to keep out the cold), voluminous tweed trousers, a plaid flannel shirt and brown suede desert boots that have seen better days: "The outfit was acceptable by any theological and geometrical standards, however abstruse, and suggested a rich inner life."

An unfortunate encounter with Mancuso, the patrolman, followed by an accident with his mother's car, forces Ignatius to get out of bed and, reluctantly, look for work. He lands a job at what may possibly be the worst clothing manufacture company in the history of fiction - not that I'm aware of any others. The office of Levy Pants is home to the deeply ineffective Gonzalez, the office manager, and the decrepit Miss Trixie, the assistant accountant who falls asleep at her desk, dreaming of retirement. Ignatius, hired to do the filing, dumps the files in the waste-basket and concentrates on inciting the factory workers to stage a palace coup. When this ends in disaster, Ignatius is fired and forced, by his mother, to find another job.

Against his better judgement, he agrees to work as a hot dog vendor. Hoping to appeal to the tourists in the French Quarter, his boss insists he wear a pirate's costume. The tourists are unimpressed, Ignatius eats most of the profits, and things, as you'd expect, end badly. Both of these jobs, by the way, are drawn from the author's experience: while at university Toole filled in for a friend working as a hot tamale vendor; he also worked for a family-owned-and-operated clothing factory.

It wouldn't be fair to call *Dunces* biographical, exactly, but we can say that John Kennedy Toole knew well the people he wrote about. The book is consistently praised for its rich depiction of the city of New Orleans and accurate representation of local dialects. Toole, like his hero, excelled academically; he won a scholarship to Tulane University and then spent a year studying English at Columbia University while teaching at Hunter College. He continued to teach right up to his death, and his colleagues and students certainly provided fodder for some of the best satire in the book. Myra Minkoff, the Jewish free-love advocate and former classmate who acts as his nemesis and muse, is as far to the left on the political spectrum as Ignatius is to the right. When his mother suggests he's leaning towards communism, Ignatius is indignant:

"Do you think that I want to live in a communal society with people like that Battaglia acquaintance of yours, sweeping streets and breaking up rocks or whatever it is people are always doing in those blighted countries? What I want is a good strong monarchy with a tasteful and decent king who has some knowledge of theology and geometry and to cultivate a Rich Inner Life."

A Confederacy of Dunces has been hailed as a comic masterpiece, and it is definitely very funny. But its hero is also one of the loneliest characters in fiction. There's a scene near the end where a group of partygoers are making fun of him as he attempts to make a speech:

"There Ignatius stood like the boy on the burning deck. . . . [He] felt as alone as he had felt on the dark day in high school when in a chemistry laboratory his experiment had exploded, burning his eyebrows off and frightening him. The shock and terror had made him wet his pants, and no one in the laboratory would notice him, not even the instructor . . . For the remainder of that day, as he walked soggily around the school, everyone had pretended that he was invisible." That paragraph says more about Ignatius, and perhaps more about the author, than a dozen pompous speeches.

Toole, like Ignatius, had a complicated and difficult relationship with his mother. She was his first fan, as mothers often are, and truly believed in his greatness. When he was young she chose his friends and kept him away from his cousins on his father's side, deciding they were too common for him to consort with. She encouraged his talents, which were prodigious, and believed him to be a genius. When her son committed suicide by the side of the road just outside Biloxi, Mississippi, Thelma Toole fell into a deep depression for two years. When she recovered, she retrieved the manuscript of *Dunces* from the top of the armoire in her son's bedroom and set out to find a publisher. For five years she was turned down by everyone, just as her son had been. Eventually, she found a writer, Walker Percy, who reluctantly agreed to read it. To his amazement, he found that she was right - the book was a masterpiece. And eventually he convinced Louisiana State University to publish it.

A Confederacy of Dunces is not the most satisfying read. The story goes nowhere and there's no proper ending. But the characters - Ignatius J. Reilly, Myrna Minkoff, Burma Jones, Miss Trixie - are among the most vivid I've ever read. The mind that created them well deserves his place in the canon of great Southern literature. A pity we lost him so soon.

Week 32: *Lord of the Flies*, by William Golding (1954)

It kept coming to me while reading Michael Wolff's *Fire and Fury: Inside the Trump White House* - the similarities between the chaos, duplicity and treachery taking place in Washington and William Golding's tale of a group of children marooned on a tropical island. *Lord of the Flies* is a world without grown-ups - as, it would seem, is the current West Wing.

Inspired by Golding's experiences during World War II, *Lord of the Flies* tells the story of a group of schoolboys who are being evacuated from England during a fictional atomic war. Their plane is shot down somewhere over a tropical island in the Pacific and only the children survive. (Why the plane, departing from England, is anywhere near the Pacific Ocean is never explained.) There has been a storm, which washed the wreckage of the plane out to sea; now, in its aftermath, two of the boys, Ralph and Piggy, meet up on the beach.

When they discover a large, cream-coloured conch shell floating among the weeds, Peggy suggests that Ralph blow into it to summon the others. With Piggy's instructions, Ralph is eventually able to create a deep, harsh booming sound that reverberates across the island. Slowly, in groups of twos and threes, the children appear out of the foliage, in various stages of undress:

"Some were naked and carrying their clothes; others half-naked, or more or less dressed in school uniforms, grey, blue, fawn, jacketed, or jerseyed. There were badges, mottoes even, stripes of color in stockings and pullovers. Their heads clustered above the trunks in the green shade; heads brown, fair, black, chestnut, sandy, mouse-colored; heads muttering, whispering, heads full of eyes that watched Ralph and speculated. Something was being done."

The assembled boys include a school choir, all dressed in black, led by a tall older boy named Jack; he and Ralph immediately stand out as natural leaders. But Ralph holds the conch, he's the one who has summoned them, and when it comes to a vote it's Ralph who's chosen to be chief. As a sop to Jack's pride, Ralph decides that Jack and his choir will hunt food for the group.

In the beginning the boys are excited to have the island to themselves -"No grownups!" But Piggy, who is sidelined because he's overweight, asthmatic and wears glasses, is more thoughtful. He reminds them that the adults, as far as they know, are all dead, having being killed in the bombing: "Nobody don't know we're here. Your dad don't know, nobody don't know--" His lips quivered and the spectacles were dimmed with mist. "We may stay here till we die."

Ralph announces that they must build a fire on the top of the mountain and keep it burning. Smoke will give a signal to any passing ship - smoke is their only hope of rescue. At this stage, the boys are fired with enthusiasm for having proper rules - meetings will be held on a makeshift platform, and the one holding the conch will speak without interruption. Rules are important, after all; in the absence of adults, rules will keep them safe.

Some of them, however, fear they're not safe. There's a beast, says one of the younger boys. It comes in the night and disappears in the morning. Although the older boys scoff and try to laugh it off, it leaves an impression. When the body of the downed pilot, trapped in his parachute, is discovered in the dark, rising and falling in the wind, the boys are led to believe the horrifying truth: the Beast is real. And it is terrifying.

The description of the hunters' first kill is a nightmare of violence and bloodlust. The pig is a sow; one moment she's dozing peacefully in the sun, nursing her piglets, the next she's being sliced and hacked and butchered to death. Afterwards, they sharpen a stick at both ends and impale the head of the sow on it, a gift for the Beast:

". . . the head hung there, a little blood dribbling down the stick. Instinctively the boys drew back too; and the forest was very still. They listened, and the loudest noise was the buzzing of flies over the spilled guts."

After this, the division sharpens between Jack and his hunters, intent on finding more pigs to kill, and Ralph's followers who want to build shelters, keep the fire going and abide by the rules of the conch. The hunters become more and more "savage", painting themselves in mud and charcoal, while Ralph and Piggy cling to what they remember of civilization. "The world, that understandable and lawful world, was slipping away." Roger, at one point, starts throwing stones at a "littleun", being careful not to hit him:

"Here, invisible yet strong, was the taboo of the old life. Round the squatting child was the protection of parents and school and policemen and the law. Roger's arm was conditioned by a civilization that knew nothing of him and was in ruins."

Jack becomes a symbol for evil . . . for why things "break up", as Ralph puts it. But Simon, the mystic, lost in a hallucinatory conversation with the pig's head - the Lord of the Flies - knows otherwise:

"'Fancy thinking the Beast was something you could hunt and kill!" said the head. For a moment or two the forest and all the other dimly appreciated places echoed with the parody of laughter. "You knew, didn't you? I'm part of you? Close, close, close! I'm the reason why it's no go? Why things are what they are?"

Simon rushes to tell the others: there is no beast, the evil is within them. He blunders into the middle of a ritual celebratory dance by the hunters and is murdered. The others - Piggy and Ralph, and the twins, Sam and Eric - tell themselves Simon's death is not their fault. They weren't part of the murderous dance that destroyed Simon. It was an accident, Piggy says. It was dark, they were scared - there's no good to be got from thinking about it. They create a new version of the facts, one they can live with. One that suits their purposes.

Right to the end, up to the moment when he realizes Jack means to kill him, Ralph calls it a game - Jack and his hunters aren't playing fair, they're not playing by the rules. Rules created by adults in a sensible, civilized society. An English society, of course, which has no use for "savage" behaviour. Piggy, holding the conch, the talisman of sense, of law and order, demands: "Which is better--to be a pack of painted Indians like you are, or to be sensible like Ralph is?"

Fear and anarchy win out. The leadership changes; in Jack, the new chief, we have a vision of authority without responsibility. Authority as it might be envisioned by a child. A spoiled, impulsive child, lacking compassion. Those who refuse to fall in with the new order are outcasts, despised and derided by the group. They are "the other"; as such, they're fair game for insults, ostracism, even death.

Sound familiar?

Week 33: *The Bell Jar*, by Sylvia Plath (1963)

"It was a queer, sultry summer, the summer they electrocuted the Rosenbergs . . ."

So begins *The Bell Jar*, with an opening sentence that foreshadows events to come. Such a sentence promises the reader we are in for a remarkable story. If only the book lived up to that promise. If only its author had lived to write other, better books. If only.

The Bell Jar was first published in London in 1963 under the pseudonym Victoria Lucas. Ostensibly, Sylvia Plath didn't want her mother and other family and friends to be hurt by the way they were pictured. Friends have said she would never have wanted the book to come out under her own name while her mother was alive.

But there were other reasons to hide behind a *nom de plume*. Plath questioned the literary value of the book. She confided to a friend that she thought of it as a pot boiler, "an autobiographical apprentice work which I had to write in order to free myself from the past". For someone who had been receiving accolades for her poems and short stories since her college days, this semi-autobiographical novel wasn't serious enough to meet her own literary expectations. In spite of the warm critical reception the book has maintained over the years - in spite of my own respect for Plath as a woman and a writer - I think her instincts were right. As a coming-of-age narrative *The Bell Jar* is not in the same class as *The Catcher in the Rye*, *A Tree Grows in Brooklyn*, or *To Kill a Mockingbird*. She had better books in her, I know - it's tragic that she didn't live to write them.

We tend to speak of Plath in hushed tones. She was a gifted poet who suffered from depression all her life. She was institutionalized on several occasions and was treated multiple times with electroconvulsive therapy. *The Bell Jar*, while not strictly a memoir, is autobiographical in all the ways that matter.

I first read it in my twenties. I had my own struggles with depression and I was profoundly affected by Plath's description of undergoing shock treatment. It seemed a barbaric procedure - it still does. But these scenes don't occur until we're more than halfway through the book. For the first hundred pages or so the writing is rather precious. It has the self-conscious cleverness of a university English major. I kept feeling I was a reluctant guest at a party of young people - students, I guess - all having what they assumed were witty, original conversations about issues that ceased to be interesting to me about three decades ago.

Esther Greenwood, a 19-year-old college student from Massachusetts, is one of a dozen young women chosen to spend a month in New York working on a fashion magazine. It's a dream opportunity: "I was supposed to be having the time of my life". Instead, Esther feels numb. She drags herself from her hotel to work and to parties and back to her hotel, feeling "very still and empty, the way the eye of a tornado must feel, moving dully along in the middle of the surrounding hullabaloo". Torn between society's expectations of the way she *should* feel and her inability to feel anything at all, she attempts to join in with the others, even resolving, unsuccessfully, to lose her virginity. When college starts that fall she can't concentrate on reading or writing, she can't sleep. Eventually she stops bathing and her mother takes her to a psychiatrist.

This is where, you would think, the story would get interesting. Having had a few sessions with smug, even urbane, psychoanalysts back in the day, I was expecting some real insight into the politics of the doctor-patient relationship. Instead we learn that Dr. Gordon is young, good-looking and conceited, and not particularly adept at reading minds. After only a couple of sessions, he recommends shock therapy. The description of the procedure is short, graphic and unvarnished - in my opinion it's one of the strongest pieces of writing in the book:

"Dr. Gordon was fitting two metal plates on either side of my head. He buckled them into place with a strap that dented my forehead, and gave me a wire to bite.

"I shut my eyes.

"There was a brief silence, like an indrawn breath.

"Then something bent down and took hold of me and shook me like the end of the world. Whee-ee-ee-ee-ee, it shrilled, through an air cracking with blue light, and with each flash a great jolt drubbed me till I thought my bones would break and the sap fly out of me like a split plant.

"I wondered what terrible thing it was that I had done."

The treatment is not a success. Voices in her head taunt her: "[You've] got the perfect setup of a true neurotic. You'll never get anywhere like that, you'll never get anywhere like that". She can't sleep - her college professor says her writing is factitious. Suicide presents itself as a way out - possibly the only way out. She tries to hang herself but can't find a place in her mother's house to tie the rope. With friends at the beach she swims out as far as she can, hoping to drown herself. But each time she dives down under the water, she bobs up again to the surface. One rainy afternoon she visits her father's grave on the outskirts of town. This seems to settle something in her mind. The next morning, after her mother leaves for work, Esther hides herself in a crawl space in the basement, swallows a large amount of sleeping pills, and slips into unconsciousness. She awakens in a hospital with no permanent physical injuries; when her brother asks, "How are you?" she looks her mother in the eye: "The same," she says. Nothing has changed.

It's at this point Plath introduces the concept of the bell jar. On her way to an expensive private hospital, courtesy of a famous novelist who's undertaken to fund her treatment, Esther knows she should be grateful. The problem is, she can't feel a thing:

"If Mrs. Guinea had given me a ticket to Europe, or a round-the-world cruise, it wouldn't have made one scrap of difference to me, because wherever I sat - on the deck of ship or at a street café in Paris or Bangkok - I would be sitting under the same glass bell jar, stewing in my own sour air."

Esther's new psychiatrist, Dr. Nolan, is young and female and although she, too, recommends electroshock treatments, she assures Esther they will be nothing like the terrifying procedure she endured at the hands of Dr. Gordon. Under Dr. Nolan's guidance, Esther experiences some improvement. She's allowed to leave the hospital from time to time and hopes to be discharged in time for the winter semester at college. As the novel ends, she enters the interview room where the hospital doctors are gathered to decide if she's well enough to be discharged. Dr. Nolan reassures her that she will be fine, but Esther isn't so sure.

"How did I know that someday - at college, in Europe, somewhere, anywhere - the bell jar, with its stifling distortions, wouldn't descend again?"

In the early morning hours of February 11th 1963, a month after the first UK publication of *The Bell Jar*, Sylvia Plath turned on the gas and put her head in the oven, having first sealed the rooms between her and her sleeping children. She was 30 years old.

As I said - if only.

Week 34: *The Postman Always Rings Twice*, by James M. Cain (1934)

When I was in my teens I read a lot. This was partly because I had *always* read a lot, and partly because I had a lot of time on my hands, being neither athletically inclined nor socially in demand. For me, there were two kinds of books: "good" books, the kind you got from the library, the kind you were happy to let your parents know you were reading - Dickens, Kurt Vonnegut, the Brontes, Joseph Heller, J. D. Salinger, John Steinbeck, Muriel Spark, John Fowles, Carson McCullers . . . Sorry. It's a long list. But you get the idea.

Then there were the - well, the not-so-good books. The kind you found snooping around in night-table drawers when you were babysitting - yes, I was *that* kind of babysitter. *Valley of the Dolls* was one of those, as was *Mandingo*, Kyle Onstott's sensationalist story of slavery in the American South. A friend's older brother introduced me to Grove Press, which is how I got my hands on the anonymous Victorian erotica *The Way of A Man with a Maid*. *God's Little Acre* was in the bottom drawer of my Dad's filing cabinet (my God, I was a snoopy kid!) along with his issues of *For Men Only* and *Stag*. I think *The Story of O* was handed around school - the dirty parts being helpfully underlined in yellow highlighter to save you having to plough through the boring bits; *Lady Chatterly's Lover* was "read" the same way. And of course *Lolita*, which, besides being about sex, was considered literature and could be found in the library.

In case you're thinking I was obsessed with sex - in which case I would ask you to name a teenager who isn't - there was a sub-category of not-so-good books that were perfectly respectable, just not on any high school curriculum. I'm talking about pulp fiction. And I don't mean the movie. The term goes back to the popular fiction magazines published in the first half of the 20th Century. Unlike the glossy, more expensive magazines, these were printed on cheap wood pulp paper, and were meant to be read and thrown away. As the magazines declined in popularity, mass-market paperbacks took their place. Available in every drugstore, bus depot and railway station in the country, they were, as the US Library of Congress puts it, "cheap, portable, disposable, and often sensational".

Most of the writers of this "hardboiled" fiction were men, and no one was harder boiled than James M. Cain. A former newspaperman who headed West during the Depression to write for the movies, Cain wrote some 20-odd novels, several of which were made into films. He claimed to make no special effort to be particularly tough, or grim, but his fiction is some of the darkest you're ever likely to come across. The reason, I think, is because he wrote people as they are, not as they should be.

His first novel, *The Postman Always Rings Twice* (1934), contains two protagonists with almost no redeeming qualities. I mean *none*. Frank Chambers, the narrator, is a drifter who turns up one morning at a roadside diner somewhere outside of Los Angeles. The owner of the place, Nick Papadakis, convinces him to stay on and help out in the garage. Frank is reluctant at first but once he catches sight of Cora, Nick's attractive young wife, he changes his mind.

Frank and Cora begin an affair, and Cora confides to Frank that she's sick of her husband, sick of being married to a man who's "greasy and makes you sick at the stomach when he touches you". When Frank suggests they run away together, Cora says she couldn't cope with life on the road. Besides, she wants to hang onto the diner. What she wants is to get rid of Nick altogether.

"You're smart, Frank," she says. "You'll think of a way. Plenty of them have. Don't worry. I'm not the first woman that had to turn hell cat to get out of a mess."

They say there's no such thing as a perfect crime; certainly, Frank and Cora's plot to murder her husband has a million holes in it. Cora, they decide, will bash Nick over the head with a homemade blackjack while he's in the bath, then push his head under the water and keep it there till he drowns. Once she's sure he's dead, she'll lock the bathroom door and leave via the window and a stepladder Frank has set up in the yard. It'll look like he slipped and fell in the bath, poor guy.

A sudden power outage and the appearance of a policeman causes the plan to go awry - Cora does manage to knock Nick unconscious, but isn't able to drown him. They call an ambulance and Nick wakes up a few days later in hospital, with no memory of what took place. The policeman has his suspicions but no substantial proof that any crime took place - or was attempted.

They've dodged a bullet. At this point anyone with half a brain would call it a day. They tried, they failed - let's move on. Unfortunately, in this case that half a brain is being shared by two hapless losers - sorry, but there's really no other word for it. Cora and Frank decide to try again, this time by faking an automobile accident. They get Nick drunk, hit him on the head, and crash the car. He dies this time, and Frank and Cora are injured but survive. All might be well except for a local prosecutor who doesn't believe their story. He manages to get them to turn on each other - Frank signs a complaint against Cora, and Cora is angry enough to make a full confession to her lawyer. Eventually, by negotiating with the companies who hold insurance policies on Nick's life, Cora's lawyer gets her a pardon and the two of them are free to marry and start a new life together.

You know, though, that these two are not going to have a fairy-tale happy-ever-after ending. Cora knows it for sure - she reminds Frank that as soon as things got rough, they turned on each other. And things will never be the same.

"We were up so high, Frank. We had it all . . . We're just two punks, Frank . . . We had all that love, and we just cracked up under it. It's a big airplane engine, that takes you through the sky, right up to the top of the mountain. But when you put it in a Ford, it just shakes it to pieces. That's what we are, Frank, a couple of Fords. God is up there laughing at us."

The ending is as bleak as you might expect. Justice is served, but with a twist. *The Postman Always Rings Twice* is a good, smart read. And, as Cain himself might have said, happy endings are overrated.

Week 35: *The Thirty-Nine Steps*, by John Buchan (1915)

"I returned from the City about three o'clock on that May afternoon pretty well disgusted with life."

This, I think, is a perfect first line. Why is he - if it is a he - disgusted with life? What's happened up to now? And what is about to happen on that May afternoon that will change things? We're immediately drawn in, and, in the case of *The Thirty-Nine Steps*, we're not disappointed.

Published in 1915, John Buchan's thriller takes place during the spring and early summer of the previous year. A European war is pending, and Richard Hannay, a 37-year-old former mining engineer, has returned to England from Rhodesia, having made a comfortable pile of money. He's been back in the "old country" for three months and is fed up with it:

"The weather made me liverish, the talk of the ordinary Englishman made me sick, I couldn't get enough exercise, and the amusements of London seemed as flat as soda-water that has been standing in the sun. 'Richard Hannay,' I kept telling myself, 'you have got into the wrong ditch, my friend, and you had better climb out.'"

He'll give it one more day, he decides; then, if nothing changes, he'll head back to Cape Town. That night, as he's unlocking the door to his apartment, he's accosted by a stranger, a nervous little man who asks to speak to him for a minute. Hannay invites him in - trusting soul, isn't he? But it was different times. Anyway, if he'd brushed him off, we'd have no story.

After ensuring that the apartment is locked, the stranger, an American named Franklin P. Scudder, lays out the details of a nefarious plot - I use the word advisedly - involving German anarchists, British military secrets, and the assassination of the Greek prime minister during his upcoming visit to London. Scudder, a kind of freelance spy, must lie low until the day of the visit, at which point he'll alert the authorities and thwart the anarchists. It's no use alerting them sooner - the prime minister's visit would be canceled and the Germans would merely find another time and place to do him in. Everything must go ahead as planned until the very last minute.

Unfortunately, Scudder's whereabouts have been discovered and his life is in danger. To throw the killers off the scent, he has faked his own death and is hoping Hannay will agree to let him hide out with him for the next few weeks. Deciding he likes Scudder and, more important, trusts him, Hannay agrees. Scudder provides a few more details over the next few days, expressing the hope that if something happens to him, his new friend will do his best to take his place. He mentions several things, in particular a Black Stone and a man who speaks with a lisp. And someone else, whom Scudder can't speak of without shuddering: an old man with a young voice who can hood his eyes like a hawk.

During this time, Scudder continues to fear for his life, and rightly so. One night Hannay returns home to find Scudder lying dead, a long knife skewering him to the floor. He's been killed because of what he knows, and Hannay figures he's next. He can't call the police, as he's now a prime suspect in Scudder's murder. His only option, he feels, is to go into hiding until he can stop the spy ring and clear his name. He boards an express train to Scotland, taking with him Scudder's notebook, which contains the details of the plot written in code.

The Thirty-Nine Steps is one of the earliest examples of the "innocent-man-on-the-run", a format that's been used many times over the years - *The Fugitive, North by Northwest* and *The Bourne Identity* come to mind. Like much of the genre, the story contains a number of fortuitous, but unlikely, coincidences. Right at the moment when our hero is about to be nabbed by either the police or the Germans, an offensive little fop named Marmaduke Jopley, whom Hannay met in London, just happens to come by in a touring-car, offering Hannay a chance to disguise himself and escape through the police cordon. Keep in mind that we're now in the Scottish highlands, more than 500 km from London and at least a two-day drive back then. And yet, here he is. How, as I said, fortuitous.

Buchan, like many English writers before him, was fond of aping the dialect of "country folk", often with unfortunate results. Here, for instance, we have a speech by a Scottish roadman - who is, of course, drunk. (My apologies to my friends of Scottish heritage):

"The trouble is that I'm no sober. Last nicht my dochter, Merran, was waddit, and they danced till fower in the byre. Me and some ither chiels sat down to the drinkin' - and here I am. Peety that I ever lookit on the wine when it was red!"

Yikes.

Still, Richard Hannay is an appealing character - a civilian everyman given the chance to be brave and selfless. You find yourself cheering for him all the way through. When Alfred Hitchcock filmed the book in 1935, he spiced it up by providing Hannay with an attractive blonde companion and replaced Scudder with a female spy named Annabella Smith. Neither of these women appear in the book; the story works quite well without them. Also, in the film, the "39 steps" refers to the German spies; in the book, it doesn't.

John Buchan was Canada's Governor-General from 1935 until his death from a stroke-related head injury in 1940. He was a prolific author, having produced almost 30 novels, seven collections of short stories, and a handful of biographies. But it's his tale of espionage, followed by four more Richard Hannay thrillers, for which he's best remembered, and deservedly so.

As writers and readers we should also be grateful for the author's legacy of his time in office: the Governor-General's Literary awards. Thank you, Mr. Buchan.

Week 36: *The Maltese Falcon*, by Dashiell Hammett (1930)

In 1934, four years after *The Maltese Falcon* was published, Dashiell Hammett wrote this of his anti-heroic, hard-boiled detective, Sam Spade: "He is a dream man in the sense that he is what most of the private detectives I worked with would liked to have been and quite a few of them in their cockier moments thought they approached. For your private detective . . . wants to be a hard and shifty fellow, able to take care of himself in any situation, able to get the best of anybody he comes in contact with, whether criminal, innocent bystander, or client."

Hammett knew what he was talking about. He'd been one himself, an operative, that is, from 1915 - 1921, working for the Pinkerton Detective Agency out of Baltimore, Spokane, and San Francisco. So when he started writing detective fiction in the 1920s, he drew on his experience to create stories that felt extraordinarily authentic. He was writing about people he knew, or knew about.

Here's the story: an attractive young woman who calls herself Miss Wonderly comes to the offices of Sam Spade and his partner, Miles Archer, looking for help. Her younger sister, Corinne, has run off with a dangerous man named Floyd Thursby. They're staying somewhere in San Francisco. Archer sets out to trail Thursby and is murdered; his body is found late that evening in an alley. Shortly afterwards, Thursby is shot down in front of his hotel. The police suspect Spade killed him to avenge Archer's death, but can't prove anything. Knowing that, Spade simply laughs it off.

The following day, Miss Wonderly leaves a message at Sam's office that she wants to see him. When he turns up at her apartment, she confesses that her real name is Brigid O'Shaughnessy, there is no sister, and she and Thursby have been working together. She's sure Thursby killed Archer but doesn't know who killed Thursby. And that's as much as she's willing to say.

"I've been bad," she tells him, "worse than you could know - but I'm not all bad. Look at me, Mr. Spade. You know I'm not all bad, don't you? You can see that, can't you? Then can't you trust me a little?"

Spade doesn't trust her, but he's attracted to her. And he agrees to help her. It eventually comes out that Brigid is involved in a complicated plot to steal a jewel-encrusted statuette, worth a fortune. Floyd Thursby was her accomplice; the two of them were originally working with Joel Cairo in Hong Kong, but decided to cut him out of the deal. Back at Spade's office, Joel Cairo turns up, offering him $5,000 to recover the bird. He believes Sam either has the statuette or knows where to get it.

In the meantime, Spade realizes he's being followed by a slim young man we later learn is named Wilmer. He, like Joel Cairo, is working for the real villain of the story, an antiques collector named Caspar Gutman. Wealthy, urbane, and obese, Gutman is obsessed with the black bird - the Maltese Falcon - whose history dates back to the mid 16th century and the Knights Templar of Malta. Gutman offers Spade $25,000 to deliver the bird to him, an offer he later rescinds, offering $10,000 instead. When the bird does fall into Spade's hands, he secures it in a storage locker and returns home to find Brigid waiting for him outside his apartment. They go inside and are met by Gutman, Cairo, and Wilmer, guns at the ready. Spade agrees to give them the bird, in return for a "fall guy" - Wilmer must be turned over to the police. This agreed to, Spade calls his secretary to bring the bird to his apartment. She does so, and Gutman frantically rips apart the packaging. Alas - it's a fake. Cairo is devastated but Gutman quickly recovers - he's spent decades searching for the bird . . . what's another year, in the greater scheme of things?

We come now to the part of the book which most will remember from the 1941 film starring Humphrey Bogart and Mary Astor - the part where Sam tells Brigid she's "taking the fall". He knows now she killed Miles Archer, he knows she killed Floyd Thursby - she's going to pay the price. "I hope to Christ they don't hang you, precious, by that sweet neck," he tells her. When she asks him why he's doing this, he says he has no choice. He may be hard-boiled and he may be a womanizer (besides sleeping with Brigid, he's been having an affair with Ivy Archer, his late partner's wife and may or may not have been romantically involved with his secretary), but he has his own, self-imposed moral code:

"When a man's partner is killed, he's supposed to do something about it. It doesn't make any difference what you thought of him. He was your partner and you're supposed to do something about it. And it happens we're in the detective business. Well, when one of your organization gets killed, it's - it's bad business to let the killer get away with it, bad all around, bad for every detective everywhere."

Hammet's been criticized for his portrayal of Cairo, the "fairy", who minces his way into the room and wears too much cologne. To be fair, though, it can be argued that including a homosexual character in a work of pulp fiction was rather brave, at the time. Cairo's sexuality is one of several aspects of the book that was downplayed in the film, in order to conform to the set of morality guidelines laid down by the Hays Code. At one point Spade strip-searches Brigid looking for a missing $1,000 dollar bill; earlier, when Brigid realizes Cairo is offering more money for the bird than she can afford, she offers to sleep with Sam. Neither of these scenes would have made it past the censors.

Having mentioned the movie - because how can you talk about *The Maltese Falcon* without mentioning Bogart and Astor? - it should be stated that John Huston's production was in most other ways faithful to the book. Like the 1931 film before it, which starred Bebe Daniels and Ricardo Cortez, most of the dialogue was lifted verbatim from the novel. And why wouldn't it be? When you have lines like "When I slap you, you'll take it and like it" why wouldn't you use them?

Unlike Sherlock Holmes or Hercule Poirot, Spade isn't particularly intelligent. That is, not more so than the average person. He makes no great claims to having a phenomenal memory, a heightened sense of intuition, or an extraordinary talent for detailed observation. What he brings to the case is a dogged determination to see it through, an understanding of human nature, and the sheer insolence to brazen it out, whatever the situation.

It's tempting to regard Sam Spade as the author's alter ego: Hammett, like Spade, was a no-nonsense, hard-drinking man's man - "spare, frugal, hard-boiled" is how Raymond Chandler described him. Even on his deathbed he refused to lie to Lillian Hellman - he refused to say he loved her.

But there are differences. Hammet was a left-wing activist who did time, in Spade's lingo, for refusing to divulge the names of Communist sympathizers. Later, his appearance before the House Un-American Activities Committee (HUAC) led to his being blacklisted. His books were removed from public libraries, screenings of film versions stopped. He became, like the many screenwriters, actors, directors, and musicians who relied on Hollywood for their livelihoods, a non-person.

Sam Spade would never have put himself in this position. It's like he told Brigid O'Shaugnessy: Sam Spade wouldn't play the sap for anyone.

Week 37: *A Severed Head*, by Iris Murdoch

Martin Lynch-Gibbon is a lucky man. He has it all: a comfortable, tastefully decorated home; a gracious, loving wife whose beauty is only just beginning to fade, and a mistress practically young enough to be his daughter. There is no question of him leaving his wife, and his mistress appears to accept that. He is, in a word, complacent. And it is his complacency - his hubris, if you will - that trips him up, throwing his life into turmoil.

A Severed Head was Iris Murdoch's 5th published novel; like her others, it's about love. But nothing so simple as the pure, unadulterated love of one human being for another, if there is such a thing. Love, for Murdoch, is far more complex, corrupted by obsession, insecurity, ego. And, in this case, incest. She was, after all, a philosopher. Her novels are preoccupied with morality, the power of the unconscious, and the fluid nature of gender and sexuality.

The character of Martin Lynch-Gibbon is one that will be familiar to Murdoch fans. Middle-aged, well-to-do, and self-regarding, he finds himself caught in a moral dilemma, thanks to a revelation by his wife, Antonia: she, it appears, is in love with her psychoanalyst. She wants a divorce, but neither she nor her therapist, Palmer Anderson, want to lose Martin. As Palmer tells him, "In a strange and rather wonderful way we can't do without you. We shall hold on to you, we shall look after you. You'll see."

Martin, for his part, is shocked by his wife's infidelity. Palmer has been his close friend; his wife, he thought, considered their marriage a happy one. At first he refuses to accept it, insisting that *this* - their marriage - is what's real. He's done nothing to deserve this . . . it's all a horrible mistake. You can't help shaking your head at the self-delusion of a man who can blithely carry on a clandestine affair for some time yet manage to feel so betrayed when his wife does the same.

In spite of his pain, Martin takes it on the chin, behaving like a gentleman, even if he doesn't feel like one. Antonia and Palmer comment on this time and again, expressing their gratitude to him for taking it so splendidly. Athough he feels he probably shouldn't be taking it "splendidly", Martin finds himself unable to detach himself from their orbit. They insist that he join them for dinner, stay the night, and allow them to help him through this awful time. Which, they assure him, will lead to him being a better, happier man.

And so begins a rather complicated, but very modern, *ménage*. Martin is unhappy but acquiescent, playing the role of the child while his wife and her lover act very much as benevolent but controlling authority figures. As for Georgie Sands, his erstwhile mistress, Martin avoids her like the plague, afraid that she might now expect something more substantial in terms of a commitment. "What I really wanted most just then," he confesses, "was to put Georgie in cold storage. It is unfortunate that other human beings cannot be conveniently immobilized."

Into this unholy alliance steps Palmer's half sister, the formidable Honor Klein. Due to arrive on the 5:57 train from Cambridge, she appears like an avenging angel - or a disapproving one, anyway. Honor seems to be the only family member who finds the current set-up distasteful. She has no use for the so-called "civilized and intelligent" way Martin has accepted his cuckoldry, and says he might have won his wife back if he'd made an effort. "Sooner or later," she says, "you will have to become a centaur and kick your way out."

When Martin does finally meet up with Georgie, she offers him the consolation and understanding he craves, but asks him to make their affair public. He can't, he says: "It would hurt Antonia so if she knew." As a kind of peace offering, he takes her back to Hereford Square, to the house he shared, until recently, with his wife. While they're looking around the place, they hear someone come in. Assuming it's Antonia, Martin shoves Georgie out the back door, only to realize the intruder is Honor Klein.

Klein, having seen Georgie's handbag on the table in the hall, confronts the young woman, worms the truth out of her, and tells her brother and Antonia that Martin has a mistress. Now it's *their* turn to be shocked and dismayed: "How can you have told such lies, Martin?" Antonia asks. "I can't conceive how you could sit there pretending to be virtuous and let us carry all the guilt. It's not like you, Martin." When Martin challenges Klein as to why she spilled the beans, she says simply she thought they should know and tells him, sarcastically, that he's heroic. "The knight of infinite humiliation. One does not know whether to kiss your feet or to recommend that you have a good analysis."

And there's more humiliation in store. Having come to the realization that he's in love with the woman he hated most, Honor Klein, Martin takes the train to Cambridge, breaks into her house, and finds her in bed with her half-brother, Palmer. Seeking consolation once again from his mistress, Martin sends Georgie a letter begging for her sympathy and understanding. She doesn't reply; instead, his brother, Alexander, calls to say he and Georgie are in love and are planning to marry. While this shocks Martin it absolutely enrages Antonia, who, it turns out, has been sleeping with Alexander for years. So Martin, poor thing, has been betrayed by his wife, his mistress, his closest friend, and his brother. And, in a way, by his best friend's half sister, if you count his unexpected passion for Honor Klein.

A Severed Head touches on several issues which were certainly taboo at the time. Incest, of course, is one - and remains so. Another is abortion. Early on we're told that Georgie became pregnant the previous year, but kindly took care of it without troubling Martin. As he puts it, "I got off with an extraordinary ease . . . I had not had to pay. It had all been quite uncannily painless." For Martin, at any rate.

By the end of the book, everyone has switched partners, something that happens rather frequently in Murdoch's tales and could be considered a harbinger of the upcoming sexual revolution. The author, after all, was no stranger to unconventional relationships. In 1956 she married the novelist and literary critic John Bayley who appears not to have been terribly interested in sex. Murdoch, however, had numerous affairs with both men and women, in particular a longstanding, passionate friendship with the writer and animal rights activist Brigid Brophy. It was an odd marriage in many ways, but it was solid. It lasted 43 years and ended only with Murdoch's tragic death from Alzheimer's.

As for the severed head, that can be interpreted in several ways . . . the marriage has been destroyed, having had its head cut off . . . various characters "lose their heads" in the course of the narrative. Specifically, though, it appears to refer to Honor Klein, the demon samurai of the story. As she tells Martin, because of who she is and what he has witnessed - the incestuous relationship between her and her brother - she's become an object of fascination for him:

"I am a severed head such as primitive tribes and old alchemists used to use, anointing it with oil and putting a morsel of gold upon its tongue to make it utter prophecies. And who knows but that long acquaintance with a severed head might not lead to strange knowledge. For such knowledge one would have paid enough."

The price, for Martin, is the loss of complacency. And that is never a bad thing, for any of us.

Week 38: *A Bend in the River*, V. S. Naipaul (1979)

"The town in the interior, at the bend in the great river, had almost ceased to exist". The name of the town is never mentioned. We are told it is located in the heart of Africa, at the end of the navigable river, just below the cataracts. The President, too, is unnamed, and usually referred to as the Big Man. Clearly, though, *A Bend in the River* is closely based on the newly independent Zaire under President Mobutu. As a story of a country and a people searching to find - or reclaim - their identity, it is fascinating, even essential, reading.

A British writer of Indian descent, V. S. Naipaul's early works were relatively light-hearted sketches set in the country of his birth, Trinidad and Tobago. *A Bend in the River*, while it contains comic elements, is a deeper and darker narrative, set in post-colonial Africa in the early 1970s. It tells the story of Salim, the son of Indian merchants living in East Africa at a time when the country is breaking its ties with Europe. Many non-African residents are anxious about the future. As Salim's wealthy friend Indar puts it, "We're washed up here, you know. To be in Africa you have to be strong. We're not strong. We don't even have a flag." When another family friend, Nazruddin, offers to sell Salim his shop at a bargain basement price, the young man jumps at the chance to break away from his family and community . . . and perhaps avoid marriage to Nazruddin's daughter, Kareisha.

The shop is located in a town in the remote interior of the country; the journey takes a week. Talking his way through frontier border guards and men with guns, it occurs to Salim that he's reversing the centuries-old trek made by slaves and their captors; like the slaves, he is, in the end, simply anxious to arrive. On arrival, he finds a kind of ghost town, "a place where the future had come and gone". The old colonial statues and buildings have been defaced or destroyed, the Europeans have left, and the Africans have fled to their tribal villages. There has been a great deal of violence. But Africa was big: "The bush muffled the sound of murder, and the muddy rivers and lakes washed the blood away."

While he waits for his customers to return, Salim makes friends with some of the others who have stayed on. He becomes close to an attractive Indian couple who run a shop across from the main hotel and has lunch with them twice a week. Shoba and Mahesh live in their own isolated world; devoted to each other, they pay little attention to the events occurring around them. Shortly after arriving, he is joined by Ali, a half-African boy later known as Metty. His family were once slaves owned by Salim's family; now they live on as servants in the family compound. Metty has been sent to live with Salim, to care for him and be cared for by him. Salim accepts that he has no choice in the matter - the tradition of care is on both sides.

One of Salim's first customers is Zabeth, an African woman believed to have magical powers, who makes the treacherous journey down the river in a dugout, several times a year. She buys razor blades, needles, enamel basins and so on from Salim and then takes them back to her village to sell. When her son, Ferdinand, comes to live in town to attend the lycée, Zabeth asks Salim to watch out for him - to act as a kind of protector to the boy. Ferdinand, who has grown up in the bush, seems ambivalent about the idea that Salim is meant to be his guide. He visits the shop once a week, as his mother wishes, but very quickly comes to prefer Metty's company to that of Salim.

After a second rebellion, white mercenaries appear and rout the troublemakers. With peace restored, the town begins to flourish. Government agencies spring up, soldiers and European visitors are everywhere - teachers, students, foreign aid workers. Salim's friend Mahesh invests in a Bigburger franchise which is a success; everyone, it seems, is making money. A large section of bush next to the river is cleared out and levelled, to make way for a new town on the site of what had been a rich European suburb. This is the Domain, a symbol of the new Africa. It is here that Salim is introduced to Raymond, a former professor and adviser to the Big Man, and his much younger wife, Yvette. Raymond, like other academics Naipaul knew at the time, has bought into the idea of a "postindependence African renaissance", and shut his eyes to the tyranny and corruption around him. Now, however, he is out of favour and has been effectively exiled from the capitol. He spends his days in a kind of limbo, working on a collection of the Big Man's speeches, waiting to be recalled to his side.

In the meantime, Salim and Yvette become lovers, a liaison that is a first for Salim; up to this point his sexual encounters have all been with prostitutes. The intensity of the relationship leads to occasional violence on his part, but breaks off only when he becomes aware that his life here, including his affair with Yvette, has become essentially meaningless. As things begin to fall apart, Salim travels to England to visit Nazruddin, who is now a landlord in London.

There he encounters other foreigners like himself, all trying to make money, all searching for somewhere better than the places they came from. He and Kareisha, Nazruddin's daughter, become engaged and he flies back to Africa to tie up loose ends.

But things have changed. The President has instituted a program of "radicalization" under which Salim's shop has been taken over by the State and given to an African. He can stay on as manager; Metty, no longer a servant, does errands for the new owner. Desperate to make money so that he can leave the country for good, Salim becomes involved in the illegal ivory trade, burying tusks in the earth under his doorstep. Metty, lost and insecure, becomes increasingly frantic to get away. He begs Salim to give him money so he, too, can leave the country. When Salim refuses, he reports him to the police. Unable to pay his fine, Salim is arrested and put in jail. A few days later, he's brought before the Commissioner, who turns out to be his former protégé, Ferdinand. He's released, thanks to Ferdinand, and smuggled out of the country on a steamer.

Claire Tomalin wrote in the *Sunday Times*, "V. S. Naipaul uses Africa as a text to preach magnificently upon the sickness of a world losing touch with its past." But what past, exactly? The continent of Africa has had many pasts. It has been colonized by Britain, France, Germany, Belgium, Spain, Portugal, and Italy. The Arab slave trade transported Africans across the Red Sea, the Indian Ocean and the Sahara Desert. The Atlantic slave trade sent them overseas, to work the plantations of the New World. It's unclear where Naipaul stands on the issue. Salim, the outsider, feels believable enough, but many of the African characters, such as Metty, are painted as somewhat malevolent, childlike creatures, unable or unwilling to accept the responsibility of independence. Ferdinand, in particular, remains a mystery. After going away to be educated, he rises quickly in the government bureaucracy, becoming very much a New Man of Africa. And yet, in Salim's eyes, he looks "withdrawn and ill, like a man recovering from fever . . . He was, after all, like other high officials. I wondered why I thought he would be different."

In awarding the 2001 Nobel Prize for Literature to V. S. Naipaul, the committee called him Joseph Conrad's heir "as the annalist of the destinies of empires in the moral sense: what they do to human beings". His human beings, as chronicled here, are unforgettable.

Week 39: *The Gathering*, by Anne Enright (2007)

Good writers don't let you off easy. They provide no pat answers - there's no riding off together into the sunset as the orchestral music swells in the background. Good writers unsettle you. They leave you with questions. They disturb your assumptions, shake you out of your comfort zone. They can be savage in their wit, ruthless in their descriptions of those they love, and unexpectedly kind towards those they don't.

Dublin-born author Anne Enright is one of those writers. *The Gathering*, her fourth novel and winner of the 2007 Man Booker Prize, is not to be read for consolation. The theme is familiar - the death of a family member brings together his surviving parent and siblings - but Enright turns it on its head. The survivors here find no comfort in death; "closure" is a word without resonance. The wounds and resentments of childhood remain; they are not washed away in a flood of repentance and forgiveness. The notion of healing has no place within this particular family - they flaunt the slights and injuries of childhood as if they happened yesterday: "This is how we all survive. We default to the oldest scar."

The narrator, 39-year-old Veronica Hegarty, begins by telling us she wants to write down what happened - or might have happened - when she was a child and she and her brother, Liam, were staying at the house of their grandmother, Ada Merriman Spillane. *Something* happened, she knows that, and it's something that matters. She will keep going back to it, writing and re-writing the story, changing the nature of the event with each iteration.

The children, ages eight and nine, were staying with their grandmother while their mother recovered from yet another pregnancy. Mammy, as they call her, gave birth to 12 children and miscarried seven times. Even for an Irish Catholic family, this was considered above and beyond the call of duty. There were sniggers at her husband's funeral; he wore himself out, they joked, "with too much shagging".

Whether it was the constant pregnancies that did it or something else, Mammy is a vague, insubstantial, clucking presence, not really meant for the role. Her children love her, although they long ago learned not to rely on her, not to trouble her when one of them got in trouble. "Don't tell your mother," their father always said, and they didn't. Veronica can forgive her mother for her lapses, which are many. What she can't forgive, she says, is the sex: "The stupidity of so much humping. Open and blind. Consequences, Mammy. *Consequences.*"

And now Liam, her favourite sibling - her partner in crime who became an alcoholic while Veronica chose marriage and suburban respectability - Liam has put stones in his pocket and drowned himself in the waters off Brighton Beach. It is Veronica who must pick up the pieces: travel to England, claim the body, and bring it back to Dublin to be buried. Grief-stricken, unable to sleep, she stops having sex with Tom, her husband. She loves him, she says, and doesn't want a divorce, but she can't sleep with him:

"So my husband is waiting for me to sleep with him again, and I am waiting for something else. I am waiting for things to become clear."

And so she spends her nights wandering through her pleasant, middle-class, suburban house, trying to reconstruct the past. The seeds of Liam's suicide, she thinks, are buried in his childhood, and hers. It has something to do with her grandmother, and the mysterious Lambert Nugent, the man Ada may have loved but didn't marry.

Thus *The Gathering* has two meanings - maybe more. There is, of course, the coming together of family members in order to bury their brother. There is also the gathering that Veronica puts down on paper - the gathering together of strands of memory and imagination in order to reconstruct the past. Enright never allows the weight of these memories, many of which are painful, to overwhelm the story. She has a lightness of touch that relieves even the darkest moments: "Suicides always pull a good crowd," she tells us, describing the mourners at Liam's funeral. Veronica imagines Ada as a whore, one of the prostitutes rescued from the streets of Dublin by the Legion of Mary, "a religious organization dedicated, in 1967, to inanity and the making of tea". She pictures Ada and Lambert having sex - "the bookie fucks the whore" is the way she puts it. Which is not, perhaps, the nicest way to be remembered by your granddaughter.

But it is, of course, all speculation. Veronica can't ever really know what did or did not take place between Ada and Lamb Nugent. Even her moment of epiphany near the end, where she suddenly recalls witnessing something that happened to Liam, something might have set him on the road to alcoholism and suicide - even that is only speculation.

In brilliant, unsparing fashion, Enright shows us the ways in which misery and humour can co-exist in families. At the risk of sounding like a Raging Feminist (goddess forbid) I want to say that a man could never have written this book. First of all, it wouldn't occur to him to write it. Nothing happens, so why would he bother? And second, the complexity of familial relationships - the way you can love your siblings while loathing their every move and wishing whole-heartedly you were an only child - it's generally women who get this stuff.

A confession here: one of the reasons *The Gathering* appeals to me is because it never condescends to give advice. Neither Enright nor her characters have any pointers to give. You won't find anyone in the Hegarty clan suggesting how you can quit drinking (which they all do, but never in front of each other). Or fix your marriage. Or save your brother. Or discover the truth.

The most you can do - the most any of us can do - is what Veronica does at the end of the book: move on with your life . . . your *real* life, the one you've been allotted. Because it is, in the end, all you have.

Last year, in an interview with the *New Yorker* magazine, Enright was asked if a story she had written was based on an actual event. "As to whether it really happen[ed]," she said, "the page is a free space. Anything can happen on the page."

The page is a free space. Yes. YES.

Week 40: *The Children's Book*, by A S Byatt (2009)

It has been said of A S Byatt that she does not wear her learning lightly. I'd go further: she has a tendency to club you over the head with it. *The Children's Book* is a bulging, behemoth of a book that frequently reads like an encyclopedia. There were times as I worked my way through this stunningly detailed story that I had the sense of being dragged unwilling through a large, eclectic museum by a well-informed but over-enthusiastic tour guide.

There are compelling stories within these 615 pages. There are men and women redefining themselves at the end of the Victorian era, children struggling to release themselves from parental expectations, family secrets that, when and if divulged, will confuse and even destroy members of the household. But these are buried, or temporarily shoved aside, by lectures (sorry, that's the only word for it) on any one of the following: German puppetry; ceramics; the rebuilding of the South Kensington Museum; the hazards of investing in South African gold; the Arts and Crafts movement; the early days of British socialism. An enormous amount of attention is given to pots and glazes, theatre design, styles of dress, and what people eat. The details are overwhelming; it makes me think there's a smaller book inside that might have worked better.

Which is not to say I didn't enjoy it. Byatt's an intelligent, compelling writer - she's incapable of writing a bad book. I just wish she'd been a little less determined to instruct.

Beginning in 1895 and stretching over two and a half decades, *The Children's Book* tells the story of Olive and Humphry Wellwood, well-to-do Fabians, art lovers, and, occasionally, sexual adventurers. They represent a class of intelligent, politically active Europeans who believed in a kind of utopia, a new order encompassing free love, votes for women, and new patterns made "by craftsmen, not by wage-slaves". Real life movers and shakers make appearances in the book: William Morris, H. G. Wells, G. B. Shaw, Rupert Brooke, Emmeline Pankhurst and her daughters. Oscar Wilde, very much the worse for wear and living in exile in Paris, is seen having a heart-to-heart with Rodin, after which he - Wilde - cadges a small loan from one of the fictional characters.

In an interview with *The Guardian*, Byatt said she started with the idea that writing children's books isn't good for the writer's own children: "There are some dreadful stories. Christopher Robin at least lived. Kenneth Grahame's son put himself across a railway line and waited for the train. Then there's JM Barrie. One of the boys that Barrie adopted almost certainly drowned himself. This struck me as something that needed investigating. And the second thing was, I was interested in the structure of E Nesbit's family — how they all seemed to be Fabians and fairy-story writers."

Like Nesbit, Olive Wellwood is a successful writer of children's fairy tales. She and Humphry inhabit Todefright, a delightful cottage in the Kentish Weald, with their five children: Tom, Dorothy, Phyllis, Hedda, and Florian (two more, Robin and Harry, will be born before the turn of the century). The Wellwood children, their cousins, and their friends are at the heart of the book and there are a lot of them - so many, in fact, that

Byatt had to create an Excel spread sheet to keep track of them. (I did the same.) Besides those already mentioned, we have Julian and Florence Cain who are the son and daughter of Major Prosper Cain, Special Keeper of Precious Metals at the South Kensington Museum (soon to be renamed the Victoria and Albert); Geraint, Imogen and Pomona Fludd, children of the gifted but seriously disturbed potter Benedict Fludd, and Philip and Elsie Warren, a young working-class runaway and his sister.

When the book opens, Olive has come to the museum to interview Major Cain for a new story she's writing. While they're talking, Tom and Julian wander off and discover a strange boy, "hay-haired, shaggy, and filthy", crouching by one of the exhibits, sketching. They follow him and find him hiding in the dark underground recesses of the museum's storerooms. When confronted, he says his name is Philip Warren. He was an apprentice in a ceramics factory but has run away. He wants to make his own pots, based on his own designs. He has no money and is half-starved but is determined not to go back to the Potteries.

After asking to see his sketches, Olive and Major Cain decide the boy has great promise. She brings him back to Todefright where he's welcomed into her lively, chaotic household. Her husband agrees to help him; together they arrange for Philip to be apprenticed to Benedict Fludd. The Fludds are an extremely odd family: the women seem strangely lifeless, while Fludd himself works so erratically the pottery is a shambles. There never seems to be enough money for food or the basic essentials. Philip stays on as an unpaid apprentice, and eventually manages to bring some order to the place, while getting the chance to create his own ceramics.

It's obvious from the beginning that there's something wrong with family life in the Fludd household. What is less obvious is that the Wellwoods, too, are deeply flawed. The adults have secrets that the children glean slowly, in bits and pieces. During a parental quarrel, Hedda hears one of them say, "I have always tried to love all your children equally, you cannot say I have not. It has not been easy, though you may think it has. You do not thank me."

This leads her to conclude what is never spoken about: their parents are not what they seem. They may not even be their parents. Such knowledge, as Byatt writes, can be dangerous:

"Knowledge is power, but not if it is only partial knowledge and the knower is a dependent child, already perturbed by a changing body, squalling emotions, the sense of the outside world looming outside the garden wall, waiting to be entered. Knowledge is also fear."

A loving but careless parent, Olive buries herself in her writing, leaving the children to their own devices. Extracts from her children's stories run throughout the book; you can almost hear Byatt exhaling as she writes these magical tales, letting herself - and the reader - off the hook for a while.

As the children grow into adolescence and maturity, they struggle to define themselves in a world that is changing every bit as much as our own. Dorothy decides she will be a doctor; Hedda becomes a suffragette; Charles joins (if that's the right word) the Anarchists, and becomes known variously as Charles and Karl, and, irritatingly, as Charles-Karl. Philip continues to make pots, his sister Elsie has a baby and raises it on her own. Tom alone, his mother's pet, the darling of the family, fails to find a role. While the others go on to university or into business, he roams the forests of his childhood, consistently refusing to say what, if anything, he wants to do. When his mother takes the family to see Barrie's new play, *Peter Pan, or The Boy Who Wouldn't Grow Up*, Tom's reaction is one of disgust. "Cardboard," he calls it. "He doesn't know *anything* about boys, or making things up."

Tom may not want to grow up but he's not alone. The adults, to some extent, are play-acting - at being parents, at being responsible. They may love their children, but they do not know them. Or they know them in ways they shouldn't.

The horrors of war put an end to the play-acting. The children march off to battle, and sacrifice their young lives on the fields and in the trenches of Flanders and the Somme. Byatt writes these hard, terrible stories in spare, precise prose that makes everything that comes before worth it.

The Children's Book is not an easy read. It is, however, an important one.

Week 41: *Infinite Jest*, by David Foster Wallace (1996)

It's never a good sign, it seems to me, when you'd rather unload the dishwasher than continue reading a particular book. Or make that dentist appointment you've been putting off. Or cut your toenails. Which, by the way, happens a lot in *Infinite Jest*, the 1996 novel by the American writer David Foster Wallace. It was a bestseller when it came out and continues to be, having sold more than a million copies. "Sold" being the operative word here. I'm inclined to think that it hasn't been read, all the way through, by more than a million readers. But I could be wrong.

Wallace is a genius. That is, he was. In 2008, he hanged himself from a rafter of his house. He's been called "one of the most influential and innovative writers of the last twenty years". His writings have influenced Zadie Smith, Jonathan Franzen, and George Saunders, to name just a few. He has a passionate, devoted, and diverse following that includes The International David Foster Wallace Society, "founded to promote and sustain the long-term scholarly and independent study of David Foster Wallace's writing". There are David Foster Wallace conferences and websites devoted to *Infinite Jest*. To say his fans are legion is almost an understatement.

What I'm saying is if you're not already one of them - if you haven't already read *Infinite Jest* - here are 10 reasons not to start:

1. The book is a joke: I like to think I have a fairly well-developed sense of humour. I like a good joke as much as the next person. But a joke that takes up 1079 pages, 96 of which are footnotes, tends to wear a little thin. To give an example, let's talk about Eschaton, a game Wallace created for the purposes of the novel. It has a ridiculously over-complicated set of rules. The chapter in which it is played takes up 21 pages. There are people – real people, I mean – Wallace fans – who have played this game, or a version of it. You can Google it. I cannot imagine that anyone with anything else happening in their life, e.g. work, family, a mortgage, toenails that need clipping, would have the time or inclination to attempt it.

And pardon me for sounding like a rube, but shouldn't a joke have a punch line? *Infinite Jest* has no punch line. No conclusion. It just . . . ends.

2.Lists: The author is addicted to them. At one point he devotes approximately 600 words (I'm guessing, I didn't count them) to the hospitals, utility companies, waste displacement facilities and liquor stores located in the town of Enfield, MA. Which is not actually Enfield at all but a fictional stand-in for Brighton, MA. This is nothing, however, compared to the gloomy radio host known as Madame Psychosis reading from a circular distributed by the Union of the Hideously and Improbably Deformed:

"The morbidly diaphoretic with a hankie in every pocket. The chronically granulomatous. The ones it says here the ones the cruel call Two-Baggers – one bag for your head, one bag for the observer's head in case your bag falls off. The hated and dateless and shunned, who keep to the shadows. Those who undress only in front of their pets. The quote aesthetically challenged."

3. The Canadian factor: I can find nothing in the literature that alludes to Wallace having a grudge against Canadians. But there are constant, gratuitous references to his northern neighbours, all of them unflattering. "Cultured Canadians tend to think vertical digestion makes the mind unkeen." "The Moms . . . has a rather spectacular thumb, plant-wise, for a Canadian." "[S]ome suicidal idiot or Canadian".

He's especially hard on Quebec, especially those living in "the blighted bowels of southern Quebec". Moncerf, Quebec, is "an asbestos-mining town ten clicks or so from the infamously rupture-prone Mercier Dam". The villainous Antitoi brothers, Lucien and Bertraund, are "Canadians of the Quebec subgenus, sinister and duplicitous but when it came down to it rather hapless political insurgents". Quebecois is a "gurgly, glotteal language that seems to require a perpetually sour facial expression to pronounce". "Sour" Saskatchewanites and "far-rightist" Albertans are also mentioned but Quebec bears the brunt of the venom. I'm assuming it's part of the ongoing joke but, like everything in this novel, it's over the top.

4. Chronology: Numbering years from 1 to 100, 1900 to 2000 and so on has worked pretty well for most us for quite some time. If you're writing a piece set in the future, maybe just avoid the year altogether – or choose one that will come to have some significance: 1984, 2001, etc. In the near future of *Infinite Jest*, the Gregorian calendar has been supplanted by a sponsorship arrangement; years are known by the name of the sponsoring company. The years before this practice are called "before subsidization", or BS (ha ha). Most of the action takes place in the Year of the Depend Adult Undergarment (YDAU); the other years are as follows, in what I think is chronological order:

Year of the Whopper; Year of the Tucks Medicated Pad; Year of the Trial-Size Dove Bar (YTSDB); Year of the Perdue Wonderchicken; Year of the Whisper-Quiet Maytag Dishwasher; Year of the Yushityu 2007 Mimetic-Resolution-Cartridge-View-Motherboard-Easy-To-Install-Upgrade For Infernatron/InterLace TP Systems for Home, Office or Mobile; Year of Dairy Products from the American Heartland; Year of the Depend Adult Undergarment, and Year of Glad.

5. The acronyms: Wallace never met an acronym he didn't love. Joelle Van Dyne, a.k.a. Madame Psychosis, was the PGOAT (Prettiest Girl of All Time) before she was (possibly) disfigured by acid and joined the UHID (Union of the Hideously and Improbably Deformed). The USA, Canada and Mexico have joined to form the Organisation of North American Nations, or ONAN (ha ha get it?). Les Assassins des Fauteils Rollents (the AFR) are a subversive group of legless French-Canadian "wheelchair assassins". E.T.A. is the Enfield Tennis Academy, the setting for most of the action; P.W.T.A. is the rival school, the Port Washington Tennis Academy; the I.B.P.W.D.W. is the International Brotherhood of Pier, Wharf and Dock Workers. I personally feel if Wallace could have gotten away with writing the entire book in acronyms, he would have done so.

6. Dissing other writers: Elizabeth Harper Neeld's *Seven Choices: Taking the steps to new life after losing someone you love* is, according to Wallace, "352 pages of sheer goo". Harold Bloom writes "stupefyingly turgid-sounding shit". Malcolm Lowry's *Under the Volcano* is "depressing". John Updike, whom Wallace once referred to as "a penis with a thesaurus", is parodied in a film called *Fun With Teeth*. Bret Easton Ellis is the "ghastly" author of *American Psycho*. (To be fair, the loathing is mutual - Ellis has called Wallace "the most tedious, overrated, tortured, pretentious writer of my generation".)

7. Tennis: As Wallace writes, during one of the many, many passages discussing the intricacies of the game, "It all tends to get complicated, and probably not all that interesting – unless you play." I don't and it's not.

8. Suicide: Wallace was obsessed with "eliminating your map", as he refers to it in the book. When not actually killing themselves, many of the characters are at least thinking about it. Dr. James Incandenza, father of Orin, Hal and Mario, otherwise known as Himself, killed himself by sticking his head in a microwave oven. (Wallace explains that yes, it can be done, in theory.) Kate Gompert, a psychotically depressed young woman, opts for suicide as a way to lessen her inner pain. Joelle Van Dyne, a.k.a. Madame Psychosis, plans her suicide meticulously; in spite of cooking up a lethal amount of cocaine, however, she's found in time and recovers. A young Czech tennis player killed himself after retiring. A successful junior tennis player decides he'll kill himself if he ever loses a match. He does, and he does.

9. Notes and errata: I have a theory – untested but firmly held – that if you can't tell a fictional story in the body of the work, you're probably not telling it properly. To the text of his narrative, which is 981 dense, single-spaced pages, Wallace adds another 388 footnotes, covering 96 pages, most of which are irrelevant, uninteresting or both. As an example, footnote 95 refers to c:\Pink2: "*Pink* being Microsoft's first post-Windows DOS, quickly upgraded to Pink2 when InterLace took everything 100% interactive and digital; by Y.D.A.U. it's kind of a dinosaur, but it's still the only DOS that'll run a Mathpak\EndStar tree without having to stop and recompile every few seconds."

"Turgid-sounding shit", you say? Yes, I think so.

10. You have, as far as we know, only one life. There are better ways to spend it.

Week 42: *Decline and Fall*, by Evelyn Waugh (1928)

This time last year BBC 2 brought to the screen a "ghastly gaggle of braying Oxford toffs", as one reviewer put it, in a delightfully-cast three-part adaptation of *Decline and Fall,* Evelyn Waugh's 1928 satire on the great and the good of England, between the wars. If you missed it, your public library will have it on DVD.

Decline and Fall is the story of an Oxford undergrad who, through no fault of his own, gets sent down, ends up teaching at a terrible prep school, falls in love with a society matron and ends up going to jail. Written before the breakdown of his first marriage, Waugh's debut novel is pure fun, lacking the darkness of later works like *Vile Bodies* and *A Handful of Dust.*

As the book opens, Paul Pennyfeather, an inoffensive divinity student at Scone College, Oxford, is set upon by members of the Bollinger Club who are rampaging through the campus, bent on destruction. They strip him of his clothes, leaving him naked in the centre of the garden quad. Charged with "indecent behaviour", our hero is expelled, causing the college porter to remark, "I expect you'll be becoming a schoolmaster, sir . . . that's what most of the gentlemen does, sir, that gets sent down for indecent behaviour".

Paul does exactly that. With no experience in teaching, and no qualifications, he lands a position as an assistant master at a dreadful preparatory school in Wales. His fellow teachers at Llanabba Castle are ridiculously inept: Captain Grimes is a one-legged pederast who frequently lands "in the soup" but is always rescued by his fellow Old Harrovians, and Prendergast is an alcoholic lay preacher who left the Church when he started having "doubts". Dr. Augustus Fagan, eccentric and ineffectual, runs the school with the help of his daughters, Flossie and Diana, and the mysterious school porter, Philbrick, who has been, depending on the story he's telling, a bank robber, an aristocrat in exile, and a con man.

During a hilariously chaotic sports day at the school, Paul meets the mother of one of his students, the beautiful and wealthy Margot Beste-Chetwynde (pronounced either "Beest Cheating" or "Beast Chained", depending on the reviewer). Margot invites him to spend the summer at King's Thursday, her country estate in Hampshire, supposedly to tutor her son, Peter, although it's obvious from the beginning that she's attracted to the handsome young teacher. As for Paul, for the first time in his life, he's in love.

King's Thursday is a centuries-old Tudor stately home, a lesser, more run-down version of Brideshead. By the time Paul arrives, it's been modernized out of recognition by yet another eccentric character - "Professor" Otto Silenus, an architect who works for Margot and is currently her lover. Silenus, who believes that factories are the only truly perfect buildings as they care for machines rather than people, has turned the estate into a Bauhaus-inspired monster of concrete, glass and aluminum. He tells Paul that Margot has twice asked him to marry her but he refused. "She would interrupt me terribly," he says. "Besides, she's getting old. In ten years she will be almost worn out."

Throughout the summer, with Otto no longer in the picture, Paul and Margot spend time getting to know each other. She throws a party to introduce him to her society friends, the "Bright Young Things" whose exploits dominate the gossip pages. One of the guests is older, fatter and much less fashionable than the others. This is the corpulent Minister of Transportation, Sir Humphrey Maltravers. He tells Paul that Margot is damaging herself, hanging around with this set:

"What Margot ought to do is marry - someone who would stabilize her position, someone,' said Sir Humphrey, 'with a position in public life."

Luckily for Paul, Margot is not in love with Maltravers or any of her other suitors. When Paul asks her to marry him, she agrees, and wedding plans go ahead full steam - new clothes, expensive gifts from Margot, a honeymoon in Corfu. Unfortunately, there's a glitch. Unknown to Paul, his fiancée's fortune stems from a thriving trade in prostitution. When Paul is caught up in her shenanigans, she flees the country, leaving Paul to be arrested and held for trial. While he's waiting for his case to come up, Peter Beste-Chetwynde visits him in his cell, telling him that if Paul agrees, Margot will marry the odious Maltravers, who is now the Home Secretary, and who will then use his influence to get Paul out of jail. As Peter says, she does feel rather guilty for Paul's predicament and, short of going to prison herself, will do anything to help.

"You can't imagine Mamma in prison, can you?" Peter says. Paul agrees - no, he can't. The penal system is made for other, lesser creatures; a woman like Margot is above it.

Hoping that his sentence will be short, Paul says he'd prefer it if Margot waited for him. The sentence that is handed down is a shock: seven years penal servitude, beginning with a month in solitary confinement. Contrary to what you might expect, these four weeks are some of the happiest of his life. He enjoys the solitude, the time for reflection, and the peace and quiet, after a summer of hectic social activity. Plus, there's a sense of familiarity about prison life; as he reflects, "anyone who has been to an English public school will always feel comparatively at home in prison".

For all its lightheartedness, *Decline and Fall* is preoccupied with themes that will recur in later novels: honour and dishonour, moral ambivalence, the tension inherent in the English class system. He knows he might have saved himself from prison by informing on Margot but he feels that would have been an ungentlemanly thing to do.

Margot doesn't completely abandon him. She organizes special food to be delivered to him in prison and eventually finds a way to get him out. After faking his own death, Paul returns to Scone College, keeping his last name and pretending to be a distant cousin of that other Paul Pennyfeather who left in disgrace. He picks up his divinity studies where he left off, relieved to be where he never should have left - on the sidelines.

In *Decline and Fall* Waugh creates an archetype he returns to again and again: a modest hero drawn into exceptional and exciting circumstances who eventually returns to his comfortable, humdrum existence. Paul Pennyfeather is essentially an outsider, as was Waugh, in spite of his privileged upbringing and his many fashionable and aristocratic friends. Much of the book is autobiographical in origin: Scone College is based on Hertford College, Oxford, where Waugh was educated. The Bollinger Club, home to the "ghastly Oxford toffs", is almost certainly designed after the notorious Bullingdon Club, whose "privileged members are known for vandalism and ostentatious displays of wealth". And the dreadful Llanabba Castle School where Paul goes to teach is a thinly disguised version of Arnold House, the Welsh school whose headmaster, "a tall old man with stupid eyes", offered Waugh a £160-a-year post teaching history, Latin and Greek. "Apparently," he recorded in his diary, "the school is so far away from any sort of place of entertainment that it is quite impossible to spend any money at all there."

When Evelyn Waugh was alive, his reputation was one of "snobbery, greed, irascibility, homophobia, homosexuality, anti-semitism, bigotry and bad manners". He was gifted with a sharp but uncharitable sense of humour and was unforgiving in print towards those he disliked. It's fair to say he had all the social prejudices of his age and only a few of the graces.

A nice man? No, not really. But a very funny book.

Week 43: *Atonement*, by Ian McEwan (2001)

Who of us are so perfect that we've never wished we could go back and do something differently? Or simply not do it at all? *Atonement*, published in 2001 and filmed six years later, is generally believed to be one of Ian McEwan's best novels. It was shortlisted for the Booker Prize and made TIME magazine's list of the 100 greatest English-language novels since 1923. It resonates, I think, because the author touches that part of us where we are the most frail, the most human - in many ways, the most corrupt. "All of us," McEwan has said, "have done something we regret. How we manage to remove that from our conscience, or whether that's even possible, interested me."

The story begins in the summer of 1935 at the country estate of an upper-class English family. Thirteen-year-old Briony Tallis, the budding novelist of the family, is awaiting the arrival of her cousins, Lola and the twins. She's written a play, *The Trials of Arabella*, and plans to rehearse it with her cousins and put it on for the family. She, of course, will play Arabella, but when it comes to reading the play with her cousins, it somehow gets away from her. Lola assumes the leading role, and Briony is reduced to the lesser role of director.

Gazing out at the garden fountain, feeling disappointed and disgruntled, she witnesses a moment of sexual tension between her older sister, Cecelia, and Robbie Turner, their housekeeper's son. Robbie has grown up with the Tallis children - Cecelia, Briony, and Leon, their older brother - and has been treated like one of the family. Taking the incident out of context, Briony mistakenly believes her sister has been insulted, even assaulted. This leads her to assume the role, in her mind, of her sister's champion. And this, in turn, is the catalyst for the misdeed that will change the course of events for her sister and Robbie, and will haunt her for the rest of her life.

The moment in the garden is transformative not only for Briony, but also for Robbie. It forces him to admit to himself that he's passionately in love with Cecelia. Back in his room, getting changed for dinner, he decides to write her a letter, apologizing for the incident by the fountain. He writes several drafts, eventually settling on one that is short, friendly, and casual. In a last minute humourous impulse, he adds a kind of postscript containing a vulgar sexual reference, then sets the letter aside and writes another, leaving out the offensive wording. Heading into the house for dinner that night, he hands Briony the envelope and asks her to deliver it to Cecelia. Immediately after giving it to her, he realizes he's given her the wrong letter, the one he wrote as a joke. The one containing the word "cunt".

Cecelia reads the letter, which has been opened; she knows that Robbie loves her and knows that Briony has read it. Robbie follows her into the library, attempts to apologize, and they end up making love. Briony enters the library and again misinterprets the situation: she thinks she's been witness to an assault. The terrible things he said in the letter, which she only vaguely understands, together with what she thinks she has seen, confirm her belief that Robbie is, in the words of her cousin, "a maniac".

During dinner, which is attended by Briony's older brother and his friend, Paul Marshall, the twins go missing, and the family institutes a search for them in the surrounding woods. Briony, searching alone in the darkness, discovers her cousin Lola being raped by a man whose face she cannot see. When questioned by the police, she tells them it was Robbie she saw. Lola, for her part, claims not to have seen her attacker, and is unable - or unwilling - to identify him. The reader has good reason to believe the assailant is Leon's friend, Paul, but that isn't confirmed until much later. Robbie is arrested, despite the protests of his mother and Cecelia, and eventually sent to prison for a crime we know he didn't commit, on the word of a thirteen-year-old girl who wants to be a hero.

After several years in prison, Robbie is released to join the British Expeditionary Force (BEF) fighting in France. Before he leaves, he meets up with Cecelia, who has become a nurse and has cut off all contact with her family, especially Briony. They share a kiss and she tells him she'll wait for him - as she's been doing all these years. The war goes badly, and the Allied troops are in retreat. Robbie, who's been wounded, marches towards the sea at Dunkirk, sustained by the memory of that brief meeting and the promise of a safe haven if he can only reach England. The wound in his abdomen festers, causing him to become increasingly delirious and confused. He finally collapses on the beach at Dunkirk and falls asleep, waiting for the evacuation to begin.

In the meantime, Briony, now seventeen, is filled with remorse for her part in what happened four years ago. She has given up her place at Cambridge and is training to be a nurse, like Cecelia. She's still writing, although maturity and experience have given her a new, modern sensibility: "The age of clear answers was over. So was the age of characters and plots . . . It was thought, perceptions, sensations that interested her, the conscious mind as a river through time, and how to represent its onward roll, as well as all the tributaries that would swell it, and the obstacles that would divert it . . . She had read Virginia Woolf's *The Waves* three times and thought that a great transformation was being worked in human nature itself, and that only fiction, a new kind of fiction, could capture the essence of the change".

I first read *Atonement* 10 years ago; it's haunted me ever since. McEwan has perfectly captured, I think, the insecurities and self-aggrandizing impulses common to adolescent girls. Briony is not an evil child, if such a thing exists, but her perspective, positioned as it is between childhood ignorance and increasing sexual awareness, leads her down a very dark path. I was thirteen once and I can relate. While I don't think I would have put others in jeopardy to make myself seem important, I can't say I wouldn't have done so, given the opportunity.

As a work of metafiction - that is, one in which the text is self-consciously aware that it is fiction - *Atonement* is actually the book Briony is writing to atone for the past. Her dilemma is this: "How can a novelist achieve atonement when, with her absolute power of deciding outcomes, she is also God? There is no one, no entity or higher form that she can appeal to, or be reconciled with, or that can forgive her. There is nothing outside her. In her imagination she has set the limits and the terms. No atonement for God, or novelists, even if they are atheists. It was always an impossible task, and that was precisely the point. The attempt was all."

Art of any kind is always about the attempt. As Browning wrote, "Ah, but a man's reach should exceed his grasp, Or what's a heaven for?" Ian McEwan, an avowed atheist, would, I think, agree.

Week 44: *Madame Bovary*, by Gustave Flaubert (1857)

Gustave Flaubert (1821 - 1880) came of age during a time of transition between the revolution of 1830 and that of 1848. It was an era of tremendous political and intellectual upheaval, a time when poets and writers like Wordsworth, Coleridge and Walter Scott denounced the rationalism of the Enlightenment, seeing themselves as champions of the marginalized and the oppressed. However, by the time Flaubert wrote his seminal debut novel, the Romantic Movement was as obsolete as the bourgeois mediocrity that had preceded it. The world was ready for a new, modern approach to literature - or so it thought. When it came down to it, though, it wasn't altogether ready for *Madame Bovary*.

Flaubert's unsentimental, and relatively sympathetic, portrayal of a married woman's adulterous affairs shocked even the most broad-minded readers of the day. The scandal that greeted the serialization of the book in the fall of 1856 lead to an obscenity trial the following January. Acquitted of the charge, Flaubert found himself with a bestseller on his hands. As you would expect.

The story begins with young Charles Bovary, a stolid, even-tempered only child, dominated by his mother and neglected by his father, who is sent to school at the age of 12 where, by dint of steady work and the lack of distractions, he does well enough to pass his exams. At his mother's urging, he studies medicine and, through her, finds a position as a doctor in a small town in Normandy, not far from Rouen. Madame Bovary

Senior also finds him a wife, a middle-aged widow named Héloïse who is some 20 years older than Charles but has an annual income of 1200 francs.

One night Charles is called out to set the broken leg of a local farmer. While there, he meets the farmer's daughter, Emma - beautiful, dainty, and well-spoken. Charles falls in love with her, and makes excuses to visit his patient as often as possible, in order to catch a glimpse of the daughter. When Héloïse dies unexpectedly (not to mention conveniently), Charles lets a decent interval pass and then begins to court Emma in earnest. For her part, she sees Charles as sufficiently handsome and well-bred to make a good husband; more than that, though, she longs to escape from the tedium of the farm, and so agrees to marry him.

For a short while, they're happy together. Charles is thrilled beyond measure to have captured such a prize - a beautiful young woman, convent educated, with a taste for luxury and refinement. But those tastes have been formed by her appetite for romantic novels; they are superficial, a little silly, and ultimately unattainable. Quite quickly Emma finds herself bored by the life of a small-town doctor and increasingly irritated by her husband, whom she sees as dull, uncouth, and uninteresting. After they attend a ball given by a wealthy nobleman, she becomes even more dissatisfied:

"At the bottom of her heart . . . she was waiting for something to happen. Like shipwrecked sailors, she turned despairing eyes upon the solitude of her life, seeking afar off some white sail in the mists of the horizon . . . each morning, as she awoke, she hoped it would come; that day she listened to every sound, sprang up with a start, wondered that it did not come; then at sunset, always more saddened, she longed for the morrow".

Thinking she needs a change of scenery, Charles gives up his practice and moves them to a larger town, where Emma gives birth to a daughter. But his wife finds no more satisfaction in motherhood than in marriage. She forms a friendship with a young law student, Léon Dupuis, who shares her appreciation for the finer things in life. Léon quickly falls in love with Emma but she, wishing to preserve the image of a dutiful wife, conceals her feelings for him. In despair, Léon leaves for Paris to continue his studies. A wealthy landowner, Rodolphe Boulanger, turns up at Charles' office and notices the doctor's pretty wife. Boulanger is a rake; he has always had mistresses, generally of the professional kind, but Emma's sweet, naive ways attract him. He launches a quest to seduce her and invites her to go riding with him for the sake of her health. Charles, of course, agrees, and Boulanger and Emma begin an affair. Now, like the heroines of her novels, she has a lover:

"So at last she was to know those joys of love, that fever of happiness of which she had despaired! She was entering upon marvels where all would be passion, ecstasy, delirium."

Emma becomes obsessed with Boulanger; she takes great risks to visit him, sending him letters every day and rushing out before daybreak to be with him. She plagues him with unexpected visits and passionate demands to the point that he finally decides she's not worth the trouble, and drops her. Emma is devastated:

"How was it that she - she, who was so intelligent - could have allowed herself to be deceived again? and through what deplorable madness had she thus ruined her life by continual sacrifices? She recalled all her instincts of luxury, all the privations of her soul, the sordidness of marriage, of the household, her dream sinking into the mire like wounded swallows; all that she had longed for, all that she had denied herself, all that she might have had! And for what? for what?"

In an agony of grief, Emma falls ill and for a while seems close to death. Charles, distraught, gives up his work, all his responsibilities, to sit by her bed and nurse her back to health. When she seems close to recovery, he takes her into Rouen to attend the opera. There they run into Léon who has completed his education and is now working in the city. The encounter revives their earlier passion for each other - they begin meeting once a week in Rouen, on the pretext that Emma is taking piano lessons there from a Mademoiselle Lempereur.

Emma believes she's in love with Léon but she's actually infatuated with the idea of love. She wants to live the life of her romantic heroines, a life of passion, beauty, wealth, and high society. Abetted by the unscrupulous Lheureux, a local merchant, she indulges her desire for luxury goods she can't afford. He allows her to buy on credit, each time renewing the account and adding to it. He also encourages her to obtain power of attorney over Charles' estate, which allows her to go even further into debt.

Léon, for his part, has his own romantic notions: "She was the mistress of all the novels, the heroine of all the dramas, the vague 'she' of all the volumes of verse. ... She had the long waist of feudal châtelaines, and she resembled the 'pale woman of Barcelona.' But above all she was the Angel!"

In describing these hapless lovers, Flaubert neither attempts to justify their adulterous relationship nor appease the reader with pious moralizing. His writing, which is astounding for a first novel in its clear, confident, and explicit prose, manages to avoid the clichés and coy intimations we find in works by Richardson and Fielding. His narrator is detached, a little cynical, and frequently amused. While Emma and Charles are strong and believable protagonists, in many ways it's the secondary characters who carry the tale. The despicable Lherueux who encourages Emma to mire herself in debt, then calls in the account and destroys her. The tedious chemist, Homais, who practices medicine without a licence and pretends to be Charles' friend, while undermining him at every opportunity. And poor Hippolyte, the stableman, who agrees to let Charles operate on his club foot and ends up having his leg amputated at the hip.

All of these are drawn with an attention to detail that feels very real and very modern. As for Emma, wrapped in her fantasies of perfect happiness with the man of her dreams, she's as believable today as she was 150 years ago. You'll find her on every episode of "Say Yes to the Dress", explaining why she deserves to walk down the aisle in a dress that costs more than some of us make in a year.

Week 45: *Howards End*, by E. M. Forster (1910)

I've always had a fondness for books about houses. *The Fall of the House of Usher* is one of the scariest (and will be reviewed here once I get up the nerve to reread it), but there are others that come to mind: *Brideshead Revisited, Bleak House, Wuthering Heights, A House for Mr. Biswas*. Houses have personalities - what would *Gone With the Wind* be without Tara? And can you imagine Mr. Rochester and Jane Eyre anywhere but Thornfield Hall? There's the wonderful Manderley, haunted by the ghost of Rebecca, and the mansion on Long Island built by Jay Gatsby, as a physical symbol of his love for Daisy Buchanan. (More on that next week.) And in Satis House, Dickens created the perfect dwelling for the wildly eccentric Miss Havisham - it's impossible to imagine her surrounded by her decaying wedding finery in a bungalow in Surrey.

Howards End is not as stately as or as decrepit as any of these; it's a cottage in the English countryside, a converted barn, actually, and loved only by the frail and ethereal Ruth Wilcox, who has lived there since she was a child. Her husband, Henry, doesn't think much of the place. It's too small - "picturesque enough, but not a place to live in". But there's a reason E. M. Forster used the name of the house for the title: Howards End is the spiritual heart of the book. It represents everything that is precious and real in an England that is rapidly reinventing itself at the turn of the 20th Century. And not, in Forster's opinion, for the better.

The Schlegel sisters give a lot of thought to these changes. Margaret, or Meg, is the oldest and she and her sister, Helen, while not rich, have enough money to indulge in literary and artistic pursuits. Cultured, artistic and well-read, they're committed to "personal relations":

"In their own fashion they cared deeply about politics, though not as politicians would have us care; they desired that public life should mirror whatever is good in the life within. Temperance, tolerance, and sexual equality were intelligible cries to them; whereas they did not follow our Forward Policy in Thibet with the keen attention that it merits, and would at times dismiss the whole British Empire with a puzzled, if reverent, sigh."

The Schlegels and the Wilcoxes appear, at least in the beginning, to represent opposing points on the spectrum. Henry Wilcox, in particular, is a man of the Modern Age. Forster refers to him as "the man who had carved money out of Greece and Africa, and bought forests from the natives for a few bottles of gin". Materialistic, pragmatic, and opinionated, he doesn't concern himself much with anything he can't buy or sell: "He lived for the five minutes that have past, and the five to come; he had the business mind". His children, Charles, Paul and Evie, are cut from the same cloth. These are the kind of people who, while not unkind or ungenerous, see humanity in terms of "us" and "them".

As different as they are, circumstances bring them together. Having met during a walking holiday in Europe, the sisters are invited to spend a few days at

Howards End. Because Tibby, their younger brother, isn't well, Margaret begs off and Helen goes on her own. During the visit, she has a brief romantic encounter with Paul Wilcox, the younger son. It turns out badly, causing embarrassment to all concerned, and the Schlegels determine to stay well away from the wealthy Wilcox family in future. Which, they assume, will be easy, seeing as they have neither friends, family, nor interests in common.

However, not long afterwards, the sisters are shocked to learn that Henry and Ruth Wilcox have taken a flat in London directly across the street. In order to avoid any unpleasantness, Helen makes an impromptu visit to her cousin, Frieda, in Germany. When Margaret goes to visit Mrs. Wilcox she learns that Paul has gone off to Nigeria and Ruth and her husband have taken the flat to be in London for their daughter Evie's wedding. The older woman talks of Howards End - the meadow, the flowers, and the giant wych-elm, "the finest wych-elm in Hertfordshire" which is thought to have magical properties. There are pigs' teeth stuck into the trunk, about four feet from the ground, and legend is that if they chew a piece of the bark it will cure a toothache.

During a Christmas shopping trip, the subject of houses comes up once again. When Meg confides that the lease is up on their house, Wickham Place, and it will shortly be sold, the older woman is horrified. On an impulse, Ruth invites Margaret to come with her to Howards End. However, just as they're preparing to board the train, Henry and Evie turn up and the visit is postponed. Not long afterwards, Ruth dies, leaving a handwritten note saying she wants Howards End to go to Margaret. Her family, assuming she was not in her right mind when she wrote it, or had been unduly influenced by the Schlegels, toss the note into the fire.

In the meantime, another figure has entered the picture. Because of a mix-up during a performance of Beethoven's Fifth Symphony, the Schlegels are introduced to an impoverished insurance clerk named Leonard Bast. Leonard has had none of the Schlegels' advantages but he, too, is interested in music and literature. In normal circumstances, their paths would never have crossed. Now that they have, the sisters take up his cause. How might the young man be helped? Encountering Henry Wilcox one night on the Embankment, they seek his advice regarding Leonard's situation. Henry says the insurance company where Leonard works is about to fail and he should get out. That information is passed along to Leonard, who quits his job, lands another, and then is let go from that one. Leonard is worse off than before, all because he listened to the Schlegels - who listened to Henry.

Gradually, Margaret and Henry develop a friendship. Although he's stuffy, two decades older than her, and not at all idealistic, she sees him as kind and well-meaning. For his part, Henry's attracted to Margaret's unconventionality. When he learns that the lease is up on Wickham Place, he offers to rent her his house in London. While showing her around the place, he proposes marriage. Surprised at how happy this makes her, Margaret considers the offer and accepts. They decide to marry in the fall, after his daughter's wedding.

In the meantime Helen visits the Basts and find them homeless, close to starving, and surviving on handouts from his relatives. Determined to embarrass Henry into doing something for them, she brings them to Evie's wedding reception, upsetting both her sister and Henry, who recognizes Mrs. Bast as the former prostitute he had an affair with years ago in Cyprus. Believing he's been set up, Henry breaks off his engagement with Margaret and Helen disappears, giving no reason for her departure and telling no one where she is. Before she leaves, however, she arranges to give Leonard a cheque for £5,000, which he, to his credit, refuses.

In *Howards End* Forster takes a hard, sometimes cynical, look at English society and the stratified nature of its hierarchy. While Helen believes that connecting with others on a personal level can break through the confines of class and social conventions, Margaret is inclined to think it's really about money. "Money pads the edges of things," she says, "there's never any great risk as long as you have money." There's an indictment here of the Schlegels and their friends: unlike the Basts, they can be as bohemian and offbeat as they like - they will always have a roof over their heads. Leonard and those like him, who make up the working poor, don't have that option.

And so we come back to the beginning: to houses. To the security of a roof that doesn't leak, walls that will not crumble, rent that will always be paid. Tragic events will occur before the story ends - and I won't spoil it for you by recounting them here. But the resolution is satisfying. As Ruth Wilcox wished, Margaret and her family restore life to Howards End; the house, like "the Dude" Lebowski, will abide.

Week 46: *The Great Gatsby*, by F. Scott Fitzgerald (1925)

"Let me tell you about the very rich," Fitzgerald once wrote. "They are different from you and me." He wrote it in a short story, "The Rich Boy", while he was waiting for *The Great Gatsby* to be published. It's worth quoting in full because it's at the heart of the *Gatsby* narrative:

"Let me tell you about the very rich. They are different from you and me. They possess and enjoy early, and it does something to them, makes them soft where we are hard, and cynical where we are trustful, in a way that, unless you were born rich, it is very difficult to understand. They think, deep in their hearts, that they are better than we are because we had to discover the compensations and refuges of life for ourselves. Even when they enter deep into our world or sink below us, they still think that they are better than we are. They are different. "

This hard, beautifully-written critique of America during the Jazz Age surprises me each time I read it. It surprises me because I think I know what it's about, and then I find something new in it - something I hadn't recognized before. This time around what seems most obvious is that this cautionary tale of frustrated ambition and excess might have been written yesterday, it so poignantly mirrors America in the time of Trump.

The story takes place during the summer of 1922, in the prosperous fictional communities of West and East Egg, Long Island. Nick Carraway, a Yale graduate originally from the Midwest, has come to New York and taken a job as a bond salesman. He rents a small house in West Egg, next door to the mysterious Jay Gatsby - mysterious because all that is known about him is that he's very rich and throws extravagant parties which he never seems to attend.

Nick's second cousin, Daisy, and her husband, Tom Buchanan, live across the bay in fashionable East Egg, home to those with "old" or inherited money. They invite Nick for dinner where he meets Daisy's girlfriend, Jordan Baker, an attractive professional golfer. While there, Jordan intimates that Tom's "got some woman in New York", which later turns out to be true. Returning home that night, Nick sees his neighbour, Gatsby, standing out in the dark, arms outstretched towards the green light at the end of the Buchanan's pier.

Shortly after this visit, Tom introduces Nick to his mistress, Myrtle Wilson. Myrtle is the wife of a local garage owner, and is about as far removed from the delicate, diaphanous Daisy as it's possible to be. She and her husband live in a desolate area between the city and the suburbs, known as the valley of ashes, which is dominated by a decaying billboard advertising the services of an opthalmologist called Doctor T. J. Eckleburg. The eyes of the doctor, reminiscent of those of Orwell's Big Brother, are "blue and gigantic — their retinas are one yard high."

Gradually, over the summer, Nick and Gatsby become friends. Nick learns that Gatsby - who used to be James "Jimmy" Gatz - fell in love with Daisy five years ago. Although she married someone else, he never stopped loving her and has dedicated himself to winning her away from Tom. Everything about him - his enormous house, his lavish parties, his unbelievable background story (which is, quite simply, unbelievable) - is geared to impress her. He has come to Long Island and bought this house because he believes he has finally become the kind of man Daisy can marry, the kind of man who will fit into her world - the world of the very rich - the world of privilege.

"The truth was that Jay Gatsby, of West Egg, Long Island, sprang from his Platonic conception of himself... [He] invented just the sort of Jay Gatsby that a seventeen-year-old boy would be likely to invent, and to this conception he was faithful to the end."

In her book *Careless People: Murder, Mayhem, and the Invention of The Great Gatsby,* Sarah Churchwell reminds us that "a mirage may be more marvelous in its way than an oasis in the desert. Gatsby's great error is his belief in the reality of the mirage; Fitzgerald's great gift was his belief in the mirage as a mirage". In this way Fitzgerald was more prescient than many of his contemporaries, including Hemingway. Half a decade before the Wall Street crash wiped out the savings of millions of investors and collapsed the fortunes of many of "the great and the good", he saw the American dream for what it was - an illusion built on hubris and corruption, already in demise.

Having waited without success for Daisy to turn up at one of his parties, Gatsby prevails upon Nick to invite her to tea, without Tom. The meeting is awkward at first, but by the end of the afternoon it seems the intervening years have fallen away and Daisy and

Gatsby are reunited. It's obvious that Gatsby believes it's just a matter of time, now, before Daisy will leave Tom and come live with him in his mansion; Nick isn't so sure.

"I wouldn't ask too much of her," he says. "You can't repeat the past."

"Can't repeat the past?" Gatsby is incredulous. "Why of course you can."

What he doesn't understand, not having been brought up with these people, is that they are meretricious and essentially venal. Nick, who knows them better, describes them best near the end of the book:

"They were careless people, Tom and Daisy - they smashed up things and creatures and then retreated back into their money or their vast carelessness, or whatever it was that kept them together, and let other people clean up the mess they had made . . ."

Myrtle, her husband George, and Gatsby are all "smashed up" in the end. Myrtle is killed by a car driven by Daisy; George, believing Gatsby is responsible, shoots him and then turns the gun on himself. Gatsby's funeral, arranged by Nick, is attended by a few servants, the mail carrier, and Gatsby's father. Of all the hundreds of socialites, debutantes, celebrities and freeloaders who came to Gatsby's parties, only one, a man known as "Owl Eyes", turns up to pay his respects.

Fitzgerald was disappointed with the response to this, his third novel. "I want to write something new," he told his editor, Max Perkins, "something extraordinary and beautiful and simple & intricately patterned". He died at the age of 44 believing himself a failure, his works forgotten. Almost a century later, *The Great Gatsby* is regularly named as one of the greatest English-language novels and sells millions of copies annually. Had it been just a memoir of the Jazz Age - fun, frivolous and decadent - it might indeed have been forgotten. It's the tragedy that keeps it fresh, the eternal struggle to be better than we are, the frustrated effort to revive the things we have lost.

"So we beat on, boats against the current, borne back ceaselessly into the past."

Week 47: *Fall on Your Knees*, Ann-Marie MacDonald (1996)

A few years ago, in an interview with *Herizons* magazine, Ann-Marie Macdonald had this to say about sexual abuse:

"The act of abuse doesn't take very long. It's often a fleeting moment in one's life, but the ripple effects - the water table is poisoned from then on, the food chain is poisoned."

She was talking about the young protagonist of her second novel, *The Way the Crow Flies,* but she might just as easily have been referring to *Fall on Your Knees,* her disturbing debut novel of ambition, heartbreak and incest. Set in Cape Breton and, briefly, in New York during the days of the emerging jazz scene, *Fall on Your Knees* deserves the accolades it's received over the years - it won the Commonwealth Writers' Prize, was chosen as Book of the Month by Oprah, and has been translated into 17 languages. It is a masterpiece. And, as is often the case with such stories, its readers are divided into two camps: those who love it and those who - well, don't.

I admit to being a member of the latter group right from the beginning. I didn't love it because of the hype - because it received so much fawning attention - and because (I'm being brutally honest here) my own first novel, released the same year, didn't. Don't let anyone ever try to convince you writers are generous, altruistic souls, happy for every success of one of their members. To paraphrase La Rochefoucauld, "It's not enough that one should succeed; other writers must fail."

Reading it now, being older and, if not wiser, at least more sanguine about these things, I'm prepared to agree with Oprah. The book is simply stunning.

At the age of 18, James Piper, a piano tuner, falls in love with the daughter of one of his clients, a wealthy, Lebanese merchant. Materia is 12, going on 13, too young to marry, and so they elope. Her father is furious, and the family disowns her. After Materia gives birth to their first child, Kathleen, James realizes he has indeed married someone who is a child in every way. Materia has no interest in being a wife or taking on any "wifely" responsibilities. More than that, she find herself unable to love the baby and leaves its care and upbringing to her husband. Eventually she gives birth to three more daughters - Mercedes, Frances, and Lily, who dies three days later. Dimly aware that there is something unnatural about James' obsession with Kathleen, Materia grows to hate him, and is comforted by a kind neighbour, Mrs. Luvovitz, who takes her under her wing, teaching her to cook and sew and generally acting as her mother.

Kathleen grows into a beautiful, intelligent young girl, gifted with a spectacular voice. James decides she will become an opera singer; he works long hours to afford her singing lessons, and encourages her to distance herself from the rest of the community - her classmates think she's a snob and turn against her. Her only friend is her father. By the time she's 14, James has become aware of the "demon" within him - his sexual attraction to his daughter - and fears he won't be able to resist it. When Great Britain declares war on Germany, he enlists, mainly to remove himself from Kathleen's presence. Materia rushes off to church, to thank Our Lady for sending the war. Unfortunately, James is only

211

able to put off temptation for so long. After earning a Distinguished Service medal for risking his life several times over, he's injured and sent home in December of 1917. Anxious to find another way to distance himself from his daughter, he arranges for Kathleen to go to New York to study with "the maestro". Her world opens up - she discovers what it truly means to suffer for her art, and what it means to fall in love. Her great adventure comes to an abrupt conclusion when an anonymous telegram informs James that his daughter has become "ensnared in a net of godless music and immorality". He rushes to New York and hauls her back to Cape Breton - nine months later she dies giving birth to twins. The story behind this, along with Kathleen's New York narrative, is revealed near the end of the book, when we're presented with the pages of her diary.

Macdonald's research is extensive but I wouldn't call it faultless. Some of the dialogue, especially in the early part of the book, sounds as though it is spoken by a teenager from the sixties: before an upcoming performance, Kathleen is so nervous, "I could puke!" She thinks her father is "so corny", a term that didn't come into popular use till the 1930s. Which was about when the term "teenager" itself began to be used, although Macdonald applies it to Kathleen in 1914. The book is full of small but annoying anachronisms: Materia, in 1898, teases James about money, calling him Rockefeller. Yes, Rockefeller was rich at that point but he wasn't a household name - certainly not in the backwaters of Cape Breton. A gifted pianist, Materia plays Scott Joplin's "Maple Leaf Rag" in the summer of 1899 - the tune wasn't published until that fall. When war breaks out and James is sent overseas, Materia prays he'll be killed "quickly and painlessly" in

Flanders. There's simply no way she could have known that the fighting would take place in that particular part of France. And don't get me started on the reference to Rudolph (as in the red-nosed reindeer) 20 years before the character was created.

But there are many things to like, even love, about this book. The bagpipes may be an acquired taste but I love this description: "A primitive reed instrument awakens something very old, and puts sorrow in a consolingly long perspective. Perhaps because grass is the oldest musical instrument for all kinds of people." More than that, though, is what I can only call the courage of the writing. There have been other tales of incest but there is nothing even mildly derivative about *Fall on Your Knees*. In my opinion, this is mainly because of the characters - they are unforgettable. The wayward Frances, who carries within her the shame of being "bad", and dies at 40 never knowing the fate of her only son. Mercedes, the good sister, whose selfless piety is a mask for utter despair: "Hope," she realizes, "is a gift. You can't choose to have it. To believe and yet to have no hope is to thirst beside a fountain." And Rose, the black, cross-dressing pianist, Kathleen's accompanist and eventually her lover. Even James, whose prurient desires have defiled both his wife and his daughters, proves himself worthy of respect in the hell of No Man's Land. Macdonald is too good a writer to let any of them, even the despicable patriarch, become a stereotype.

Fall on Your Knees is as richly-layered, as eccentric, and as haunted as the Cape Breton landscape. And almost as beautiful.

Week 48: *A Farewell to Arms*, by Ernest Hemingway (1929)

I always want to slap Hemingway's women. They never seem like fully realized characters. Unlike the men, who, while they may not always be admirable, at least are recognizably human. Hemingway believed that women, along with politics, drink, money and ambition, ruined a writer. So it's not surprising that his women tend to fall into two categories: bitches, like Margot Macomber*, who find ways to humiliate their husbands, and seductress-victims who are "understanding" of the men who abuse them.**

My favourite, if I had to pick one, is Brett Ashley, the aristocratic love interest in *The Sun Also Rises*. Brett, too, is a bitch, but an interesting character, and the closest Hemingway ever came to writing a woman I might like to sit next to at dinner.

He could be very sentimental about his women. Catherine Barkley is a good case in point. She's a nurse, and a good person. It helps that she's beautiful. In the hands of another writer she'd be a strong, engaging character, and when we first meet her she is just that. Once she falls in love, however, she becomes somebody else altogether.

A Farewell to Arms is set in Italy during the final years of the First World War. Lieutenant Frederic Henry, the narrator, is an American ambulance driver with the Italian army based in a town near the Austrian front: "The town was very nice and our house was very fine." (It's lines like this that inspired the annual "Bad Hemingway" writing contest which ran from 1977 to

2005.) When he meets Catherine, she's mourning the death of her fiancé who was killed in the battle of the Somme. She should have married him, she says, before he left:

"He could have had anything he wanted if I had have known. I would have married him or anything. I know all about it now. But then he wanted to go to war and I didn't know."

Henry, who's had plenty of brothel sex, has never been in love. It takes him a while to fall in love with Catherine, although he lies to her and tells her he loves her. When he's wounded in the knee and sent to a hospital in Milan, Catherine - who has been transferred there - comes to see him. It's then that he realizes he's in love with her; their liaison has grown from being a game to take their minds off the war to a proper love match. From this point on, Catherine becomes a typical Hemingway love object:

"I'll say just what you wish and I'll do what you wish and then you will never want any other girls, will you? . . . I want what you want. There isn't any me any more. Just what you want. . . . I'm good. Aren't I good? You don't want any other girls, do you? . . . You see? I'm good. I do what you want."

People in love say all kinds of silly things. What's galling is that it's always the women who say them. Like a feudal lord, Henry accepts her oaths of allegiance but never makes any of his own. They spend all their free time together and eventually the inevitable occurs: reluctantly, she tells him she's pregnant. Being a Hemingway gal, of course, she assures him she doesn't want him to worry about it:

"I'll try and not make trouble for you. I know I've made trouble now. But haven't I been a good girl till now? . . . You simply mustn't worry."

Meanwhile, there's a war on. The Germans and Austrians launch an offensive, and the Italians are forced to retreat. Henry, back in action with his knee repaired, travels with some other drivers, two Italian engineering sergeants, and two frightened young girls. When the sergeants abandon the drivers when their car gets stuck in the mud, Henry shoots one of them, and another driver finishes him off. Further up the road, the Italian military is singling out officers and shooting them, blaming them for the series of defeats. Henry, too, is pulled aside - believing he's about to be executed, he jumps into the river and escapes.

At this point, Henry has made his own "separate peace", as he puts it. He's done with the war, a conflict he never fully embraced. He believes in doing his duty, and has earned himself a medal for his courage. But the rhetoric of war, words like "sacred", "glorious", and "sacrifice", embarrass him:

"We had heard them, sometimes standing in the rain almost out of earshot, so that only the shouted words came through, and had read them, on proclamations that were slapped up by billposters over other proclamations, now for a long time, and I had seen nothing sacred, and the things that were glorious had no glory and the sacrifices were like the stockyards at

Chicago if nothing was done with the meat except to bury it."

Having escaped death by drowning, Henry makes his way to Stresa, where he reunites with Catherine. If the Italians discover his whereabouts, he'll likely be arrested - maybe shot - for desertion. Knowing that, he and Catherine flee to Switzerland, rowing across the lake in a storm. They arrive safely and are arrested shortly after landing; however, as they carry both passports and money they aren't detained for long. A soldier drives them to Locarno, where their money helps them secure provisional visas. They rent a cabin in the mountains overlooking Montreux and spend the next few months in a kind of honeymoon state, making plans for the future and trying not to think about the war.

As the time nears for Catherine's delivery, they move to Lausanne to be close to the hospital. Three weeks later she goes into a long, painful, protracted labour. Drunk on nitrous oxide, she assures him she's not going to die, and Henry, the atheist, bargains fervently with God to let her live. The baby, delivered by Caesarian section, is stillborn; Catherine continues to hemmorhage and dies on the operating table. Her death, like that of the child, like that of the thousands of young men who are dying every minute of this war, is predestined:

"If people bring so much courage to this world the world has to kill them to break them, so of course it kills them. The world breaks every one and afterward many are strong at the broken places. But those that will not break it kills. It kills the very good and the very gentle and the very brave impartially. If you are none of these you can be sure it will kill you too but there will be no special hurry."

Darn it all anyway. The man could write.

*"The Short Happy Life of Francis Macomber"

**Liz, in "Up in Michigan"

Week 49: *The Electric Kool-Aid Acid Test*, by Tom Wolfe (1968)

In 1967, at the peak of the Summer of Love, Tom Wolfe set out to chronicle the adventures of Ken Kesey and his followers, the Merry Pranksters. All he knew about Kesey at that point was that he was "a highly regarded 31-year-old novelist and in a lot of trouble over drugs". Five years earlier he'd achieved bestsellerdom with *One Flew Over the Cuckoo's Nest,* which was made into a play the following year; in 1964 he followed that up with *Sometimes a Great Notion,* which has been described as the quintessential novel of the Northwest.

Wolfe, who died last week at the age of 88, was no slouch, either, having honed his writing skills as a regional newspaper reporter and coming to prominence with *The Kandy-Kolored Tangerine-Flake Streamline Baby*, a collection of essays that heralded the advent of New Journalism. Wolfe probably felt there was no one better placed than he to get inside the story and bring it to life. And he was right. Kesey and Wolfe were a perfect fit. As *The Guardian's* Jarvis Cocker has said, it was a case of "someone seeking new ways to tell stories described by someone else seeking to find a new form of journalism."

The Electric Kool-Aid Acid Test, published in 1968, is an as-if-first-hand account of the Pranksters' journey across the country in a colourfully-painted school bus named "Further". The way Wolfe writes it, it's difficult to believe he wasn't there, embedded with the Kesey troupe, right from the beginning. But he wasn't. His first meeting with Kesey is three years later, when

Kesey's released from the San Mateo County Jail after serving six months for marijuana possession. At that point he embeds himself with the Prankster contingent, and interviews just about every individual connected with the "journey" including, of course, Kesey himself. Using flashbacks, poetry, and changing points-of view, Wolfe translates the psychedelic experience with a versimilitude that is almost uncanny. He doesn't just describe tripping on acid . . . the encounters with the Hell's Angels . . . the music of the Grateful Dead. He makes you *feel* it.

The saga begins on a three-acre property in the California redwoods, where Kesey and his entourage - his wife Faye, their children, and an increasing number of followers - experiment with mind-expanding drugs, most notably LSD. Kesey had been introduced to acid and mescaline a few years earlier, when he volunteered to take part in government studies to supplement his income. A charismatic and dynamic individual, Kesey quickly becomes a kind of psychedelic warrior, the evangelistic leader of drug-fueled revolution which spreads from his estate near La Honda to the San Francisco Bay area and, eventually, across the country to New York. They buy an old school bus, slather it in Day-Glo paint, and set off to drive across the country. As luck would have it, Neil Cassady turns up and offers to do the driving. This would appear to be a gift from Heaven; to have the driver/hero of Kerouac's *On the Road* conduct them on their soon-to-be historic journey is an obvious sign that they are the direct and rightful inheritors of the tradition of the Beats.

The goal of the bus trip (which sounds like a nightmare, by the way, if only for the lack of any washroom facilities) is partly to get Kesey to New York in time for the publication release of *Sometimes a Great Notion*. Beyond that, they plan to meet up with the Acid Culture guru himself, Timothy Leary, and the League for Spiritual Discovery, based in Millbrook, New York. High on speed, driving with one hand and keeping up a running commentary on - well, on everything, Cassady drives while the Pranksters take turns filming the trip, which results in over 100 hours of pretty random footage. When it's finally edited - somewhat - it's 30 hours long and only Cassady stays awake long enough to see it.

The rendezvous with the Leary cohort is not a success. The Pranksters are put off by the subdued, almost monk-like nature of the Millbrook adherents. They'd expected to be greeted with wild jubilation; instead, as Wolfe puts it, there's a general vibration of "We have something rather deep and meditative going on here, and you California crazies are a sour note".

Back in California, the Pranksters set out to turn on the masses. They stage a series of Acid Tests: light-and-sound events featuring the Grateful Dead and Big Brother and the Holding Company, offering Kool-Aid laced with LSD. In the middle of the fun and mayhem, Kesey and Mountain Girl are caught and charged with smoking marijuana. Kesey fakes suicide and escapes to Mexico, where he hides out in Manzanillo on the Pacific coast, and is joined by a few of the others. After eight months of living with increasing paranoia, Kesey returns to the States with a new mission: drugs have taken them along the path to enlightenment, but it's time to move on. As you might imagine, the idea of giving up drugs doesn't go down well with the "togglecoat bohemians, boho slugs, lumpen beatniks" and "the jellybeancocked masses". An Acid Test Graduation is planned for October 31, 1966, but The Grateful Dead, Bill Graham, and other influential people pull out of the deal at the last minute. The event goes ahead, on a much smaller scale, with only the Pranksters themselves buying into the whole thing.

Afterwards, Kesey is arrested on the previous drug charge and sentenced to six months in jail. Before he begins his stretch on the work farm, he moves his family to Oregon, and sets up house on his brother's farm. Neil Cassady dies by a railroad track outside San Miguel de Allende, and the painted school bus, "Further", is resigned to the "swamp", a wet, low-lying area behind the Kesey family farm.

Wolfe himself never took acid. He believed it was far too dangerous and he had good reason to think so. He felt he could tell a better story by "saturation reporting", staying with his subjects and observing them for long periods of time. He wasn't immune to Kesey's charm, but the book is not a hagiography. What comes through, time and again, is the absolute, overwhelming egomania of the Pranksters, only thinly disguised as a search for enlightenment. Satori through abandoning every vestige of responsibility. Not for nothing did he come up with the phrase the "Me Generation".

But there are some wonderful moments: the Hell's Angels roaring up Highway 84, descending in all their awesome badness on the peace-loving Pranksters. Cathy Casamo, stoned out of her gourd, racing from the bus without a stitch on, and immortalized in "head" lore as Stark Naked. The denizens of Haight-Ashbury circa 1966 - Jack the Fluke, "a laughing grizzly

Irishman with a beard like an Airedale"; Owsley Stanley, the paranoid acid genius; Terry the Tramp, of Hell's Angels fame. Not to mention the Pranksters themselves: Mountain Girl, Doris Delay, The Hermit, June the Goon, Marge the Barge, Freewheeling Frank the Hell's Angel, Cassady flipping his sledgehammer, Babbs, Gretchen Fetchen, George Walker, Zonker with his Arab headdress playing Torrence of Arabia. And Kesey himself, "the elder statesman of psychedelphia", in his buckskin shirt and red Guadalajara boots.

The things that bother me, rereading the book, are exactly what disturbed me back in the 60s. The way women are portrayed, for example, as very minor characters in the psychedelic journey, even when they're married to the hero, or about to give birth to his child. And the attitude of the "heads" towards those who are working to make political change:

"Some kid who could always be counted on to demonstrate for the grape workers or even do dangerous things like work for CORE in Mississippi turns up one day— and immediately everybody knows he has become a head. His hair has the long jesuschrist look. He is wearing the costume clothes. But most of all, he now has a very tolerant and therefore withering attitude toward all those who are still struggling in the old activist political ways for civil rights, against Vietnam, against poverty, for the free peoples. He sees them as still trapped in the old 'political games,' unwittingly supporting the oppressors by playing their kind of game and using their kind of tactics, while he, with the help of psychedelic chemicals, is exploring the infinite regions of human consciousness".

Much of it seems almost quaint - the fervent belief held by so many at the time that "mind-expanding" drugs would lead to a new and better society. But the writing itself is powerful, intense, visceral, absolutely engaging. As a counterculture document *The Electric Kool-Aid Acid Test* stands with *On the Road, Slouching Towards Bethlehem,* and *Fear and Loathing in Las Vegas.* As Siskel and Ebert used to say, "Two thumbs up!"

Week 50: *Portnoy's Complaint*, by Philip Roth (1969)

"So. Now you know the worst thing I have ever done. I fucked my own family's dinner."

That line, one of the most memorable in modern literature, appears about halfway through Philip Roth's humorous, sexually explicit monologue, which is prefaced by the following clinical definition: "Portnoy's Complaint: A disorder in which strongly-felt ethical and altruistic impulses are perpetually warring with extreme sexual longings, often of a perverse nature". Given the nature of those "extreme sexual longings", the sexually-molested-dinner event shouldn't come as a shock. But it does.

Alexander Portnoy is an unmarried, sexually frustrated, guilt-ridden American Jew who's come of age at the dawn of the sexual revolution. It's tempting to see him as Roth's alter ego: when Alex begs his therapist to help make him a man - "Enough being a nice Jewish boy, publicly pleasing my parents while privately pulling my putz!" - we can hear the voice of the respectable boy from Newark, New Jersey, demanding to be heard. The fact is, though, that it's Roth's gift as a writer that convinces us his characters cannot be completely fictional. We believe in them the way we sometimes believe in an actor's onscreen character. Rock Hudson was gay, you say? But didn't he make love to Doris Day?

Framed as a therapy session, the book has Portnoy confessing every lustful urge, every shameful, intimate recollection to his psychoanalyst, Dr. Spielvogel. The roots of his dysfunction are, of course, embedded in his childhood, raised as he was by a loving but chronically constipated father and an intensely controlling mother. All of Alex's neuroses, we are told, come down to his mother. Sophie Portnoy is, without doubt, the archetype of the Jewish mother: nagging, meddling, manipulative, and emasculating. (I'm reminded of a Jewish friend of mine whose mother called out, just as he was leaving to hitch-hike across Europe, "Don't take any rides from strangers!")

Desperate to please her, while inwardly rebelling against her, teenage Alex, the model student, the perfect son, finds release in masturbation on an almost heroic level. Self-abuse is seen as a subversive act; he "whacks off" at every spare moment. Anything, it seems, can serve as a prop for his favourite hobby - an empty milk bottle, a sock, a baseball mitt ... even a piece of raw liver. (Hence the assault on the family's dinner.)

Locked in the bathroom, Alex fantasizes about *shiksas* - blonde, blue-eyed, all-American girls, preferably well-endowed, who call him "Big Boy" and demand that he "beat it to a red hot pulp". In this way, young Alex is not so very different from any other teenage boy on the planet. Well, apart from the liver, perhaps. But most young boys grow up. At least, I'd like to think they do. Alex does not. Two decades later, he's still conflicted, still self-loathing, and still beating it to a pulp. Except now, instead of dreaming about mindless fucking and jerking off into his baseball mitt, 33-year-old Alex is bedding as many *shiksas* as he can find.

None of them, however, are good enough. When he finally meets Mary Jane Reed, the beautiful model (and possibly ex-call girl) who fulfills every one of his fantasies, he's still not satisfied. She's dumb, for one thing - what's a nice Jewish man with an IQ of 158 doing with a girl who's functionally illiterate? And so he dumps her in Rome, after first engaging in a threesome with a prostitute - twice. "You've made me as degraded as you!" she cries. Which is precisely the point. A self-hating character like Alex can't simply fuck women, he has to find ways to demean them.

We'd call Alex a sex addict today, or worse. In the wake of Harvey Weinstein et al we don't have much time for men who need to debase women in order to pump up their egos. There's a scene near the end where Alex does his best to rape a young Israeli woman; only the fact that he loses his erection ("I can't get a hard-on in this place," he moans) prevents him from carrying it out. As for his mother - well, 50 years on Sophie doesn't seem nearly as awful as we thought she was. At least she *cares*. At least she *pays attention*. And surely we're past all that baloney about castrating mothers causing impotence in their sons. We *are* past it, aren't we?

When it was published in 1969, the *New Yorker* hailed it as "one of the dirtiest books ever published". And it may be. But *Portnoy's Complaint* is more than literary porn. Its "lust-ridden, mother-addicted" protagonist raises questions about what it means to be a man, what it means to be Jewish - what it means to be alive in America in the 20th century. *The Guardian*'s Chris Cox has argued that the reason the book stands up so well, so many years later, is because it "transcends its own vulgarity . . . by using sex to explore pretty much everything else: history, culture, identity, religion, politics". One of its most poignant scenes is the death of 15-year-old Ronald Nimpkin, another "good Jewish boy" who lives in Alex's building. "You couldn't look for a boy more in love with his mother than Ronald!" the women say after Ronald is found dead, hanging from the shower head. In a particularly brilliant Rothism, he's written his mother a note and pinned it to the collar of his shirt: "Mrs. Blumenthal called. Please bring your mah-jongg rules to the game tonight. Ronald."

Roth went on to become one of the most awarded authors in America. He received the Pulitzer Prize in 1997 for *American Pastoral* and in 2001 in Prague he was awarded the inaugural Franz Kafka Prize. He wrote - brilliantly, in my opinion - right up to the moment he decided to stop, five years ago, at the age of 80. "I did what I could with what I had," he said. Unlike some of his compatriots, he knew when to quit.

Irving Howe, who hated the book, dismissed it as "an assemblage of gags". The worst thing anyone could do with *Portnoy's Complaint*, he said, was to read it twice. Well, *I* read it twice and I loved it. Forgive me, Irving, but with all due respect, I think you're a bit of a schmuck.

Week 51: *The Elegance of the Hedgehog*, by Muriel Barbery (2006)

When I was 23, I brought a copy of *Ulysses* with me to Greece and carried it around for five weeks. I never actually got around to reading it, but carrying it with me made me feel a cut above my fellow backpackers, most of whom were toting copies of *Catch-22*, *Siddhartha*, and *The Hobbit*. All good books, definitely. But for sheer difficulty, I'll still put James Joyce in the top 10, if there is one.

My point is that there are books we read because they make us feel smarter. They are not necessarily the books we read for pleasure.

Muriel Barbery's 2006 publishing phenomenon (it has sold more than two million copies and been translated into 40 languages) is an amalgam of both. Its references to phenomenology, Japanese art-house films, and the works of the Dutch masters flatter the reader while the surprising and insightful observations that appear on every page surprise and please us. Barbery's genius is to have put these pronouncements into the mouths of two very unlikely narrators: a squat, middle-aged, rather ugly concierge of a Paris apartment, and a precociously literate 12-going-on-thirteen-year-old girl.

Renée Michel, the concierge, is 54 years old. She has been a widow for 15 years and for the past 27 she's been the concierge at number 7, rue de Grenelle. All her life she's been poor, plain, and of no consequence. The people she works for, the wealthy inhabitants of this *hôtel particulier*, pay her no more attention than they would any other hireling. She exists to keep the townhouse clean, take messages, answer the door. The idea that she might have an interior life, especially one that is complex, sensitive, and astute, is scandalous.

But Madam Michel has a profound inner life. Lacking any formal education, she's studied and read practically everything worth studying and reading. Her cat is named Leo after Tolstoy, her favourite author; she adores 17th century Dutch painting, Japanese arthouse movies, and the music of Purcell and Mahler. She listens to opera, waxes ecstatic over *Death in Venice*, and has read enough of Edmund Husserl to conclude that phenomenology is a fraud - "nothing more than the solitary, endless monologue of consciousness". All of this, however, she keeps hidden from the other inhabitants of the building, who are, almost without exception, rich, superficial, and bourgeois in every sense of the word.

Hiding herself is not just important - it's essential, as she sees it. Having never had reason to expect anything from the world, she wishes simply to be left to enjoy her books, her music, and her dark chocolate in peace. She opens up only to Manuela, the Portuguese cleaning woman, with whom, on Tuesdays and Thursdays, she shares tea and conversation.

Barbery is not "just" a novelist, if there is such a thing - before quitting her job to write full time she was a philosophy professor. In an interview in 2007, shortly after the book came out, she said that in creating the character of Renée Michel she was "inspired by the idea of a reserved, cultured concierge who turned stereotypes on their head and at the same time created a compelling comic effect". She does the same thing with the second narrator: Paloma, the youngest daughter of the Josses, who occupy the fifth floor of the building. Paloma is unlike almost any other 12-year-old you're likely to meet. She shares many of Renée's values, and harbours a deep disgust for the superficiality of those of her family. Her mother is conventional and useless, her sister is a "walking disaster", and her neighbours are privileged snobs. She's also like the concierge in that she, too, hides her real nature from those around her. If her parents and teachers knew how exceptionally gifted she really is, she "would never have a moment's peace".

Unable to see anything worthwhile in the life she is living, Paloma has decided to commit suicide on the 16th of June, the day she turns 13. She is quietly stealing her mother's sleeping pills, one at a time. When the day comes she will use them to kill herself - after first setting fire to the apartment. In the meantime, she is keeping two diaries, one called "Journal of the Movement of the World" in which she records her observations of the world around her; the other is called "Profound Thoughts" in which she sets down her reflections on art, poetry, people and herself.

Profound Thought No. 9 provides us with the title of the book:

"Madame Michel has the elegance of the hedgehog: on the outside she's covered in quills, a real fortress, but my gut feeling is that on the inside, she has the same simple refinement as the hedgehog: a deceptively indolent little creature, fiercely solitary - and terribly elegant."

The Elegance of the Hedgehog, for the first half of the book, is really a series of philosophical essays. As a novel, it only comes into its own with the appearance of the delightful Kakuro Ozu, a wealthy, middle-aged businessman who moves into the building and forms a friendship with Renée. He sees in her the cultured, perceptive individual she is; in his company she comes out of her shell and thrills to fine Japanese cuisine while discussing, in no particular order, Yasujiro Ozu (a distant relation), Tolstoy, exile and the irreducibility of culture.

"For the first time in my life," she tells herself, "I have made a friend."

And yet. While Kakuro appears oblivious to their differences in social standing, Renée is all too aware of how it must seem to others. How ludicrous, that such a wealthy, refined, and successful gentleman would seek out the company of a servant. When he invites her to have dinner with him on his birthday, she turns him down. Paloma, who has witnessed this refusal, pushes her to explain herself. And so we learn about Lisette, Renée's beautiful older sister, who had the temerity to demand more out of life, and was punished for it. The lesson she learned was: if you want to survive, keep your head down. Don't fraternize with those who are not of your class.

Barbery suggests that society conspires to prevent us from ever really seeing other people: "We never look beyond our assumptions and, what's worse, we have given up trying to meet others; we just meet ourselves. We don't recognize each other because other people have become our permanent mirrors." When Renée finally allows herself to be seen, to be recognized for the perceptive, unique individual she is, she experiences a level of happiness that borders on ecstasy. And Paloma, observing this transformation, finds a reason to go on living. Change is possible, after all, and there is beauty in this world.

If I were being hypercritical, I'd say that Barbery's characters strain the limits of credibility. I can believe, to some extent, in a self-taught concierge who reads Proust; I find it more difficult to believe that an adolescent girl, even one as intelligent as Paloma, can be as familiar with 16th century poets as she is with manga, can discuss Vermeer and Racine and Japanese haikus, and regularly listens to Glenn Miller before setting off for school in the morning.

But novels are all about suspending disbelief, and once you do that, you can accept almost anything.

Week 52: *The Fall of the House of Usher; The Pit and the Pendulum*, by Edgar Allan Poe (1839 and 1842)

The Fall of the House of Usher is 19 pages long. *The Pit and the Pendulum* is even shorter. By the standards of your average novel, these hardly make the grade. But, as David Rush writes in my edition of *1001 Books You Must Read Before You Die* - a title that seems especially menacing this week - these works deserve inclusion "because it is simply impossible to imagine the modern novel without considering Poe's masterful writing".

I need to state here and now that I've never been a fan of the genre, in books or on film. Case in point: I was so traumatized by descriptions of Hitchcock's *Psycho* that I only saw the film a few years ago - on TV, at a safe distance from the television set, with my eyes squeezed shut during the shower scene.

So, yes, when it comes to horror I'm a wuss. I attribute it to an overactive imagination combined with a lifetime of watching the news: there are enough scary things happening in real life without going out of your way to pay money to see them.

When I was 11, my best friend - I'll call her Bonnie, because that was her name - loved horror flicks. She was a tomboy and an athlete and I don't think she had a nervous bone in her body. She coaxed me into going with her to see *The Fall of the House of Usher*, the first of Roger Corman's popular series of films based on the stories of Edgar Allan Poe. I don't remember much about it because I had my eyes shut during the scary bits - which comprised most of the movie.

The next year, as if I hadn't learned my lesson, Bonnie persuaded me to see *The Pit and the Pendulum*. I kept my eyes open and had nightmares for a week.

Between 1960 and 1965, Corman made eight films loosely adapted from Poe's stories; if they were your introduction to Poe, as they were mine, you want to keep in mind that the key word here is "loosely". They were meant to be low-budget horror flicks, and they were that, but they had Corman at the helm - who directed some 55 films, including *The Little Shop of Horrors* - and starred the inimitable Vincent Price. They were well-made, for the most part - especially *The Masque of the Red Death* - but they didn't have much to do with the books.

To get back to those, I have a bone to pick with the *1001 Books* editors: if the reason for including Poe is because of his influence on the modern novel, it would make more sense to include either *The Murders in the Rue Morgue* or *The Purloined Letter*. Or both. With these stories, and his amateur sleuth, the Chevalier C. August Dupin, Poe created the template for the modern detective novel. He wrote the rules, really: the concept of the armchair detective who outwits the local police; the object hidden in plain sight, invisible to everyone except, of course, the armchair detective; the concept of solving a crime by observation and deduction. Sir Arthur Conan Doyle called him "a model for all time", and who are we to argue?

Poe's horror tales, on the other hand, draw on the Gothic horror tradition begun by Horace Walpole in the 18th century and continued by Mary Shelley, Washington Irving, and a host of others. Dark and suspenseful as they are, they're not groundbreaking. And if you've seen one dank, rat-infested, medieval dungeon - well, you've seen them all.

Set in Toledo, Spain, during the last days of the Inquisition, *The Pit and the Pendulum* features an unnamed narrator who falls into a swoon after being found guilty by a tribunal of white-lipped, black-robed judges. When he awakes he's in a damp, airless chamber, so dark he cannot see his hand in front of his face. At first he fears he's been locked in a tomb, but as he slowly feels his way around the walls it becomes apparent that he's been placed in one of Toledo's infamous dungeons. After he comes within inches of falling into a deep, circular pit, he realizes that this was supposed to be his fate - to fall into the abyss and drown.

Once again, he loses consciousness. This time, when he awakes, he finds he's been strapped down to a wooden frame, facing the ceiling. Now there is just enough light to allow him to see that a large pendulum with a razor-sharp edge is suspended directly above him. It swings slowly back and forth, and begins to descend towards his chest. At the last moment, with the aid of the scraps of meat left out for him, he attracts the attention of the rats swarming up from the pit. They crawl over his body, chewing away at the straps that tie him down, and he's able to slip free just in time.

The pendulum is raised to the ceiling, and the walls of the dungeon become red-hot. They begin to close in, pushing the prisoner closer to the edge of the pit. Just as he's about to lose his foothold and fall to his death, there's a blast of trumpets and the sound of voices shouting. The walls retreat, and an arm catches him just before he falls: "The French army had entered Toledo. The Inquisition was in the hands of its enemies."

With *The Fall of the House of Usher* Poe gives us another unnamed narrator, one who arrives at the end of "a dull, dark, and soundless day" at the home of his childhood friend, Roderick Usher. Usher has written to him, begging him to come and see him in order to help alleviate some kind of mental disorder. The house itself, which stands on the brink of a "black and lurid tarn", is ancient, its stones covered in fungus. Although the outer walls appear intact, he notices a barely perceptible fissure extending from the roof of the building down to the foundation.

His friend is glad to see him but is obviously not well:

"Surely, man had never before so terribly altered, in so brief a period, as had Roderick Usher! . . . The now ghastly pallor of the skin, and the now miraculous lustre of the eye, above all things startled and even awed me. His action was alternately vivacious and sullen. His voice varied rapidly from a tremulous indecision . . . to that species of energetic concision . . . which may be observed in the lost drunkard, or the irreclaimable eater of opium, during the periods of his most intense excitement."

Usher confides to his friend that he suffers from a nervous affliction, made worse, he says, by his sister's illness. The lady Madeleine is gradually wasting away, to the despair of her doctors, who can find neither a cause nor a cure. Her death, Usher says, will leave him "the last of the ancient race of the Ushers".

Not long afterwards, Usher announces that his sister has died. He plans to bury her temporarily in the tombs underneath the house in order to keep her body away from the sinister designs of the physicians. As grave-robbing was a fairly common practice on the part of medical students, especially when the cause of death was "interesting", the narrator agrees to help carry her body down to the small, damp, subterranean vault. At this point, he learns that the lady Madeleine and her brother were twins - something you'd assume he'd know, seeing that he and Roderick have been friends since boyhood.

But to continue:

A week goes by and Roderick become more and more uneasy. One stormy night, when the narrator cannot sleep, Roderick comes to his door in a state of complete agitation. He leads him to the window; looking out, they see that the house and grounds are enveloped in a strange, luminous vapour. In an effort to distract him, the narrator offers to read aloud. While he's reading, he hears noises that match the descriptions in the books - the cracking and ripping of a wooden door, a dreadful, unnatural shriek, the clanging of a metal shield falling to the floor. He leaps to his feet and rushes to where his friend is sitting, rigid and staring at nothing, speaking softly and quickly, as if to himself.

"We have put her living in the tomb," he says. And then: "I tell you that she now stands without the door!"

The door blows open and there stands the lady Madeleine, blood on her robes, her emaciated figure showing signs of some terrible struggle. With a low moan, she falls onto Roderick, and brings him lifeless to the ground. Fearing for his life, the narrator flees the building. He turns to see the house, in the light of the "full, setting, and blood-red moon" begin to crack along its fissure, eventually crumpling into the waters of the tarn.

A prolific genius, Poe was one of the most influential American writers of all time. His stories play on our deepest fears and anxieties - he knew about the dark bits at our core and brought them to life in ways that remain relevant today.

As Stephen King has put it, "Poe's The Man. What more can I say?"

Week 53: *Eugene Onegin*, by Alexander Pushkin (1837)

It's often said that only those who know Russian can fully enjoy Alexander Pushkin's masterpiece, *Eugene Onegin*. They may be right. But until the time when you or I can read the original, I recommend Charles Johnston's translation, published in 1977 by Viking Press. For a non-Russian speaker like myself, it gives a sense of the beauty and originality of the phrasing. Written in the form of a poem, *Onegin* is at once playful and deeply serious; Johnston captures the humour, the irony, and the pathos of the story. He also, in his translation, has cast the narrative in what is known as the *Onegin* stanza, a form of sonnet invented by Pushkin and substantially different from the traditional Shakespearean and Petrarchan sonnets.

I'm not a poet and if you want to learn more about this verse form, you can go online and check it out. Apart from stating that the *Onegin* stanza is almost impossible to accomplish in English, I'll say no more about it. Except that Johnston seems to have done it, and done it astonishingly well.

Pushkin's story is deceptively simple: Eugene Onegin, a handsome, worldly young man, adept at seducing young women and casting them aside, grows jaded and bored with high society, and retreats to an estate in the country left to him by his uncle. While there he makes friends with a neighbour, a good-looking young poet named Vladimir Lensky who embodies all the youthful ideals Eugene has discarded. Lensky is romantic and naive and deeply in love with Olga Larin, the beautiful but rather thoughtless daughter of a local landowner.

Onegin, curious to get a glimpse of the girl, accompanies him to dinner at the Larin home. While there he notices Olga's older sister, Tatyana, and suggests to his friend that while Olga is pretty but essentially shallow, her sister is more interesting.

At 17, Tatyana is shy, quiet, and reserved, and capable of an intensity of feeling that rivals any poet. From an early age she's devoured romantic novels, especially those by Samuel Richardson and Jean-Jacques Rousseau, and when she meets Eugene Onegin she sees in him the embodiment of the dark, brooding Romantic hero. After waiting in vain to see or hear from him again, she writes him a letter in which she declares her passion. He doesn't respond and so she writes to him again, and then again. When they do finally meet up, he lets her know politely but in no uncertain terms that he's not in love with her and marriage between them will never happen. He also, rather condescendingly, gives her some advice about keeping her emotions under control in the future.

Tatanya is devastated. She can't sleep, can't eat . . . her whole being is focused on Eugene, to the exclusion of any other possible suitors. One night she dreams that a large black bear chases her, then carries her into a house full of monsters having a party. The host of the party is Onegin, who appears as a kind of demon. Olga and Lensky enter the room and Onegin, furious, picks up a carving knife and appears to kill Lensky. She awakes anxious and uneasy and searches a book for answers but receives none. Several days later Lensky invites Onegin to attend Tatyana's name-day celebration, insisting it will be a small affair, just a few family and friends. It turns out to be a large, noisy party, with half the county in attendance. Angry at

Lensky for tricking him into coming, Onegin decides to take his revenge by flirting with Olga and monopolizing her for the entire night. Believing he's been gravely insulted, Lensky challenges his friend to a duel; Eugene, who now regrets his actions, feels compelled to respond in kind. They meet at the appointed place, raise their pistols, and shoot. Lensky falls to the ground; by the time Eugene rushes to his side, the young poet is dead. After a brief period of mourning, Olga marries a cavalryman and Tatyana, still brooding over Eugene, is persuaded to travel to Moscow to stay with an aunt. There she's brought to one social event after another, with the aim of finding her a husband. She hates the city and pines for the natural beauty of the countryside. As for Eugene, he's overcome with guilt and remorse over Lensky's death, and has left the country.

When he next sees Tatyana, she's a composed, sophisticated young matron, married to a fat, older military man and living in St. Petersburg. There seems to be almost nothing left of the shy, vulnerable country girl he once rejected. Now it's his turn to fall in love, and his turn to be rejected. He writes to her, but she doesn't reply - writes again, and again. Just as Tatyana wrote to him. He spends the winter in seclusion, reading his books. As spring appears, he goes to her home and finds her in tears, reading his letters. Now she confesses that she loves him as much as she ever did, but she will not allow him to ruin her. She is married, and plans to stay that way. And there Pushkin leaves them - Tatyana, mature and strong within herself, Eugene Onegin alone and distraught.

Tatyana Larin is probably the best-loved character in Russian literature. She feels very real, much like Jane

Austen's Elizabeth Bennet - a strong, complicated young woman who refuses to fit into a mould. Pushkin, I think, adored her, the way a writer comes to love a character he's created who lives life on her own terms. He's reported to have said to a friend, while writing the end of *Onegin:* "Do you know, my Tatiana has rejected my Eugene. I never expected it of her." Don't you love that?

As for Eugene Onegin, he and Pushkin have much in common - educated, articulate, and wealthy - but Onegin is essentially hollow at the core, something that could never be said about the author. In an unhappy twist of fate, Pushkin's own life ended when he fought a duel with his brother-in-law over his wife's affections. He was 37.

Week 54: *Sons and Lovers*, by D. H. Lawrence (1913)

I've always felt that if you're going to read D. H. Lawrence, you should start with *Sons and Lovers,* his seminal tale of passion, domestic conflict, working-class aspirations, and poverty. Set in the Nottingham coalfields at the turn of the last century, it's a story of becoming - becoming a man, an artist, a lover. The hero, Paul Morel, is closely based on Lawrence himself. Like Paul, Lawrence's father was a semi-literate miner who married an educated woman who quickly became dissatisfied with her husband and placed her hopes and aspirations on her children - her sons in particular. As one of her biographers has said, "She needed her children to make up for the disappointments of her life."

Lawrence began working on this, his third novel, at a time when his mother was ill with cancer (she died before it was finished) and he used it to lay out in detail his admiration for his mother, her contempt for his father - which was shared by her son - and their deep, abnormally intense relationship: "[S]he was the chief thing to him, the only supreme thing". At one point, near the end of the book, he stoops to kiss her and she cries, "I've never had a husband - not really."

But back to the story. Gertrude Coppard, the refined daughter of "a good old burgher family", meets and falls in love with a rough-hewn, handsome, and engaging young miner named Walter Morel. He quite literally sweeps her off her feet; they marry, move into a rented house, have children. Very soon, she sees her marriage as a crashing failure; they have little money and nothing in common. To her chagrin, she, who had reason to expect more out of life, has been reduced to the meagre existence of a miner's wife.

She shifts her affections to her son, William, who is so attached to his mother he is burdened with guilt when he attends a fair without her. Eventually he leaves for London, where he does well and is engaged to be married to a pretty but shallow young socialite. When he dies of pneumonia, his mother is understandably devastated - she's lost everything that made her life worth living.

Almost everything. Because there's still Paul, who is as handsome and bright as his older brother but is also gifted with a sensitive, artistic nature. She turns her attention to him, monitoring his every move, encouraging his artistic endeavours and urging him to believe in his art. It goes without saying that she's not going to be fond of any young woman who threatens this relationship. When his friendship with the beautiful, sensitive, and spiritual Miriam Leivers grows into a love affair, platonic though it is, Mrs. Morel sees it as a threat:

"She is one of those who will want to suck a man's soul out till he had none of his own left," she said to herself; "and he is just such a gaby as to let himself be absorbed. She will never let him become a man; she never will."

Which is ironic when you consider that if anyone is determined to keep Paul under her thumb and stunt his manly growth, it's his mother.

Paul's feelings about Miriam waver. In their passion for nature and books, they are soulmates. There are ideas he can share only with her. But Miriam isn't interested in a sexual relationship. She wants to live her life, with him, on a higher, spiritual plane, and he often feels suffocated to the point of hating her. Through her, he becomes friendly with another woman, Clara Dawes, who is estranged from her husband. Clara intrigues Paul partly because of her beauty - she's tall and blonde, rather statuesque - and partly because of her reputation as a suffragette. Clara is older than Paul, and sexually mature. Wary of each other at first, they eventually become lovers. With her, he experiences physical passion for the first time but eventually concludes that Clara really still "belongs" only to her husband.

I was an English lit major back in university, and my fourth year was dominated by "the men": Lawrence, Hemingway, Faulkner, and Fitzgerald. Lawrence came first, coming to maturity before the First World War, but he set the tone. At the time, I remember being impatient with him, for all kinds of reasons. First of all, I disliked the way he hated his women in between bouts of loving them. And while I appreciated - and still do - his superb descriptions of the open, hilly countryside of his childhood, his worship of nature-with-a-capital-N felt overblown . . . overwritten. Anthony Burgess calls him an animist, "as prepared to believe in the Aztec Quetzalcoatl as in the Greek Aphrodite". In his biography of Lawrence he refers to his "mysticosensual relationship between man and the earth - specifically, Laurentian man and the Laurentian earth - a little hard to accept and rather easy to parody".

When it comes right down to it though, I think the sexual intensity of the mother-son relationship that lies at the heart of the novel embarrassed me. A kind of psychological incest is hinted at - if there is such a thing. As a child Paul loves to sleep with his mother, which isn't that unusual, but as adults they behave like sweethearts. He swears he loves her above any other woman, she is his only love. Her sons, first William and then Paul, are her surrogate husbands; they will never be able to truly love any woman as long as she is alive.

Reams have been written about Paul Morel and his mother and I'm sure none of it would come as a surprise to the author. Psychoanalytic theory was in its infancy but Lawrence would have been aware of Freud's Oedipus complex, and he certainly understood that his relationship with his mother was unusual. When she was dying he wrote to a friend:

"We have been like one, so sensitive to each other that we never needed words. It has been rather terrible and has made me, in some respects, abnormal."

The death of his mother leaves Paul adrift, bereft of any kind of rudder . . . totally without purpose. He has broken off his relationships with the two women who loved him - Miriam who wanted to sacrifice herself for him and Clara who desired a mature, stable relationship. As he leaves Miriam for the last time, he wonders where he will go. He calls out for his mother - "She was the only thing that held him up, himself, amid all this" - and you feel he's dangerously close to giving up entirely.

Thankfully, he doesn't. In the final paragraph of the book, Paul makes the decision not to give in to "the darkness", and walks resolutely toward town.

Week 55: *The Shining*, by Stephen King (1977)

It says a lot about what you view as literature when you're surprised to find Stephen King included in a list of *1001 Books You Must Read Before You Die*. But he's in there. And he deserves to be, if only for *The Shining*, his disturbing tale of marital tension, telepathy, and madness. As there is likely not an adult in the English-speaking world who hasn't seen Stanley Kubrick's 1980 adaptation, I feel compelled to let you know - for those who haven't read it - the movie is quite different from the book. In some ways, it's better, in that the movie had Jack Nicholson as Jack Torrance, Shelley Duvall as his wife, and Kubrick at the helm. In the film, Nicholson's mental deterioration is shocking and undeviating; the book, on the other hand, is more of a psychological thriller, posing some difficult questions. Such as: What, exactly, is madness, and where does it come from? There are certainly external forces at work here (more about those later), but are the seeds of insanity simply buried within us, waiting for conditions to ripen and allow the madness to bloom.

The book begins with Jack Torrance, a writer and a recovering alcoholic, being interviewed for a job as the winter caretaker for the The Overlook Hotel, a secluded mountain resort in the Colorado Rockies. Jack hopes that the isolation will give him a chance to finish a play he's been working on but the fact is, this job is a last chance for him to save his marriage. Although Jack's a loving husband and father when he's sober, when he's drunk he can be abusive and violent. Once he accidentally broke his son's arm; an argument with a student which ended in fisticuffs lost him his job as a teacher. Wendy, his wife, has considered leaving him but now that he's stopped drinking, she's agreed to try again in spite of her misgivings.

Their five-year-old son, Danny, is a bright, thoughtful child with the ability to "see" things . . . things that happened in the past, and things that may or may not take place in the future. His clairvoyance lets him hear his parents' thoughts, listen in on their whispered conversations. He knows about his father's drinking - the BAD THING, he calls it - and worries about a possible DIVORCE. His "invisible friend", Tony, is often part of Danny's visions; as the Torrances are making plans to leave Boulder for his father's new job at the hotel, Tony shows Danny a series of dark images involving destruction, blood, and the word REDRUM, pronounced "red rum". "Be careful, doc," Tony warns him. Be careful.

As you might expect, given the author, The Overlook is perhaps not the ideal location for three people to be snowbound for the better part of the winter. First of all, once the snow falls, the hotel and its inhabitants will be completely cut off. The nearest town, Sidewinder, is 25 miles away, and the roads are closed in the winter. The phone lines are likely to be down, leaving only the CB radio as a method of contacting the outside world.

Also, the hotel has a grim history. According to the manager, an "officious little prick" named Ullman, a previous caretaker named Delbert Grady went crazy and murdered his wife and two daughters, before killing himself with a shotgun. A woman committed suicide in Room 217. There've been so-called "ghost sightings" over the years, which Ullman brushes off as hysterical nonsense, but it gives everyone, including the reader, a chill.

The Torrances arrive at The Overlook on the last day of the season. Guests are departing, staff are getting ready to pack up and leave. The manager gives them a tour of the hotel, during which they meet the chef, Dick Hallorann, who shares some of Danny's psychic gifts. Recognizing the gift in Danny, he takes the boy aside and tells him his grandmother called it "shining". He explains that there are some bad things in the hotel, but they can't hurt him. Just look away, he says. But if ever there is real trouble, Danny should send out a call to him, telepathically, and if Dick hears it, he'll come.

Once Dick and the rest of the staff leave, the Torrances are left alone in the large, empty hotel. Jack attends to the chores he's been assigned, the most important being keeping an eye on the boiler in the basement. He's been warned that if the pressure is allowed to build, the whole place could blow "sky-high". Wendy cooks and cleans, and keeps her promise to Hallorann to keep the kitchen in mint condition.

Danny plays with his toys, and does his best to keep hopeful, in spite of occasional feelings that all is not well. He knows his father is struggling not to drink, and that his mother worries about both of them. He begins to "see" things - frightening images like blood and spattered brain tissue on the walls of the Presidential Suite . . . a dead woman in the bathtub of Room 217 . . . a firehose that turns into a snake. He's not the only one - while trimming the topiary hedge animals, Jack notices that they're quietly changing positions and appear to be about to attack him. He writes it off as something similar to the DTs, although he hasn't had a drink for months.

Eventually it becomes clear that Danny's psychic presence is exciting the supernatural activity that already exists in the hotel. The Overlook becomes a character in itself, a demonic force that seeks to subsume the child by working through the father. Long-dead characters - Grady, the demented caretaker, Lloyd, a phantom bartender, Lorraine Massey, the suicide - appear in various forms and urge Jack to "correct" his wife and son. The hotel bar, dry as a whistle, appears to him to be stocked with every kind of booze imaginable. He gets drunk and once he's drunk, he's not Jack the responsible father any more . . . he's Jack the monster we remember from the film. *"Here's Johnny!"* (That line, by the way, never appears in the novel.)

In his excellent book on the craft of writing (*On Writing,* Scribner: 2000), King describes his teenage fascination with horror movies, in particular the string of Roger Corman films loosely based on Edgar Allen Poe. I reviewed two of them, *The Pit and the Pendulum* and *The Fall of the House of Usher*, three weeks ago. A third, one of Corman's best, is *The Masque of the Red Death,* Poe's tale of a group of nobles who take refuge in an abbey in order to escape a fictional plague sweeping the country. King includes an excerpt from that story right at the beginning of the book. The point of the excerpt becomes clear when Jack, poring over old newspapers and scrapbooks stored in the hotel's basement, comes across an invitation to a masked ball, dated August 29, 1945. "Dinner Will Be Served At 8 P.M. Unmasking and

Dancing At Midnight". Jack, however, never gets to see behind the mask. And in the end, it destroys him.

Stephen King has made no secret of the fact that he was disappointed with Kubrick's version of *The Shining*. He hated Shelley Duvall in the role of Wendy - Duvall is an acquired taste, I agree - calling her "one of the most misogynistic characters ever put on film". But it's the character of Jack that veers most noticeably from the novel. As King says, the character has no arc: "When we first see Jack Nicholson, he's in the office of Mr. Ullman, the manager of the hotel, and you know, then, he's crazy as a shit house rat. All he does is get crazier. In the book, he's a guy who's struggling with his sanity and finally loses it. To me, that's a tragedy."

I agree. There's a psychological depth to the book that never comes across in the film. In the novel, we learn that Jack's alcoholism and anger issues stem from an unhappy childhood with a terribly abusive father. Throughout the book he is constantly trying not to become the person his father was and is truly horrified in a final lucid moment when he realizes he's about to kill his son. "Run away," he tells Danny. "Quick. And remember how much I love you." In the film, Jack never has a moment's remorse - when he finally freezes to death in the snow we can only heave an exhausted sigh of relief.

Five years ago, Stephen King wrote a sequel to *The Shining*. It's called *Dr. Sleep* and it catches up with Danny as an adult, psychologically traumatized by the events at The Overlook. King said it was a "return to balls-to-the-wall, keep-the-lights-on horror". It won the 2013 Bram Stoker Award for Best Novel.

I plan to read it. One of these days.

Week 56: Absalom, Absalom!, by William Faulkner (1936)

There are writers whose books take you into another place and hold you there, from the opening sentence until the moment, finally, when they release you. Alice Munro and the fictional town of Jubilee, Ontario. Harper Lee and Monroe County, Alabama. John Steinbeck and the Golden State of California.

William Faulkner set all but four of his novels, and 50 short stories, in Yoknapatawpha County, which was inspired by and based on Lafayette County, Mississippi, where he spent most of his life. He called it his apocryphal home, and wrote about it with the kind of somatic understanding that comes from knowing a place better than you know yourself. *Absalom, Absalom!* is one of the most difficult of these works, not only because of its structure - it's told entirely in nonchronological flashbacks by a series of unreliable narrators - but also because of the language. Which is powerful and rhythmic but wrapped in long, unwieldy sentences that can frequently run to a page or longer. The difficulty is compounded by the references to "niggers", a word that appears so often you are tempted to simply close the book and move on. But the very use of such words, tossed out so casually and frequently, underlines the brutality of a country whose economy was based on the labour of slaves. Cursed by it, as Faulkner has said.

First published in 1936, *Absalom, Absalom!* tells the story of Thomas Sutpen, who came out of nowhere and established a dynasty, only to have it fall to pieces within his lifetime. The story is told, first of all, by

Quentin Compson, who is 20 years old in 1910 and attending Harvard University. Quentin has a Canadian roommate named Shreve, and through a series of exchanges Quentin tries to explain the South to this foreigner, this cheerful young man from a cold climate who can't possibly know what it's like to be born and bred south of the Mason-Dixon line. Quentin begins by telling Shreve about a summons he received the previous summer from his elderly aunt, Rosa Coldfield. Miss Rosa never married; she has "the rank smell of female old flesh long embattled in virginity". The house she lives in is "unpainted and a little shabby, yet with an air, a quality of grim endurance as though like her it had been created to fit into and complement a world in all ways a little smaller than the one in which it found itself". Rosa has nourished a bitter hatred of Thomas Sutpen for more than 40 years and she wants to tell Quentin the reasons. She has something else in mind, as well, although we don't get to hear about that until very near the end of the book.

As Rosa tells it, Sutpen rode into town one day in 1833 accompanied by a "wild" band of slaves and a French architect who'd been somehow coerced into working for him. Through means that were legal but not necessarily ethical, he bought 100 square miles of land from a local tribe and spent the next two years building a cotton plantation and a large, ostentatious mansion. Who he was - who his people were and where they lived - was a mystery. He was a handsome but cold man, with no inclination for friendship, but he did make one friend shortly after arriving: Goodhue Compson, Rosa's father. When his mansion was built and it came time to marry, Sutpen chose Compson's older daughter, Ellen. Within a few years Sutpen, who was pretty well universally disliked and even feared, was well established within the local aristocracy and had fathered two children, Henry and Judith, with Ellen, and another daughter, Clytie, with one of his slaves.

After listening to Rosa's version of Thomas Sutpen's story, Quentin sits with his father and they go over it, the story of Sutpen and his legacy. We learn that Rosa's anger towards Sutpen goes back to the time when, after Ellen died, he proposed to her. But in doing so, he offered her such an outrageous insult she walked away and never forgave him.

But it isn't until much later that we learn that Sutpen was born into poverty in the backwoods of West Virginia (which wasn't West Virginia until a half century had passed). He ran away when he was 14 after being snubbed by a well-dressed Negro who turned him away from the door when he was trying to deliver a message. Having heard about the West Indies during the short period when he attended school, Thomas gets it in his head that one could go there and, if one was courageous and shrewd, one could become rich. He finds a ship, lands in Haiti, and becomes the overseer of a French sugar plantation.

After showing great courage in subduing a slave revolt in 1827, Sutpen marries the plantation owner's daughter and fathers a son. (It should be mentioned, I think, that there were neither slaves nor French plantations in Haiti at this time. In 1791 the slaves revolted and by 1804 the independent republic of Haiti was the first black national state of the Americas.) After the child is born, Sutpen learns that he's been tricked: his wife, Eulalia Bon, has negro blood. Sutpen renounces her, hands over his fortune to her as compensation, and leaves. The child, however, will reappear 30 years later.

At the age of 20, his son Henry goes to college at the University of Mississippi where he meets the handsome, sophisticated, and laconic Charles Bon, who is eight years older. Henry looks up to Charles, aping his style and manner of speaking, and they become close friends. In his letters home, Henry talks about his new friend, how much he admires him and so on, and Ellen, who lives in a kind of perpetual fantasy, decides that Charles and Judith will marry. That Christmas, Henry brings Charles home for a visit, and Sutpen recognizes him as the son he left behind in Haiti. Without acknowledging this to anyone, he forbids the marriage - primarily, one would think, for reasons of incest, but as it turns out, given the time and the place, the greater crime is miscegenation, or "race mixing".

When Sutpen eventually tells Henry the truth - that Charles is his half-brother - Henry says he doesn't believe it. He refuses to abandon his friend, repudiates his birthright, and leaves. Shortly afterwards, the Civil War breaks out; Charles and Henry enlist together, and for four years Henry struggles to convince himself that incest is acceptable, under certain situations. What he doesn't know, and we learn later, is that Charles has realized early on that Sutpen is his father. He's been waiting all this time for some sign of recognition from Sutpen that yes, he is his son. If Thomas will only do that, Charles will refuse to marry Judith, will leave and never return.

But Thomas is incapable of giving him even that. Instead he seeks Henry out and informs him that Charles has black blood. He knows that this, more than incest, will convince Henry to take direct action to prevent the marriage. And he's right.

The tragedy is that Henry, more so than Judith, truly loves Charles. He sees him as a kind of heroic figure. And he's not wrong: at one point, during battle, Charles saves his life. So the fact that it's he who must do his father's bidding and destroy his friend makes the final outcome even more painful.

The title, being a direct reference to the biblical story of King David and Absalom, his third and favourite son, may lead you to think of Faulkner as a "Christian writer". He has, in fact, been called that. But he wasn't. At least, not in the sense of preaching Christianity. Far from it. But he used it, as all writers use what they know. He once put it this way: "The writer must write out of his background. He must write out of what he knows and the Christian legend is part of any Christian's background, especially the background of a country boy, a Southern country boy. My life was passed, my childhood, in a very small Mississippi town, and that was a part of my background. I grew up with that, I assimilated that, took that in without even knowing it. It's just there. It has nothing to do with how much of it I might believe or disbelieve—it's just there."

Much of what we learn about Sutpen is speculation; while Quentin, his father, Miss Rosa and even Shreve attempt to translate the thoughts and intentions of characters who died before the story begins, we can never be sure if we, the readers, are meant to place any faith in their telling. Faulkner is writing myth, and debating what is true and what is not seems beside the point.

What we can say, though, is that all of his characters, young and old, are damaged. Even Quentin, a young man distanced by three generations from the darkness of those times, appears to be succumbing near the end. "I am older at 20 than a lot of people who have died," he tells Shreve. He knows the terrible truth about the South - he may not have lived it, but he carries the burden. And yet, at the very end, when Shreve asks him why he hates the South, Quentin denies it, quickly and immediately. "I don't hate it, he thought, panting in the cold air, the iron New England dark: I don't. I don't! I don't hate it! I don't hate it!"

Week 57: *Keep the Aspidistra Flying*, by George Orwell 1936)

Only in a book compiled by an English editor, with the assistance of a team of writers, editors, critics, and reporters who are also, for the most part, English, would George Orwell's third novel, following on the heels of *Burmese Days* and *A Clergyman's Daughter*, have made a list of *1001 Books You Must Read Before You Die*.

It's not that *Keep the Aspidistra Flying* is a bad book - it's pretty good, actually, and paints a vivid picture of a kind of genteel poverty that is harrowing, the more so for being based on some of his own experiences recounted in his memoir *Down and Out in Paris and London*. It's a good read - I enjoyed it. But does it really belong on a list of the most important English-language novels ever written? Side by side with *War and Peace*? *Anna Karenina*? *One Hundred Years of Solitude*? Probably not.

Orwell himself wasn't happy with the book, once it was published. In a letter to George Woodcock on 28 September 1946 he noted that it was one of the two or three books of which he was ashamed, saying he wrote it only because he needed the money. Which isn't the worst reason for writing. Especially if you're Orwell. This is the writer, after all, who would go on to give us *Animal Farm* and *Nineteen Eight-Four*.

The story takes place in England in the 1930s and centres around Gordon Comstock who, at the age of 29, has declared war on money. Intelligent, well-educated, and poor, Gordon is obsessed with the idea that everything - *everything* - revolves around money; as the song says, money makes the world go around:

"For after all, what is there behind, except money? Money for the right kind of education, money for influential friends, money for leisure and peace of mind, money for trips to Italy. Money writes books, money sells them. Give me not righteousness, O lord, give me money, only money."

If only he had money, he thinks, he'd have the time, the freedom, to write. Money would give him the right connections so that he would publish in the right places and come to the attention of the right people. "Serve the money-god," he says, "or go under." And so he chooses to go under.

Gordon is the last male in a line of respectable but dull, ineffectual family members who have never, since Gran'pa Comstock made his fortune, succeeded at anything. They are not an "old" family, "merely one of those families which rose on the wave of Victorian prosperity and then sank again faster than the wave itself". His parents and older sister, Julia, have invested all their hopes and dreams for the future in Gordon. He's bright - gifted, even - and shows literary promise. "He alone had it in him to 'succeed'". And so they spend what money they do have making sure he goes to an expensive public school, where he's tormented by the other boys for not being rich. Julia, who idolizes her younger brother, goes to work at a tea-shop, contributes to the family income, and saves her pennies for gifts for Gordon. At seventeen Gordon drops out of school, cadges off his sister for a while, and finally - grudgingly - accepts a job in the accounts department of the New Albion Publicity Company. Here he meets Rosemary Waterlow who eventually becomes his girlfriend.

While there, a slim volume of Gordon's poetry is published to mildly positive reviews. Word gets out that the accountant is actually a poet and Mr. Erskine, the managing director, promotes him to the position of copywriter. He does well in this job - so well that they raise his salary, which you'd think would be a good thing.

But it's not. Gordon is terrified of Making Good, "to sell your soul for a villa and an aspidistra!" He resents having to work for a living, and resents those who don't. He decides that what he wants is not a good job, like the one he has at the New Albion, but one that will keep him fed and sheltered without claiming his soul. And give him the time to complete his poetic opus, *London Pleasures*. Through his friend Ravelston, the wealthy left-wing publisher of *Antichrist* magazine, he's hired as an assistant at a dilapidated, second-hand bookshop: "The hours were long, the pay was wretched - two pounds a week - and there was no chance of advancement". It's exactly the kind of job he's looking for.

Surprisingly, it seems that living in a wretched bedsit in a slummy part of town, never having enough money to socialize or treat Rosemary to a decent dinner, and putting up with a nosy, penny-pinching landlady is not the Paradise you would think. The job is boring and in the evening when he does get back to his room he's either too tired, too cold, or too hungry to write. And his obsession with money intensifies. Everyone, he believes, despises him for not having money. He's convinced that Rosemary, who says she loves him, would agree to have sex with him if only he had money. She urges him to go back to New Albion - Mr. Erskine has said he'd consider taking him back. As she puts it, "We can't afford principles, people like us."

But Gordon is determined not to give in. He won't take a better-paying job, and he won't let Rosemary or Ravelston help him out. His pride, however, doesn't prevent him from continuing to "borrow" from Julia, although he hates himself every time he does it.

Gordon is profoundly depressed, and increasingly neurotic. A day out in the country turns into a nightmare when he and Rosemary end up at an expensive hotel, shamed into ordering a meal they can't afford and being humiliated by a supercilious waiter. Afterwards, they attempt to make love for the first time but Rosemary stops him when she sees he hasn't brought a condom. Even this, according to Gordon, is all about money: "You say you 'can't' have a baby . . . You mean you daren't; because you'd lose your job and I've got no money and all of us would starve."

As absurd and self-pitying as he seems, there is something rather noble in Gordon's war against money. Especially when the cost of noncompliance is so high: there was little unemployment insurance and no national health care. Falling between the tracks could, and often did, lead to disaster.

It's just that he goes about it in such a hapless manner. He professes to despise capitalism but, unlike Orwell, he's not interested in turning his literary talents to working for social justice. I'm convinced that the main reason George Orwell didn't care much for this book is because he didn't particularly like its hero.

But the story is the one that most closely mirrors Orwell's life at the time. He, too, was a struggling writer - although more gifted than Gordon - and he, too, worked part-time in a London bookshop. Orwell didn't believe he'd ever be successful in his lifetime, which made him able to relate to the sublimely unsuccessful Gordon.

The book received mixed reviews; Cyril Connolly felt all the talk about money kept it from being a proper work of art. And readers objected to the grimness of the story, which is only partly relieved by the ending - Rosemary gets pregnant, Gordon goes back to his "good" job at New Albion, and the two of them get married. In another book that might be seen as a happy ending. But, after Gordon's diatribes against bourgeois conventions, it seems anticlimactic and rather sad.

The term "Orwellian" has come to mean the dark face of the future, as described in *Nineteen Eighty-four*. But these days, at a time when the Money God reigns supreme and young people are facing overwhelming student debt and outrageous housing costs, *Keep the Aspidistra Flying* may actually be more relevant.

Week 58: *The Shipping News*, by E. Annie Proulx (1994)

It's nice every now and then to correct the experts, don't you think? My edition of *1001 Books You Must Read Before You Die* states that Edna Ann Proulx didn't start writing fiction until she was in her fifties. Which makes it sound as if she was in real estate or accounting and then, rather unexpectedly, started writing award-winning books. (In 1993 she won the PEN/Faulkner Award for *Postcards*; *The Shipping News*, which came out in 1994, received the National Book Award, the Heartland Prize from *The Chicago Tribune*, the *Irish Times* International Fiction Prize, and the Pulitzer.)

The fact is, her first published work of fiction was a science fiction tale called "The Customs Lounge" which appeared in September 1963, when she was 28. She had another the following year in *Seventeen* magazine, which I must have read as I devoured *Seventeen* and never missed an issue. (I still have vivid memories of Colleen Corby who appeared on an unprecedented 15 covers and was featured in the magazine's fashion spreads almost every month.) But back to Proulx.

I read somewhere that she wrote *The Shipping News* as an experiment. After the success of *Postcards*, which has been called a true American tragedy, her editors suggested she write something with a happy ending. If that was her intent, I'm not sure she succeeded. Although happiness is a subjective emotion and one person's fairytale ending is someone else's nightmare. This is not to say *The Shipping News* is a gloomy novel - it's filled with humour, bizarre and quirky characters, jokes . . . situations that will make you laugh out loud. But the ending is a kind of truce, an uneasy period of calm before the next storm lashes the coast.

The protagonist, Quoyle, is an unlikely hero. An overweight, lumpish 36-year-old who lives in the town of Mockingburg in upstate New York. He has a "head shaped like a crenshaw, no neck, reddish hair" and "features as bunched as kissed fingertips". He also has an abnormally large chin, which he frequently tries to hide with his hands. We never learn his first name. Quoyle is lonely and desperately unhappy. His selfish, unloving parents favoured his abusive older brother and convinced him he was, and always would be, a failure. Hi sole friend is a cheerful copy editor named Partridge, who works at the local paper and is an excellent cook. Aside from his daughters, Bunny and Sunshine, Partridge and his wife Mercalia provide Quoyle with his sole companionship.

His marriage, as such, is a farce. Petal is an attractive but nasty piece of work who will sleep with anybody and everybody, and does, making Quoyle's life a misery. In spite of her malicious taunts he sticks with her to the end, which happens when she and her lover, running away to Florida, are killed in a car crash. (The fact that Petal sells the girls to a paedophile before running away seems a bit over the top; you get the sense that Proulx wants to ensure that if we had any vestige of affection for this woman, this will be sure to snuff it out.) In spite of everything she put him through, Quoyle grieves for his dead wife, believing she was his one and only chance of experiencing love.

Quoyle struggles to keep his little family together until his aunt, Agnis Hamm, turns up and convinces him to accompany her to Newfoundland. His wife is dead, his parents have committed suicide . . . there's nothing to keep him in New York. She's homesick and she wants to see the old family home, if it's still standing. With help from Partridge, Quoyle lands a job on *The Gammy Bird,* a small newspaper in Killick-Claw, and he, his daughters, the aunt, and her old dog Warren set off for "the Rock". (The death of Warren, by the way, is incredibly touching. I cried when I read it, and, as you know, I'm a hard-bitten book reviewer. I don't know much about E. Annie Proulx but I bet she owns a dog. Or did.)

Through Agnis and various townsfolk, Quoyle learns a good deal about his ancestors, a colourful if disreputable bunch who mostly made their living as wreckers, luring ships onto the treacherous rocks and helping themselves to the cargo. Disliked by their neighbours - a feeling that was mutual, it seems - earlier Quoyles towed the family home miles from Killick-Claw to a remote, desolate outpost overlooking the foggy northern coast. They settled it on the point of a bluff overlooking the ocean, and tied it down with cables to prevent it from rocking in the wind. The aunt is overjoyed to find that the house, which has been empty for more than 40 years, is still standing, although it's gravely in need of repair. While she gets builders in to make the place habitable and prepares to get her ship upholstery business up and running, Quoyle goes to work at the newspaper.

In my opinion, *The Gammy Bird* is one of the best things about this book. Owned and edited by Jack Buggit, a local fisherman, the newspaper flies in the face of anything and everything pertaining to good journalism. It specializes in car wrecks, sexual abuse stories, and typos. Buggit knows what his readers want: "We run a front-page photo of a car wreck every week, whether we have a wreck or not. That's our golden rule. No exceptions." Quoyle, who is deathly afraid of water and whose wife was killed in a car accident, is assigned to the car wreck beat and the shipping news. For someone with little or no experience, he writes surprisingly well. Almost inadvertently, he transforms the shipping news from a list of ships in harbour into a popular weekly column.

While Quoyle is the hero, every other character has a story. We learn about the aunt's lifelong partner, Irene Warren, for whom her beloved dog is named, and the fact that she - the aunt - was sexually abused as a child by her brother, Quoyle's father. Bunny, Quoyle's older daughter, suffers from nightmares, has a particular terror of white dogs, and may be gifted with second sight. Buggit, Quoyle's boss, prefers fishing to newspapering but has a definite eye for a story. Over the years he's rescued many people from drowning but the sorrow of his life is that he was unable to save his son, Jesson, who died at sea. And angry, demented old Nolan, Quoyle's only living relative, squirrelled away in his hermit's lair, leaves bits of knotted twine around Quoyle's house, as a warning. Oh, and he owns a white dog.

Proulx takes a slow, almost glacial approach to her narrative. Long periods where nothing much happens are punctuated by events that take the story in new, unexpected directions. Quoyle discovers a suitcase floating in the water, containing the severed head of one of his aunt's clients, who left without paying for her services. A goodbye party for Nutbeem, one of Quoyle's colleagues, goes awry when the drunken guests, in an effort to prevent him from leaving, hack his boat to pieces. Near the end, the old Quoyle home is yanked off its moorings in a storm and disappears without a trace. Considering the time, effort and money she put into fixing it up, the aunt takes it pretty well. "'I'll get over this,' she said. 'I've always been good at it. Getting over things.'" And she has - she's survived sexual abuse, the death of her partner, the loss of her dog. She'll move to St. John's where her shop is, build a summer home on the site of the house. "As usual," Quoyle thinks, "the aunt was way out front and running."

The best parts of the story - the parts where you feel Proulx is on a roll, so to speak - are the stories, the oral histories, rollicking tales of shipwrecks and marital mishaps, spontaneous monologues that capture the flavour, the almost surreal humour of the islanders. I had it in my head, before reading *The Shipping News*, that it was a love story. There is love, eventually, between Quoyle and Wavey Prowse, the "tall and quiet woman" with a troubled past and a son with Down syndrome. But the real love affair is between the author and Newfoundland - the landscape, the inhabitants, the weather. And the water. It's to be expected that a story set in this part of the world would feature the ocean so consistently, in all its manifestations. Drownings are a regular occurrence - Quoyle himself comes close to drowning near the end, and his editor, Jack Buggit, actually does drown. And comes to life again, in his coffin at his own wake.

I feel I need to say something about the writer's use of metaphor. They are convoluted and somewhat perplexing, and they tend to get in the way of the story. "Waves struck with the hollowed basso peculiar to ovens and mouseholes." Um, what? You keep coming up against "taught thighs like Chinese bridges" and "eyes like willow leaves" and you find yourself stopping to wonder, what does a willow leaf look like again? Exactly? Some are just awful: "The bay crawled with whitecaps like maggots seething in a broad wound." But then, a few lines later: "The waves pouring onshore had a thick look to them, a kind of moody rage." When it works, it works.

Week 59: *The Vicar of Wakefield*, by Oliver Goldsmith (1766)

"I was ever of opinion, that the honest man who married and brought up a large family, did more service than he who continued single, and only talked of population."

And so, from the very first line of his narrative, Dr. Primrose, the vicar of Wakefield, lets us know that his first priority is his family. It is because of them the good vicar makes innumerable sacrifices, is brought into penury, forced into debtor's prison, and, eventually - because this is a story of good triumphing over evil - is restored to physical and financial health. The story, like much of what was written at the time, is replete with lashings of sentimentality and morality, and contains enough unlikely coincidences to satisfy a Spanish soap opera. But because it was written by Oliver Goldsmith, it is humorous, ironic, and charitable towards its characters. And, like *She Stoops to Conquer*, it's a classic.

Goldsmith was an 18th century Anglo-Irish poet, essayist, novelist, and playwright who rose from humble beginnings to enjoy the friendship of such notables as Samuel Johnson, Edmund Burke, and Sir Joshua Reynolds. His writing was prolific, even for the times, and no one doubted his gifts. But those closest to him confessed they were regularly confounded by his behaviour. Stocky, pockmarked, and physically unattractive, he couldn't open his mouth without putting his foot in it. He envied the celebrity status of other writers - and, I would assume, their money. He regularly made a fool of himself, even when he wasn't drunk, borrowed money from his friends, and gave away what he had. He also had a lively sense of fun and was universally deemed to be excellent company. Horace Walpole called him "an inspired idiot"; Dr. Johnson declared, "No man was more foolish when he had not a pen in his hand, or more wise when he had." Had he spent his money more wisely and drank less, he might have lived to reap the financial rewards of a gifted scribe. As it was, he died young (age 46) owing something like £2,000, much of it in gambling debts.

The story of how *The Vicar of Wakefield* came to be published has been told many times. According to Dr. Johnson, it came about like this:

"I received one morning a message from poor Goldsmith that he was in great distress, and, as it was not in his power to come to me, begging that I would come to him as soon as possible. I sent him a guinea, and promised to come to him directly. I accordingly went as soon as I was dressed, and found that his landlady had arrested him for his rent, at which he was in a violent passion: I perceived that he had already changed my guinea, and had a bottle of Madeira and a glass before him. I put the cork into the bottle, desired he would be calm, and began to talk to him of the means by which he might be extricated. He then told me he had a novel ready for the press, which he produced to me. I looked into it and saw its merit; told the landlady I should soon return; and, having gone to a bookseller, sold it for sixty pounds. I brought Goldsmith the money, and he discharged his rent, not without rating his landlady in a high tone for having used him so ill." (Taken from Washington Irving's biography of Oliver Goldsmith.)

The novel was *The Vicar of Wakefield*, and Johnson had sold it to Francis Newbery. It remained unpublished for four years; Newbery was so doubtful about its worth that he hedged on it by selling a share to a Salisbury bookseller. When it was finally published in 1766 it was not what you'd call an overnight success. Critics and readers were mostly indifferent, but steadily over the years it rose to become the most widely-read novel of the 19th century.

The plot is fairly simple: Dr. Primrose and his family - his wife, Deborah, his daughters, Olivia and Sophia, and his four sons, George, Moses, Dick and Bill - enjoy a comfortable existence mostly due to a family inheritance, which allows the vicar to donate to charity the £35 he receives as his annual salary. His son George is engaged to be married to the wealthy Arabella Wilmot, but on the eve of their wedding the vicar is informed that the merchant banker who holds his money has declared bankruptcy and left town. When Dr. Primrose, believing it's the ethical thing to do, tells Arabella's father about their reversal of fortune, the wedding is called off. George, who's been educated at Oxford, leaves for London; the rest of the family move to a smaller house on land owned by Squire Thornhill.

The Squire is known to be something of a rake, while his father, Sir William, is famous for his fairness and generosity. The vicar encourages his family to be cheerful in spite of their reduced circumstances, and for a while they make the best of it, making friends with a handsome but penniless young man, Mr. Burchill, who saves Sophia from drowning. She's attracted to him but Deborah, her mother, who's ambitious for her daughters to marry well, discourages any liaison. Squire Thornhill turns up and captivates the family with his manners, good looks and flattery and eventually Olivia runs away with him.

Dr. Primrose sets off to find his daughter and bring her home. He falls ill, spends three weeks recovering at an inn, and then continues on his journey. Falling in with a traveling theatrical troupe, he meets up with a gentleman who invites them back to his mansion for a dinner party. The house turns out to belong to Arabella's uncle who informs him that his niece is still in love with George but is now engaged to be married to Squire Thornill. As for George, he ran into trouble after fighting a duel for his so-called friend the Squire and has now joined that very theatrical troupe as an actor. When the Squire sees that George and Arabella still have feelings for each other, he finds him a job in the West Indies. Not suspecting him of ulterior motives, George happily goes off to seek his fortune.

Later, Dr. Primrose stops for the night at an inn where, amazingly, his daughter Olivia is also staying. They embrace joyfully and Olivia confesses to her father that she's made a terrible mistake: her marriage to the Squire was a sham - the minister wasn't a minister and her husband isn't her husband. In fact, he's had several previous "marriages" and now plans to compound his villainy by marrying Arabella for her fortune.

The vicar takes her home but they arrive to find the house in flames. All members of the family survive but everything except a few books are lost in the fire. Still, the vicar remains incurably optimistic. When the evil Squire demands the rent be paid, the vicar is forced into debtor's prison where he lectures his fellow prisoners on their need to repent. Olivia's health declines and she's reported to have died. George, who has returned from the West Indies, seeks to revenge his sister, is charged with attempted murder, and is brought to the same prison to await trial. And Sophia is abducted by persons unknown and taken away in a carriage.

Just when all seems lost, Mr. Burchill turns up and saves the situation. He rescues Sophia, and informs the family that Olivia is not really dead and he is not really Mr. Burchill. In reality, he's the good Sir William Thornhill, who travels the country in disguise. Why he waited this long to reveal himself is beyond me but better late than never. The sham marriage between Squire Thornhill and Olivia wasn't a sham, actually - the Squire's servant tricked him and hired a legitimate minister - so Olivia has not been disgraced. George hasn't wounded anyone - that was a trick on the part of the Squire - so he's now free to marry Arabella, who rejects the Squire as an unmitigated cad. A double wedding winds things up: George marries Arabella, and Sir William marries Sophia. And the reader breathes a sigh of relief.

At least, this reader did.

Week 60: *Veronika Decides to Die*, by Paulo Coelho (1998)

In 1999, Paulo Coelho wrote an essay for the *London Telegraph Review* in which he discussed the time he spent in mental institutions in the 1960s, during Brazil's military dictatorship. At the time, he wrote, "the word 'artist' was synonymous with homosexual, communist, drug addict, and layabout." Coelho, who was 18, had artistic aspirations; not knowing where to begin, he joined an amateur theatrical group and began experimenting with drugs and radical politics. When his parents realized this was more than a passing phase - that he was not following the career path they had laid out for him - they had him admitted to a psychiatric hospital, "for his own good".

"And thus began my journey through various psychiatric hospitals. I was admitted, I was given all kinds of different treatments, and I ran away at the first opportunity, traveling around for as long as I could bear it then going back to my parents' house. We enjoyed a kind of honeymoon period, but after a while I again started to get into what my family called 'bad company,' and the nurses reappeared."

His mother and father were not monsters; Coelho makes it clear they acted out of love for their son, and in later years never forgave themselves for having him committed. But the three years he spent in and out of Rio de Janeiro's Dr Eiras Sanatorium provided the inspiration for *Veronika Decides to Die*, his 1998 novel which, like his other books, was a New York Times best seller and has been translated into dozens of languages. The theme of the book is madness - what is it, and who are the madmen, and women? Madness, he concludes, is the name we give to those who refuse to conform. And the real madmen - and women - are the ones who hide their differences within a facade of normality.

At this point I think I need to self-disclose: I'm not a fan of new-age homilies disguised as novels. When I pick up a book that's trying to send me a "message", I get prickly. If I want to be preached at, I'll go to church. I'm probably one of the few people who has yet to read *The Alchemist*, Coelho's inspirational fable about a Spanish shepherd boy who travels to the pyramids of Egypt in search of a treasure. Just seeing the word "inspirational" on the cover puts me off.

Having said that, I didn't absolutely hate this book. (Second self-disclosure: a reader on Amazon.com once started her review of my novel, *Displaced Persons*, with those words. Safe to say, I read no further.) *Veronika Decides to Die* is set in Ljubljana, the capital of Slovenia, a few years after the break-up of Yugoslavia. Veronika, a 24-year-old librarian, is smart, educated, attractive, and has had her share of lovers. However, she sees no point in continuing to live, with death waiting for her at the end of a long, meaningless life. And so she decides to kill herself.

She swallows a large dose of sleeping pills and wakes up in Villete, a notorious psychiatric hospital established a few years earlier in an abandoned army barracks. The doctor informs her that she has damaged her heart and will be dead within a week. Hearing this, Viktoria begins to have some regrets for trying to kill herself. At first she's intimidated and rather frightened by the other inmates, but gradually she becomes intimate with three of them - Zedka, Mari, and Eduard. Her interactions with these three lead her to question what it means to be crazy.

Zedka, who has a loving family but cannot shake the image of a past lover, is being treated for depression. She says insanity is the inability to communicate your ideas:

"It's as if you were in a foreign country, able to see and understand everything that's going on around you but incapable of explaining what you need to know or of being helped, because you don't understand the language they speak there.' 'We've all felt that.' 'And all of us, one way or another, are insane.'"

Mari, a wife, mother, and successful lawyer, has chosen insanity as an escape from an unbearable present. For years she's suffered from devastating panic attacks. When her husband can no longer care for her, she enters Villete and is treated for depression. When she learns she's been asked to resign from her law firm, she asks the doctor to keep her in the asylum, insisting she's not cured. Older and wiser than Veronika, Mari talks openly about sexual pleasure and masturbation. She advises Veronika to spend what little time she has left discovering her true sexuality. "Even if you have only two days to live," she says, "I don't think you should leave this life without knowing how far you can go."

Eduard, the son of rich and powerful parents, is being treated for schizophrenia. We learn that he, like Coelho, developed a passion to become an artist. He began to fill the house with strange people, "all of them badly dressed and with untidy hair, who listened to horrible music at full blast - endlessly drinking and smoking and showing a complete disregard for basic good manners." Pressured by his parents to bury his ambitions, he lost touch with reality and was admitted to Villete; now he never speaks and appears to be unaware of his surroundings.

Veronika begins to see that being a mental patient means gaining the freedom to do whatever you want without consequences. She plays the piano again, something she hasn't done in years, and, finding herself attracted to Eduard, decides to follow Mari's advice. Assuming that Eduard isn't aware of her or anyone else, she strips naked in front of him one night and masturbates herself to orgasm, several times.

Of all the characters in the novel, I found the head psychiatrist, Dr. Igor, the most puzzling. At times he seems to be compassionate and truly interested in the welfare of his patients - at other times he's completely callous and just a little off his rocker. He tells Veronika she's going to die and gives her injections that simulate the effect of heart attacks, simply for the purpose of proving his theory: an awareness of death encourages people to live more intensely.

Which seems to be true. Veronika, facing death, decides she wants to live. Other patients, observing Veronika apparently approaching death, re-evaluate their own lives. Mari asks to be released . . . Eduard finds the courage to leave the asylum. And Veronika discovers a new appreciation for the world around her and doesn't die. Happy endings all round. And just a little banal.

Veronika Decides to Die is about the importance of accepting your differences in a society that pressures its members to conform. Which is good advice and may or may not serve as a hopeful inspiration to some.

Enough said.

Week 61: *The Virgin Suicides*, by Jeffrey Eugenides (1993)

I can't absolutely confirm it, but as it's been told to me over the years, I was taught to read at the age of three by my mother. She was tired, it seems, of my constant demands: "Read me a story." And so she taught me to read to myself. And to my sisters.

And though I can't remember asking to be read to, I've always loved it. Years ago, when I was working in radio and spending a lot of time in my car, I listened to books on tape, borrowed from the library. The three-hour drive from Calgary to Edmonton, with a quick coffee break in Red Deer, felt much less tedious when accompanied by the voice of Sissy Spacek reading *To Kill A Mockingbird*.

I don't do a lot of long-distance driving these days, and had almost forgotten what a pleasure it is to be read to. When the story is engaging, and the person doing the reading does it well. My 8-CD version of *The Virgin Suicides*, Jeffrey Eugenides' 1993 debut, is performed by Nick Landrum, who provided the voiceover for "Dexter". Based in Brooklyn, Landrum has the perfect voice for story-telling. Just the right inflections - not too dramatic, but with the kind of intonation that draws you right inside the story. Be sure to check him out on Bob Dylan's *Chronicles - Volume One*. He will not disappoint.

So, back to *The Virgin Suicides*. The basic premise of the story can be put pretty simply: in the space of a single year, five teenage girls, all from the same family, commit suicide. Thirteen-year-old Cecilia is the first.

She slashes her wrists with her father's razor and is found in the upstairs bathroom, clutching a laminated picture of the Virgin Mary to her chest. (Yes, it's a bit "on the nose" as the Brits like to say - predictable, if you like . . . lacking nuance. But the Lisbon girls are Catholics; they attend church every Sunday and there's a crucifix in every room. So it makes sense.) Cecelia survives this attempt, but a week later, during a party her parents are giving for her, she goes upstairs and throws herself out her bedroom window. She dies, impaled on a spike of the iron fence that surrounds their yard. Before the year is out, her older sisters - 17-year-old Therese, 16-year-old Mary, 15-year-old Bonnie, and 14-year-old Lux - will follow suit. Therese overdoses on pills, washed down with gin; Mary, who survives her first attempt, succeeds two weeks later, taking an overdose like her older sister; Bonnie hangs herself, and Lux dies of carbon monoxide poisoning, parked in the garage.

It's a shocking story, told with irony and, frequently, with humour - although I disagree with the critics who hailed it as "wickedly funny". It can be read as a critique of social mores but works best, I think, as simply a good story well told.

The setting is the town of Grosse Pointe, Michigan, in the 1970s, an affluent suburban community populated by middle-class residents fleeing the "rot" of the city. The auto industry is deteriorating, young men are dying in Southeast Asia, and the "new right" is mobilizing in defense of traditional family values. In the leafy streets of Grosse Pointe the residents feel safe from the changes occurring in the outside world - the very sterility of the town protects and isolates them.

On the surface, the Lisbons appear to conform to the community norms. Mr. Lisbon teaches math at the local high school, Mrs. Lisbon is a stay-at-home mom. It's not until the death of Cecelia, who was always something of a misfit, that cracks begin to appear in the household. As you might expect, Mr. and Mrs. Lisbon attempt to safeguard their remaining daughters. Curfews become more strict - the girls become more isolated. Bonding with each other, they are virtually excluded from any other kind of social life. Fourteen-year-old Lux, the prettiest and liveliest of the sisters, rebels. She forges notes to get out of gym class, climbs up on the changing room lockers to smoke, and has a string of brief sexual liaisons. When the girls are allowed to attend a high school dance, Lux stays out all night, coming home in the morning in a taxi, alone. Mrs. Lisbon is horrified - the girls are taken out of school and not allowed to leave the house. Lux is forced to burn her rock records but retaliates by having sex with random men and boys on the roof of the house while her parents are asleep.

All of this is told through the lens of a group of neighbourhood boys, who narrate the story in the first-person plural. Obsessed with the Lisbons, even somewhat in love with them, they spy on them, gossip about them, and, occasionally, are allowed some access to the girls' inner lives:

"We started to learn about their lives. Coming to hold collective memories of times we hadn't experienced. We felt the imprisonment of being a girl. The way it made your mind active and dreamy and how you ended up knowing what colors went together. We knew the girls were really women in disguise, that they understood love, and even death, and that our job was merely to create the noise that seemed to fascinate them."

So this is what you need to know about the book: while it's ostensibly a story about five teenage girls, it's actually a story about adolescent boys. Which is what makes it palatable. The author is not trying to write about women; if he was, there'd be plenty to complain about, as there often is when men write from a female perspective and vice versa. (I'm not saying it can't be done, just that it's often done badly.) *The Virgin Suicides* is not about women, it's about the way men, especially young men, view women. The boys are seduced not so much by the girls themselves but by what they represent. Young, white, blonde girls on the verge of womanhood. And blood. It doesn't get much better.

We never get to see the girls up close - like the boys, we're kept out of their bedrooms, out of their inner thoughts. Eugenides does this deliberately, in order to keep us at a distance, in the way the boys are always across the street, speculating, guessing, surmising, but never really knowing. I found it frustrating, partly because one effect of that distance is to keep us from caring, too much, about the girls. If I'm going to spend 8.75 hours listening to a story about five young women, I'd like to feel something when they die.

Why they kill themselves is never spelled out, in so many words. It's been argued that they are imprisoned in a paradox: on the one hand, they're eroticised by the outside world, as represented by the narrators; on the other, their burgeoning sexuality is squelched by their mother's puritanical dictates. But this is not uncommon - most young women struggle with the pressure to conform to sexual stereotypes that would not be embraced by mom and dad. Thankfully, most of them don't choose suicide.

I think we're not meant to know the reason. Eugenides has said the point of the book is about the unknowability of suicide, "the fact that you can never pinpoint the reason why someone commits suicide". In the end, it's the boys themselves who, as men, come closest to what feels like the truth: "Something sick at the heart of the country had infected the girls."

It might have been written today.

Week 62: *American Rust*, by Philipp Meyer (2009)

Since his debut novel was published in 2009, Philipp Meyer has been likened to Steinbeck and Salinger, Faulkner and Hemingway. In 2010 the New Yorker rated him one of the 20 best novelists under 40. The accolades are appropriate, keeping in mind that Meyer, writing at the tail end of the Great American Dream, has a different take on what drives us to be who and what we are. I wouldn't call him cynical, exactly, but his unsentimental clarity makes for a pretty grim read.

American Rust takes place in what used to be the industrial heartland of America. The fictional town of Buell was once a thriving Pennsylvania steel town; now, like communities throughout the northeast, its old stone houses are boarded up and abandoned, its shops are empty, its factories shut down. Many of the residents have fled, hoping to find work in other parts of the country. Those who have jobs, even minimum wage ones like those on offer at Wal-Mart, are lucky. Others live on welfare, deal drugs, or both. Still others go back to the bush, living much as hunter-gatherers did hundreds of years ago. The whole town, for the most part, is on "the other side of the tracks".

"The work was all in the Midwest now, taking down the auto plants in Michigan and Indiana. And one day even that work would end, and there would be no record, nothing left standing, to show that anything had ever been built in America. It was going to cause big problems, he didn't know how but he felt it. You could not have a country, not this big, that didn't make things for itself. There would be ramifications eventually."

These are the thoughts of Billy Poe, former high-school football star currently in jail, waiting to appear in court for a crime he didn't commit. In a stream of consciousness style reminiscent of Faulkner, Meyer presents the narrative from several points of view, alternating between Poe, his friend, Isaac English, Isaac's sister, Lee, Poe's mother, Grace, and Bud Harris, the town's police chief and Grace's sometime boyfriend. Each of these characters, vividly drawn and intensely real, gives us insight into what happens when market forces drive a community into the dirt.

The book opens with 19-year-old Isaac heading out of town, on his way, he thinks, to California. Recently graduated from high school, Isaac is a mathematical genius and should, under normal circumstances, be studying at one of the Ivy League colleges, like his older sister, Lee. But 5 years ago his mother committed suicide, his sister left for Yale, and Isaac chose to stay home to care for his father, who is confined to a wheelchair after a workplace accident. Now Isaac is on the road, like Kerouac, with $4,000 in his pocket - stolen from his father's desk. His plan is to ride the rails west and become a student of physics at UCLA Berkeley.

Before you start feeling sorry for his dad, you need to know that Henry English is by no means an ideal father. He treats Isaac much as he did his wife, which was not well, favouring his daughter and putting her needs and aspirations well above those of his son. And while Isaac loves his sister, he resents the fact that she was able to leave so easily while he felt compelled to stay.

On the way out of town, Isaac stops at the trailer where Poe lives with his mother, and urges his friend to come with him. The two boys were best friends in high school, although they were an unlikely combination: Isaac was small, skinny, all brains, Poe was handsome, twice the size of Isaac, and a natural athlete. A few years ago, Poe saved Isaac's life. After his mother's suicide Isaac went out to the frozen lake where she drowned and jumped in. Poe risked drowning himself, diving under the ice and rescuing his friend.

Now, however, Poe has given up. Having turned down offers of college football scholarships, he sees no future for himself, and lacks the ability to leave and make a go of it somewhere else. And so he lives with his mother, drinks heavily, and gets into fights.

Grudgingly, he agrees to accompany Isaac as far as the train yards. By nightfall they arrive at an abandoned car factory and decide to bed down for the night. Poe gets a fire going and they settle in, only to be interrupted by three homeless men who have made the factory their temporary home. A fight breaks out and Isaac ends up killing one of the men, a large Swede named Otto. The boys flee, leaving behind two pieces of telltale evidence: Isaac's backpack, which he stashed in a nearby field, and Poe's high school football jacket, which bears his name and player number. When they try to go back the next day to retrieve the jacket, they find Bud Harris and his partner, Steve Ho, waiting for them.

Harris has already found the jacket, and recognized it as belonging to Poe. He's helped the boy before, as a favour to Grace; now, as much as he wants to avoid hurting Grace, he believes Poe, who has a history of violence, killed the Swede and will have to pay the price. He drives the boys back to town, advising them to stay inside for the next few days. "Stick around," he says, "where I can find you."

Isaac is sure he'll be charged with murder. Even though it was mainly self-defence - one of the men was holding a knife to Poe's throat - it was Isaac who threw the rock. He retrieves his pack from the field where he left it, and heads east towards Pittsburgh. In the meantime, Lee returns to Buell hoping to get her father into a care home and take Isaac out of there. She and Poe rekindle their high school sexual relationship; during a night of love-making Poe tells her it was Isaac, not him, who killed the man. He refuses, however, to tell the authorities, and when he's arrested and put in jail he stays silent. He knows he could save himself by telling the truth, that it was Isaac who killed Otto, but he won't.

Poe's taken to a maximum security prison where every murderous cliché you can imagine is firmly in place. Simply staying alive means walking an impossible tightrope between rival gangs of convicts. Unwittingly, he manages to anger just about everyone in the prison, and is attacked and almost killed. He wakes up in hospital, hooked up to an IV, tubes sticking out of him, in a great deal of pain. "After a minute it occurred to him: I am alive."

Lee, having been told the truth, is torn between her love for her brother and her moral imperative to do what is right. She is, after all, a law student. In the end she swallows her guilt, deciding to sacrifice Poe to save Isaac. Grace, who loves her son, believes she's made all the wrong decisions. If she'd left Buell when she'd had the chance, none of this would have happened. Harris, who wants to wash his hands of the boy, is conflicted as well. He loves Grace, and knows this is going to destroy her. In the end, he makes a decision to go against everything he stands for and save her son.

Some judicious editing might not have been a bad thing. *American Rust* is heavy on introspection and there are times when you want the characters to stop thinking and *just move on*. But all that deep thinking has a purpose: Poe comes to see that he's not the coward he thought he was. He saved Isaac once before - by keeping silent, he will save him again.

As for Isaac, after spending two weeks in the wilderness, battling the cold, near starvation, and hostile strangers, he knows he cannot allow his friend to take the fall for something he did. He makes his way back home to Buell, resolved to turn himself in and accept the consequences. But when he goes to the police station, Harris refuses to hear his confession. Before Isaac can say anything, Harris tells him that the men who witnessed the murder are dead - the implicit message being: they were bums, they won't be missed. Poe will be set free; Isaac, who killed a man, will not have to suffer the consequences.

Harris watches Isaac leave and thinks about the fact that Poe had been stabbed and nearly died, but refused to tell on his friend. And Isaac, who might have got away scot-free, came back to confess.

"Both of those boys were worth saving, he thought. That is something you wouldn't have known."

Yes, *American Rust* is "relentlessly pessimistic", to quote one reviewer, but then so is *The Grapes of Wrath*. Meyer, though, has no Tom Joad in his story. The time for moral heroes has come and gone - in a deteriorating society, everything can be rationalized. Even murder.

Week 63: *The Master*, by Colm Tóibín (2004)

Colm Tóibín's novel is a hybrid - not totally fiction, not purely biography. The proper name for it, I think, is creative nonfiction, although there are so many interpretations of that genre that it's difficult to categorize. *The Malahat Review* awards its Constance Rooke Creative Nonfiction Prize to "the best work submitted to the magazine's annual contest for a genre that embraces, but is not limited to, the personal essay, memoir, narrative nonfiction, social commentary, travel writing, historical accounts, and biography, all enhanced by such elements as description, dramatic scenes, dialogue, and characterization." Making CNF, in my humble opinion, an exciting, even exhilarating, venture for both writer and reader.

In the case of *The Master*, Tóibín has chosen to inhabit the consciousness of Henry James, one of the greatest novelists in the English language. I'll leave it to the James scholars to say whether or not he pulls it off, but I will say that Tóibín draws a compelling portrait of a complex individual whose ambiguous sexuality both informed and hindered his writing. It also makes me want to reread James. So watch this space.

Tóibín has chosen as his time frame the five-year period which James' earlier biographer, Leon Edel, calls the treacherous years. It begins in January 1895 with the staging of "Guy Domville", a mortifying disaster that effectively ended James's relationship with the theatre, and ends in October 1899 with Henry - as Tóibín refers to him - beginning work on the masterpieces of his later years: *The Wings of the Dove, The Ambassadors,* and *The Golden*

Bowl. Having left America to settle in Europe as a young man, Henry is now in his 50s and living mainly in London. The restless, rootless life of an expatriate is beginning to weigh on him. He's accomplished a great deal as a writer, but his books, which were never read by the masses, are dwindling in popularity. His attempt to find a new audience through drama has proved a failure. And, it has to be said, he's lonely.

In the aftermath of the public humiliation caused by the failure of his play, Henry escapes to Ireland, where he's the guest of Lord Wolseley, Commander-in-Chief of the army. There he's waited on by an attractive young corporal named Hammond, who seems to be willing to be more than a manservant if Henry will give the word. Henry, being Henry, says nothing. Back in London, he learns that Oscar Wilde is going to trial, an event he views it with a kind of fascinated horror. He has no love for Wilde, who, in terms of discretion, is his polar opposite, and finds his behaviour outrageous and appalling. Still, like everyone else, he wants to know the details.

In many ways, *The Master* is a story of ghosts. Dead friends and family members haunt Henry James - or rather, as a writer, he haunts them. Two women in particular occupy his thoughts: one is his sister Alice, who died of breast cancer at the age of 43, and the other is his cousin, Minny Temple, an attractive, energetic young woman who died in 1870 when she was only 24. She was the model for Isabel Archer in *The Portrait of a Lady*; he will return to her again as Milly Theale in *The Wings of the Dove*. Now, almost 30 years after her death, he wonders: does he prefer her dead to alive, so he can write her the way he wished her to be? "He could control her destiny now that she was dead, offer her the experiences she would have wanted, and provide drama for a life which had been so cruelly shortened". It's thoughts like these (if indeed Henry had them) that reveals a pretty cold, bloody-minded nature - reveals him, in other words, as a born writer.

As for his sister, Alice, she was aggressive and intelligent and possessed an acerbic wit. In her own words, she was born a few years too soon. Overshadowed by her brothers, she chose - or was chosen by - illness, and spent most of her life in bed, cared for first by her parents, then by Henry, and finally by the educator, Katharine Peabody Loring. Henry, while feeling that he failed his sister by not inviting her to live with him, firmly believes he had no option. Alice would have been too much of a distraction - the work comes first.

Work, in fact, comes before everything: before family, before pleasure, before intimacy. The people he meets, especially those he cares for, are important mainly because of what they bring to his writing . . . what he can use. The Henry James we read in this book is happiest "alone in his room with the night coming down... and pen and paper and the knowledge that the door would remain shut until the morning came and he would not be disturbed".

In terms of a plot, there's not much to hang your hat on. He travels, attends social evenings, and makes peace with William, his older brother. In 1897 he leases and eventually buys Lamb House in Sussex, where he lives for most of the rest of his life. He brings his longtime servants with him and ends up having to sack them for drunkenness. That same year his close friend,

Constance Fenimore Woolson, commits suicide, and he faces accusations from another friend that he might have saved her if he'd visited her in Venice as he promised. He does return to Venice to help clear out her apartment; while there he takes part in a rather bizarre ritual which Tóibín definitely did not invent: with the assistance of her favourite gondolier, he rows out to the deepest part of the Venetian lagoon and, one by one, drowns all of her dresses.

Tóibín, who's never made a secret of his own homosexuality - why should he? - gives full rein to his subject's repressed homoerotic leanings. He imagines the conflict Henry experienced as a young man lying naked next to his friend, Oliver Wendell Holmes. He refers, in passing, to his long-ago passion for Paul Joukowsky, a handsome young man he met in Paris. And late in the book, on a visit to Rome, he describes Henry's meeting with the young Norwegian-American sculptor, Hendrik Andersen, with whom he falls in love and to whom he remains devoted until his death.

For decades Henry James's descendants fought to keep his sexuality a secret. The cat was let out of the bag for good in 1990 when Eve Kosofsky Sedgwick proposed that we read James as "a gay writer whose efforts to remain in the closet gave him his style". Her argument, Tóibín writes, "removed James from the realm of dead white males who wrote about posh people. He became our contemporary".

Colm Tóibín's to be commended, I think, for not trying to mimic James's style. For those who find "the Master" hard going at times - and here I'm referring to the individual, not the novel - this is a good thing. *The*

Master is an intelligent, remarkable novel about a writer, dead for a century, who deserves to continue to be read.

Week 64: *The Portrait of a Lady*, by Henry James (1881)

Having previously posted a review of *The Master*, it seems fitting to go to the source this week, and take a look at the classic novel that gave rise to Henry James's reputation as "the master". *The Portrait of a Lady*, first published in 1881, was his first in-depth exploration of a theme that would occupy him for decades: the impact of the Old World, i.e. Europe, on the character of the New - that is, America. In this case, the New World is represented by Isabel Archer, a free-spirited, intelligent young woman who lives with her widowed father in Albany, New York. As James wrote in his notebook, "The idea of the whole thing is that the poor girl, who has dreamed of freedom and nobleness, who has done, as she believes, a generous, natural, clear-sighted thing, finds herself in reality ground in the very mill of the conventional." This is the tragedy of *Portrait*; it is also, in its treatment of the psychological conflict she experiences, what makes it a very modern novel.

As the book opens, Isabel's father has died, leaving her, if not penniless, then close to it. Her maternal aunt, Lydia Touchett, arrives on the scene, determined to "do something" for the girl. She invites her to come back with her to England, where they will stay for a time before going on to the continent. The idea appeals to Isabel; she has a desire to leave the past behind her - to begin afresh. She agrees to accompany her aunt who is as unconventional in her way as her niece. Aunt Lydia lives apart from her husband, Daniel, who is very rich and owns Gardencourt, a large estate not far from London. On arrival, Isabel meets her elderly uncle, her cousin, Ralph, and Ralph's friend, the wealthy Lord

Warburton, all of whom are immediately taken with the striking young woman. Warburton is so taken, in fact, that within a few weeks he proposes marriage. Isabel turns him down - she wants to see the world for herself . . . marriage to Warburton would make her feel like "some wild, caught creature in a vast cage".

Warburton is not the first man she's rejected: Caspar Goodwood (and who wouldn't reject a man with such a hapless name?) is the son of a wealthy American mill owner. At one point Isabel gave him reason to believe she might marry him, but by the time she left America she had changed her mind. She likes Caspar, but has no desire to marry him. Or anyone else. Her journalist friend, Harriet Stackpole, thinks she's making a mistake. She follows Isabel to England, bringing Caspar with her. Her point in coming is to get material for a series of feature articles about Europeans; Caspar makes the journey in order to pursue his offer of marriage.

During her stay at Gardencourt, Isabel and Ralph become close friends - it seems obvious that Ralph is in love with Isabel but even if she wasn't his cousin it's unlikely anything would come of it. Ralph is very frail and there are intimations that he hasn't long to live. His father, too, becomes ill while she's there and decides to leave some of his fortune to Isabel. Ralph asks him to leave her a great deal more. He wants her to have half his own inheritance, so that she might be completely independent and free to live life as she chooses. The elder Touchett agrees, making Isabel, when he dies, a wealthy woman.

James lets us know that, for someone as innocent as Isabel, this sudden windfall is not necessarily a good thing. Harriet Stackpole believes the money will change her: "The peril for you," she says, "is that you live too much in the world of your own dreams - you are not enough in contact with reality - with the toiling, striving, suffering, I may even say sinning, world that surrounds you. You are too fastidious; you have too many graceful illusions. Your newly acquired thousands will shut you up more and more to the society of a few selfish and heartless people, who will be interested in keeping up those illusions."

Isabel and her aunt leave for Florence, where Aunt Lydia lives the greater part of the year. Here she introduces her niece to her close friend, the much-esteemed Serena Merle. The two women hit it off immediately: "Isabel had never encountered a more agreeable and interesting figure than Madame Merle". James tells us, "She knew how to think - an accomplishment rare in women". What Isabel doesn't see is that Madame Merle is calculating and devious, and her affection for the younger woman has a great deal to do with her fortune. She arranges for Isabel to meet her friend, Gilbert Osmond, another American living abroad. Gilbert is a widower whose wife died in childbirth, leaving him to raise their daughter, Pansy. Together, Gilbert and Madame Merle conspire to make Isabel fall in love with him in order to get their hands on her fortune.

Gilbert Osmond is, to all intents and purposes, a dilettante. He has no career, no name, no position, no money - nothing but an attitude of otherworldliness which Isabel buys lock, stock and barrel. She sees him as pure in thought, too noble to concern himself with such mundane activities as making money. Ralph, however, is not deceived. He perceives that "under the guise of caring only for intrinsic values Osmond lived exclusively for the world. Far from being its master as he pretended to be, he was its very humble servant, and the degree of its attention was his only measure of success. He lived with his eye on it from morning till night, and the world was so stupid it never suspected the trick". When Ralph learns that Isabel has agreed to marry Osmond, he's appalled and tells her so. But nothing will deter her. She sees marrying Osmond as doing something great, something generous, and looks forward to a blissful union - a meeting of minds. They marry and settle in Rome and within a year she sees him for what he is - cold, egotistical, and cruel. Although she's become fond of his daughter, she is desperately unhappy.

Why, then, does she stay with him? Divorce was not uncommon, especially among the wealthy, and if that wasn't an option it was considered quite acceptable to simply live apart. You might as well ask why any woman - or man, for that matter - stays in a disastrous relationship. Isabel has her reasons, and James is too sophisticated a writer, in the best sense of the word, to give us any easy answers. Isabel not only stays but, near the end, when the truth is revealed to her - that Madame Merle and Osmond were lovers once upon a time, and that Pansy is actually Merle's daughter - she doesn't flee the marriage. Near the end, her aunt sends a telegram: her cousin Ralph is dying back in England. Against her husband's wishes, Isabel travels back to Gardencourt, and spends the last few days at his bedside. Caspar Goodwood turns up again and, knowing something of her misery, makes an impassioned plea for her to renounce her marriage - to stay in England, or return to America with him. You find yourself rooting for him - "Go on, Isabel, do as he says - leave the bastard!" She's moved by his words but tells him to go. And when he comes to Gardencourt the next morning, he's informed that Mrs. Osmond has left for Rome.

The ending is ambiguous: will she really stay with her husband, knowing what she knows about him - feeling as she does? Papers have been written on the subject . . . scholars have argued that it's in her nature to accept the consequences of her actions, however dire they may seem. Others have said she's heading back to rescue Pansy, who's been confined to a convent by her father for daring to love the wrong man. I choose to believe she's going back to put an end to her marriage in a suitable, if conventional, manner. She will most likely need to buy him out, but she won't worry about that. Like Rome and its ruins, she has suffered and survived. She was happy before she was rich, and she will be happy again:

"She saw herself, in the distant years, still in the attitude of a woman who had her life to live, and these intimations contradicted the spirit of the present hour. It might be desirable to die; but this privilege was evidently to be denied her. Deep in her soul - deeper than any appetite for renunciation - was the sense that life would be her business for a long time to come. And at moments there was something inspiring, almost exhilarating, in the conviction. It was a proof of strength - it was a proof that she should some day be happy again. It couldn't be that she was to live only to suffer; she was still young, after all, and a great many things might happen to her yet."

Week 65: *The Namesake*, by Jhumpa Lahiri (2002)

A baby boy is born in Cambridge, Massachusetts, to Bengali immigrants, recently arrived from Calcutta. The child is given a pet name while his parents wait for his proper name to arrive in a letter from home. The letter never arrives, and the boy grows up resenting his pet name, which is Gogol, after the Russian author. He goes to school, endures adolescence, falls in love, and marries. His father dies, his mother learns to live alone, and the boy, now a young man, comes to terms with his heritage.

It's a simple story, on the surface, written in deceptively simple prose. The author, Jhumpa Lahiri, plays no games with the reader. We see none of Tom Wolfe's verbal acrobatics. There are no unreliable narrators à la Gillian Flynn. Yet *The Namesake*, her 2002 novel exploring the immigrant experience in America, is so intensely readable - her characters so engaging - you don't want the story to end.

Born and raised in Calcutta, Ashima is married to Ashoke Ganguli, a man she first spoke to on her wedding day. They leave for New England directly after the wedding, barely knowing each other. Each day, while he studies for his engineering doctorate, Ashima deals with the daily challenges of adapting to a new country. Bereft of her parents, aunts, uncles, and friends, she trembles at the thought of raising her child in a cold, foreign city, surrounded by strangers.

"For being a foreigner, Ashima is beginning to realize, is a sort of lifelong pregnancy - a perpetual wait, a constant burden, a continuous feeling out of sorts. It is an ongoing responsibility, a parenthesis in what had once been ordinary life, only to discover that that previous life has vanished, replaced by something more complicated and demanding. Like pregnancy, being a foreigner, Ashima believes, is something that elicits the same curiosity from strangers, the same combination of pity and respect".

When their son is born, Ashima and Ashoke delay giving him a proper name. The honour of that has been given to Ashima's grandmother; until they receive her letter they will call him by his pet name. These pet names, used by family and friends are a Bengali tradition - early in the book, we learn why the Gangulis call their son Gogol:

Seven years earlier, Ashoke is on a train, reading a book of short stories by the Russian author, Nikolai Gogol. He gets into conversation with a stranger, an older man named Gosh.

"Do yourself a favor," Gosh says. "Before it's too late, without thinking too much about it first, pack a pillow and a blanket and see as much of the world as you can. You will not regret it. One day it will be too late."

Shortly after that, there's a terrible accident: the train derails, Gosh is killed, and Ashoke is discovered in the wreckage only because a rescuer sees a page of the book fluttering in his hand. After recovering from his injuries, Ashoke makes a decision to follow Gosh's advice. He applies to MIT, receives a fellowship, and leaves for America. Two years later he returns to Calcutta in order to find a wife. While waiting in the delivery room for Ashima to deliver their child, Ashoke thinks again of the fact that it was only because he was sitting up reading while the others slept that he was not killed like the others. It was Gogol, the Russian writer, who saved his life. Hence, the pet name, Gogol, for his son.

Ashoke lands a professorship at MIT, their daughter Sonia is born, and the family moves to the suburbs. Ashima, who doesn't drive, misses being able to walk with everywhere with her children. Slowly, she and Ashoke make friends with other Bengalis in the area, and Friday night gatherings become a regular occurence. While their parents socialize, the children watch TV in the basement rec room or play board games upstairs.

And everybody eats.

The preparation, sharing, and consuming of food is a recurring motif. At the very beginning we see Ashima standing in the kitchen, recreating a popular Indian street snack. As a baby, Gogol is introduced to the world not by baptism but by Annaprashana, a Hindu rite of passage marking the child's first intake of food other than milk. The list of foods mentioned makes one's mouth water: samosas, chicken curry and rice, tandoori, pakoras, mincemeat croquettes, lamb korma, sweet yogurt and pantuas. For the immigrant Gangulis, food, prepared in the traditional manner, is more than a way to satisfy hunger - it's a lifeline to their culture.

Growing up in New England, Gogol always feels like an outsider. He's shy, bookish and artistic, and he hates his name. Before he sets off for university, he officially changes it to Nikhil; his family and their friends will continue to call him Gogol but he'll be Nikhil, or Nik, to everybody else - including his first serious girlfriend, an art student he meets on the train to Boston. He and Ruth date for a year but after she goes away to Oxford to study for a semester the relationship becomes strained and they break up. During this time Ashoke finally tells his son the story of the train accident that led to the pet name, Gogol.

After graduating from Yale, Nikhil attends design school at Columbia, then lives uptown and works for a firm in Manhattan. Here he meets Maxine, who's moved back to live with her parents in their spacious, cosmopolitan townhouse. Gerald and Lydia Ratliff are everything the Gangulis are not: wealthy, sophisticated, and extremely liberal. They welcome Nikhil into the household and he virtually lives there, going back to his apartment only occasionally to check his phone messages and his mail. The ease of this lifestyle seduces him - he makes excuses not to visit his parents. When Ashoke is leaving for an extended trip to Cleveland, his mother asks him to come for the weekend, in order to say goodbye. Instead, Nikhil drives up to New Hampshire, to spend time with Maxine and her parents.

Shortly before Christmas, his father, who is still away in Cleveland, dies of a heart attack. Nikhil is devastated by grief and remorse and Maxine, who genuinely cares for him, is unable to comfort him. He takes a month off from work and spends it at home with his mother and sister, surrounded by the friends and neighbours who knew his father. When his family travels to Calcutta to spread his father's ashes, he refuses to let Maxine come with them. This leads to a series of arguments and a few months later, he steps out of her life altogether.

The following year, under pressure from Ashima, Nikhil agrees to call a childhood friend. Moushumi was one of the youngsters who attended the Friday night gatherings. Now she's a graduate student in French literature, recently returned from Paris and recovering from a broken engagement. Neither she nor Nikhil expect to be attracted to each other - the date is simply to satisfy their parents - but they are. Very quickly, they fall in love and marry, amused to find themselves doing exactly as their parents have always wished - marrying a Bengali.

It doesn't last. Nikhil doesn't care for her friends, especially Donald and Astrid, who were friends of Graham, Moushumi's ex. Moushumi becomes restless, and begins to wonder if she made a mistake, jumping into marriage this way. An affair with an old boyfriend leads to a divorce, and she moves back to Paris. That Christmas, Nikhil comes back home to help his mother. Ashima has sold the house where she raised her children - where she has lived for 27 years - and is going back to Calcutta. For the foreseeable future she will spend half the year with family in India, and half with her daughter and son in the States.

"For the first time since her flight to meet her husband in Cambridge, in the winter of 1967, she will make the journey entirely on her own. The prospect no longer terrifies her."

This Ashima, once the trembling immigrant, now drives the roads of New England. She has an American passport, a driver's licence, a social security card. She is the doyenne of a large group of friends who will be devastated when she leaves. She has, in other words, made a life for herself in the "cold, foreign city".

As Nikhil contemplates saying goodbye to his mother he wonders how his parents managed it: ". . . leaving their respective families behind, seeing them so seldom, dwelling unconnected, in a perpetual state of expectation, of longing. All those trips to Calcutta he'd once resented - how could they have been enough? They were not enough".

He ponders the random events, the unforeseen incidents, one leading to the other, beginning with his father's accident on the train, all those years ago. Nikhil had tried to correct that randomness by changing his name. But he was only partially successful: "Things that should never have happened, that seemed out of place and wrong, these were what prevailed, what endured, in the end."

As I say, a simple story. But powerfully told.

Week 66: *The Line of Beauty*, by Alan Hollingurst (2004)

Not having read anything by Alan Hollingurst until now, it took me a while to get into the rhythm of his 2004 Booker Prize-winner, *The Line of Beauty*. Quite a while, actually. It wasn't until halfway through that I began to see the point of 438 pages devoted to some of the most superficial, fatuous, and entitled characters, young and old, you're ever likely to meet.

What I eventually realized was that this otherwise conventional novel is very funny, and if you accept "the gayness of the narrative position", as the author has described it, and are prepared to follow it through all its explicit homoerotic adventures, you end up with a sharp, insightful picture of a ruthless decade. Not to mention a vivid description of gay sex before the terror and prejudice of AIDS put an end to that particular freewheeling, no-holds-barred lifestyle.

It's the summer of 1983, "the last summer of its kind there was ever to be". Twenty-year-old Nick Guest has graduated from Oxford with a First in English and is about to begin postgraduate studies at University College London. The focus of his doctoral thesis is Henry James - which gives him the opportunity to drop bits of the Master into conversations, a kind of showing off which becomes more than a little annoying. As in, "[He] spoke, as to cheek and chin, of the joy of the matutinal steel" when referring to someone who's well-shaven.

A side note: I seem to be all about James these days. Three weeks ago I wrote about *The Master,* by Colm

Tóibín; the following week it was a review of *The Portrait of A Lady*, and now we find him turning up in a novel that might have been written by James himself, had he been born a century later. But that's it for now. Unless Salinger sneaks James into *Franny and Zooey* (next week's read), we're done with the Old Master for the moment.

In spite of his Oxford credentials, Nick is from middle-class stock. He attended university on scholarship, giving him a chance to rub shoulders with the sons and daughters of England's elite. One of these, Tobias Fedden, has become a close friend. Nick has long had a crush on Toby, who's straight, and ends up invited to stay with his family in their spacious Notting Hill home. Toby's father, Gerald, is an MP - Conservative, of course - and has recently been elected member for Barwick, Northamptonshire, the fictional home of Nick's parents. Nick admires Gerald, but nurtures a suspicion that "there might be something rather awful about him". The money in the family - and there's a lot of it - comes through Toby's mother, Rachel.

As the story opens, Nick has been left on his own to watch over Toby's sister, Catherine, while Toby and his parents holiday in France. Catherine, or "Cat", is a troubled young woman with a history of self-harming. She has periods of manic energy, when she's lively and upbeat, followed by dark episodes of depression. Nick talks her through one of these periods and when her parents come back they suggest he stay on; Cat's become attached to him and he is, after all, a friend of Toby's.

If ever there was someone in a position to survive merely on charm and goodwill, it's Nick. Without ever seeming to do anything to earn it, he gains the trust of Gerald and Rachel, who treat him, for the most part, like one of the family. While it's likely they're aware that he's gay, it's never mentioned - not till the end when things turn sour for Nick and his benefactors.

So far, Nick's sexual adventures are all fantasy. He has yet to actually have sex, although he dreams about it all the time. Through a personal ad he meets the vastly more experienced Leo Charles, a black man from Willesden, who lives with his mother. As Nick is too timid to bring Leo back to the Feddens', and they can't have sex at Leo's, they're restricted to conducting their affair on the fringes of park paths, public toilets, and side streets. Nick falls in love with Leo and tells him so; Leo is less effusive but obviously cares for Nick. He brings him home to meet his mother and sister, and takes him to meet "old Pete", a former lover who is now middle-aged and sick.

AIDS isn't actually mentioned until we meet up with Nick three years later, in the summer of 1986. Nick is now openly gay and has fallen in love with another Oxford friend, Antoine or "Wani" Ouradi. Wani, the son of a Lebanese millionaire, is, in Nick's view, "beautiful as a John the Baptist painted for a boy-loving pope". He's deeply in the closet, keeping his coke-fuelled threesomes a secret from his parents, his friends, and, most of all, his fiancée. He treats Nick to expensive gifts, money, and drugs, and hires him as his editorial assistant for the luxury magazine they plan to launch.

The name of the magazine is "Ogee", a rather ugly word for the beautiful double-S curve used in architecture. The ogee is the "line of beauty" used in the title, but it has other meanings: there's the dip and swell created by a man's lower back and buttocks, and there are, of course, the lines of cocaine used to keep the party going.

Hollingurst has an impeccable eye for character, and an ear for dialogue particular to class. Sir Maurice Tipper and his wife Sally are particularly gruesome: he's an asset-stripping millionaire with no interest in anything but money . . . she's smug, self-satisfied, and easily shocked. Together they make for unpleasant but necessary houseguests; Gerald dislikes them but sees them as valuable business contacts.

As awful as they are, the Tippers are only two in a host of unlikable individuals. One of my personal favourites is Toby's grandmother, Lady Partridge, a wealthy harridan who could easily stand in for Bertie Wooster's Aunt Agatha. Attending Rachel and Gerald's 25th anniversary party, she finds herself seated beside Wani's father: "Nick knew it was upsetting for her to sit next to what she always called an A-rab, but something seemed to kindle in her too at the closeness of so much money". Margaret Thatcher, reverently referred to by Gerald as "The Lady", has a cameo appearance here: Nick, high on cocaine, asks her to dance. To his surprise, and Gerald's chagrin, she agrees.

The party, of course, has to end, and it doesn't end well for any of the characters, gay or straight. Lovers get sick, friends die, and the powerful Feddens become the focus of scandal - only partly due to the homosexuals they harbour in their midst. Gerald's shady dealings are leaked to the press, and he's forced to resign. On the home front, Rachel gets wind of his affair with his secretary but decides to stick with him, good Tory wife that she is. Nick does better than most, which seems a shame considering he's a morally ambivalent, social-climbing hanger-on. Wani, who's about to die, leaves him a large property in Clerkenwell, and so far he's escaped the HIV plague. It's early days, though; as the novel ends, Nick is waiting, once again, to be tested.

In one of the book's best moments, Nick, after being told that Leo has died, remembers seeing him at a club, earlier that year. The shock of recognition is followed by an instinctive fear of being accosted - he leaves by the back way, his hand on the shoulder of a new acquaintance, "turning a blank gaze across the room to find the little woolly-hatted figure . . . who had once been his lover."

Cool, a little callous, and sad, it pretty much sums up this funny, furious, bittersweet book. Read it, if you haven't.

Week 67: *Franny and Zooey*, by J. D. Salinger (1955 and 1957)

In his dedication at the beginning of *Franny and Zooey*, J. D. Salinger appeals to William Shawn, his "editor, mentor, and (heaven help him) closest friend", to accept this "pretty skimpy-looking book". It is, in fact, rather skimpy, being a short story and novella under one cover. Both appeared earlier and separately in *The New Yorker*, "Franny" in 1955 and "Zooey" two years later. Together, they work as a novel, partly because "Zooey" picks up exactly where "Franny" leaves off. It's hard to imagine one without the other.

After the publication of *The Catcher in the Rye* (1951), J. D. Salinger devoted most of his fiction to the Jewish-Irish Glass family from New York City. There are seven of them, not including Les and Bessie, the parents, but by the time we come to *Franny and Zooey* two have already died: Seymour, the eldest, committed suicide on his honeymoon ("A Perfect Day for Bananafish"), and Walter died in Occupied Japan in late fall of 1945. Buddy, generally thought to be Salinger's alter ego, is now the oldest sibling. He lives in upstate New York, teaches English at a rural women's college, and is the one who writes the stories. Waker, Walt's twin, is a Roman Catholic monk of the Carthusian order; Beatrice, or "Boo-Boo", is a suburban homemaker living in Westchester County; Zachary Martin, or "Zooey", is an actor, and Franny, the youngest, is a 20-year-old college student and actress.

All seven of the Glass children, at one time or another, were panelists on a radio show called "It's a Wise Child". They are, without exception, precociously intelligent, although Seymour was the true savant of the family, becoming a professor at Columbia at the age of 20.

As the book opens, it's the fall of 1955, the weekend of the big Yale football game. Franny arrives by train to spend the weekend with her boyfriend, Lane Coutell, who meets her at the platform. The plan is to grab something to eat and then attend the match, but during lunch it becomes apparent that all is not well. Instead of eating, Franny smokes cigarette after cigarette and talks about how sick she is of her teachers, how college is such an incredible farce. Lane, who is monopolizing the conversation with the details of a paper he's written, finally begins to notice: "You've got a goddam bug today - you know that? What the hell's the matter with you anyway?"

All Franny can offer is apologies for being "off" at the moment. She excuses herself, goes to the ladies' room, and cries for a full five minutes. When she returns, she tells him she's dropped out of the play she's been doing, because she's sick of everything:

"I'm just sick of ego, ego, ego. My own and everybody else's. I'm sick of everybody that wants to *get* somewhere, do something distinguished and all, be somebody interesting. It's disgusting - it is, it *is*. I don't care what anybody says."

If this sounds familiar, it should. Who can forget Holden Caulfield, who left his private school because he was surrounded by "phonies"? It's one of Salinger's favourite themes, in life as well as his art; he holed up in New Hampshire for decades partly to get away from the phonies. (Several memoirs* have been written showing that Salinger might have been something of a phoney himself, but that's for another review.)

Eventually, Franny begins talking about a book she's carrying with her, *The Way of a Pilgrim*. She tells Lane she took it out of the library and it's well overdue, and then goes on to explain that it's the story of a simple man who becomes obsessed with the instruction in 1st Thessalonians that we should pray without ceasing. He travels the world, looking for someone who can tell him how a person can do that - pray without ceasing - and eventually meets a Russian monk who teaches him the Jesus prayer: "Lord Jesus Christ, have mercy on me". The monk explains that if you say it over and over again it will become automatic and unconscious and eventually you will get to see God. After telling Lane all of this, Franny excuses herself from the table, heads towards the ladies' room, and faints.

When she comes to, she's lying on a couch in the manager's office, with Lane sitting beside her. He tells her not to worry about the game, or the cocktail party they were planning to attend and goes off to hail a cab. Franny lies there looking at the ceiling. As her story ends she begins to mouth the words of the prayer, over and over again, without making a sound.

Zooey's story, which begins the following Monday, finds Franny collapsed on the sofa in her parent's apartment on New York City's Upper East Side. She is alternately crying and mumbling and is apparently having some kind of nervous breakdown. Her brother, Zooey, is in the bathtub, smoking cigarettes and reading a letter from his older brother, Buddy, written four years ago. In it Buddy talks about his students, mentioning that he has 38 short stories to mark: "Thirty-seven of them will be about a shy, reclusive Pennsylvania Dutch lesbian who Wants To Write, told first-person by a lecherous hired hand. In dialect". He apologizes for the years when he and Seymour force-fed Zooey and his sister a steady diet of religion and philosophy and tells him he should go ahead and become an actor.

Zooey's mother comes into the bathroom, smokes at least a dozen cigarettes - everybody in this family smokes - the place must stink to high heaven - and shares her worries about Franny. When she mentions the book Franny's brought with her, *The Way of a Pilgrim*, Zooey recognizes it as one that belonged to Seymour. He gets dressed, seeks out Franny on the sofa where she's huddled with the family cat, and gives her a pep talk that includes disparaging the "Jesus prayer" and calling her selfish. Not surprisingly, this upsets her even more. Zooey then goes into Seymour's room, and calls Franny from the bedroom phone, pretending to be Buddy. She sees through this, but doesn't hang up. Zooey then shares stories from their "freakish" upbringing, and concludes with something Seymour once told him about the need to live with optimism and love. When they hang up, Franny is finally calm; she lies in bed, smiling, and falls into a dreamless sleep.

In terms of action, that, in essence, is the story. It's not that nothing happens . . . it's that what does happen is all internal. Generally rendered in dialogue. "We don't talk," Zooey says, "we hold forth. We don't converse, we expound. At least I do. The minute I'm in a room with somebody who has the usual number of ears, I either turn into a goddam *seer* or a human hatpin."

It's not unusual - in fact, it's necessary, I think - for a writer to become attracted to the characters he creates. In Salinger's case, he was in love with the Glass family. All of them, even Bessie, who is used as a kind of verbal punching bag by most of her children. An ex-vaudevillian, Mrs. Glass has fingers "of an extraordinary length and shapeliness", and the "comely" legs of a former dancer: "The feet were extraordinarily small, the ankles were still slender, and, perhaps most remarkable, the calves were still firm and evidently had never been knotty". As for Franny, "Her skin was lovely, and her features were delicate and most distinctive. Her eyes were very nearly the same quite astonishing shade of blue as Zooey's but were set farther apart, as a sister's eyes no doubt should be." Zooey, besides being the most handsome of the seven siblings, possesses the "somewhat preposterous ability to quote, instantaneously and, usually verbatim, almost anything he had ever read, or even listened to, with genuine interest".

We are meant to adore this family, even envy them, in spite of their peculiarities. Or because of them. They are so intelligent, so attractive, so well-read. And also so completely neurotic. It's here, I think, where Salinger's literary canon stumbles, just a little. He loves them too well; he asks nothing of them but that they should exist. And talk. And talk. Aside from committing suicide, he never asks them to *do* anything. They *are* the plot. And if you love them, or are at least prepared to appreciate them, you will come to *Franny and Zooey* again and again and find something new to delight you.

If, however, you find them intensely irritating and just a tad self-obsessed, you may give this a pass.

And miss a great story by an American genius.

At Home in the World, by Joyce Maynard (1998) tells the story of her affair with J. D. Salinger. He was 53, she was 18. The critics trashed the book and she received death threats. In *Dream Catcher: A Memoir* (2001), Margaret "Peggy" Salinger wrote about life with her reclusive father. She, too, received death threats.

Week 68: *Lolita*, by Vladimir Nabokov (1955)

In his otherwise self-serving piece in *Harper's*, the disgraced American broadcaster John Hockenberry says one thing I agree with entirely: "I feel absolutely certain that Lolita would never be published today".

No, it probably wouldn't. This is, after all, a book about a middle-aged man raping an adolescent girl. Several times a day, for more than two years. I can't imagine anyone, even a writer as respected as Vladimir Nabokov, successfully pitching such a story today. Can you?

Martin Amis calls it a "cruel book about cruelty". It is that. While waiting in jail on a charge of murder, a professor of mixed European extraction, whose pseudonym is Humbert Humbert, writes his memoir, *The Confession of a White Widowed Male*. In a (fictional) foreword written by one John Ray, PhD, we learn that Humbert died before the trial got underway, and the object of his obsession, Lolita, died in childbirth the same year. So right off the bat we know that this is a book about sex and death . . . the two things that Woody Allen said come once in a lifetime.

As a protagonist, Humbert is not particularly loveable - or even likeable. In the hands of another writer, he would be just what he is: a disgusting, perverted creep. Also in the hands of anyone else, *Lolita* would be pornographic. It's not. There isn't a four-letter-word in the entire narrative, and not a single actual full-on description of any of the many disgusting things Humbert proudly crows about doing to his little sex slave. Your maiden aunt could read *Lolita* without blushing; she might, however, wish to throw up.

The story is this: after losing his mother at a young age, Humbert is raised by his wealthy father and enjoys a perfectly happy childhood. At the age of 13 he falls in love with Annabel, a lovely young girl who dies of typhus, leaving him with a lifelong preference for adolescent girls. As a young man, he frequents prostitutes, preferring those who at least look as if they might be below the age of consent. Sick of his obsession, and worried about his sanity, he marries a Polish woman of his own age. The marriage falls apart, he has a mental breakdown, is incarcerated for a time in a psychiatric hospital, and, on his release, migrates to America. There he finds himself in the fictional New England town of Ramsdale, lodging with Charlotte McCoo and her daughter, Delores. Charlotte calls her daughter Lo, and Humbert privately adjusts this to Lolita.

Delores/Lolita is a 12-year-old "nymphet", an adolescent girl who, in his mind, oozes sexuality. He fantasizes about her in his diary, flirts with her, surreptitiously fondles her now and then. Lolita likes him, even flirts back at times, and uses him as a sounding board about her antagonistic relationship with her mother. Charlotte, for her part, has fallen in love with Humbert - he is, after all, "a great big handsome hunk of movieland manhood" (his own description of himself). After sending Lolita off to summer camp Charlotte writes him a letter confessing her feelings and begging him to leave the house if he doesn't feel the same. Perceiving a way to stay close to Lolita, Humbert responds by proposing marriage. Charlotte agrees, but tells him that when Lo comes home from camp, she plans to send her away to boarding school.

At this point, you can almost hear Humbert grinding his teeth in frustration. He contemplates murdering Charlotte but settles for buying sleeping pills with which to sedate her and her daughter so he can fondle Lolita in the night. Before the summer ends, however, Charlotte is dead: having found his diary, she becomes enraged, tells him he'll never see her daughter again, and scribbles several letters to friends describing him as a monster. Rushing out of the house to mail them, she's hit by a car. Now there's no one to stand in his way. Humbert picks Lolita up from camp, and tells her her mother's been hospitalized. Together they set off on an extended excursion, criss-crossing the country in Charlotte's old beater, driving by day and spending night after night in endless dreary motels.

To be fair to the old pervert, while planning to have his wicked way with the girl he doesn't want to actually traumatize her. His plan is to knock her out with sleeping pills so she remains unconscious of his predations. Happily for him, this doesn't prove necessary: Lolita has already lost her virginity at camp and is, at least in the beginning, a willing sexual partner. She makes him pay for it, though. Every kiss, every caress, every fuck (my word, not his) comes at a price. Humbert doles out dresses, shoes, ice-cream sundaes, movie tickets. Nothing is too good for his darling.

As for Lolita, we learn almost nothing about her. We never really know her, because Humbert doesn't know her. And we live in Humbert's head. This is the brilliant, awful, unbearable thing about reading this book: Nabokov drags us - kicking and screaming, perhaps - into Humbert's head, Humbert's world view. We know he's a monster - he frequently describes himself as such. He fetishizes her . . . drools over her . . . maybe even loves her. But he knows her less well than those campers who spent a month with her that summer when she was still, to all intents and purposes, a child.

He loses her eventually, as we knew he must. Another middle-aged man, a well-known playwright named Clare Quilty, has stolen her heart and in the end she runs away with him. When we next hear from Lolita, two years later, she is 17, pregnant, and in desperate need of money. She's also married, although not to Quilty, who kicked her out when she refused to take part in his pornographic films. Seeking vengeance, Humbert tracks Quilty down at his mansion in Ramsdale, where he's living the life of a drug-addled sybarite. In a manic, ridiculous scene, Humbert shoots Quilty, several times, then allows himself to be arrested.

Readers may ask why, considering her loathing for the man, Lolita didn't run away from Humbert earlier. Some have speculated that she may have loved him. I doubt it. To me, Lolita is suffering from "Stockholm syndrome", the psychological alliance a hostage develops with her captor. With her mother gone, Humbert is all she has. He tells her repeatedly that if she leaves, if she goes to the police, she'll end up a ward of the state - in an abusive foster home, most likely. Or worse, in a reformatory. She stays, and goes along with it all, until her White Knight carries her off. By this time, however, her ideas of love and manhood are so distorted she fails to recognize him as just another pervert.

Near the end, when Humbert, a sick, broken man, languishing in jail for murdering the other sick man who stole his Lolita, thinks back on all of this, he feels the judge should sentence him to at least 35 years, not for murdering a man who was as corrupt as he, but for rape. Self-awareness has dawned on Humbert Humbert . . . finally. Too late for the childhood he destroyed.

Week 69: *Of Mice and Men*, by John Steinbeck (1937)

"Guys like us, that work on ranches, are the loneliest guys in the world. They got no family. They don't belong no place . . . They ain't got nothing to look ahead to."

This is the story that George tells his friend Lennie over and over again. The life of an itinerant ranch hand, living hand to mouth, hustling work where he can find it. But he and Lennie are different: they have each other. And together they will save their money and buy a few acres of land with a shack on it, and a couple of outbuildings, and raise chickens, and pigs, and grow their own food.

"An' live off the fatta the lan'!" Lennie shouts. Because he knows the ending to the story - George has told it many times.

This is their dream. To live on their own small property, with no one to tell them to shove off, no one to boss them around. Lennie, who is big, enormously strong, with the intellect of a child, believes George implicitly. A few more jobs and they'll have their stake; they'll buy a place and quite roaming from ranch to ranch. And Lennie will tend the rabbits.

George is smart. He knows how to plan ahead, how to get along with the jerkline skinner, "the prince of the ranch". He may be small in stature but he knows how to think, how to find work and how to get them out of there when trouble's brewing. George knows that Lennie, who is simple and impulsive, is a liability, but he knows Lennie will do as he's told. If he gets into trouble, as he's done before, he will come back to a place by the river, and hide in the brush till George comes to get him. That much Lennie will remember.

What George can't control is the pretty, wayward young wife of the boss' son, Curly. The only woman on the ranch, she's lonely - Curly, with his hair-trigger temper and his nasty, suspicious nature, isn't much company. So she hangs around the bunkhouse, flirting with the men, making a nuisance of herself. And Lennie likes to touch nice things.

He did it before, in Weed. Touched a girl's dress and wouldn't let go - held on even harder when she screamed. The girl cried rape and the two men only just escaped being lynched. Now there's another ranch and another girl. And nothing good can come of it.

John Steinbeck, who was born and grew up in Salinas, California, drew on his own experiences to tell this tale of migrant farm workers. He dropped out of college without taking a degree and spent several years working on farms and ranches in the Central Valley. In 1936 he wrote a series of newspaper articles about the shocking conditions experienced by workers in California's migrant labour camps - whole families lacking proper shelter, food, or running water; he followed it up the next year with *Of Mice and Men*, a tragic novella based on those lives.

What gripped me the first time I read it, and continues to hold me each time I go back to it, is the straightforward, no-nonsense storytelling. We know the author has a message, but unlike some of his contemporaries, or even his own work of later years, he doesn't hit you over the head with it. He lets his characters go about their business, trying to keep their heads above water, with all the odds stacked against them. It's a dark, hopeful, and hopeless description of what it means to be human.

By the time Steinbeck was awarded the 1962 Nobel Prize for Literature he had written twelve novels, four novellas, a half dozen nonfiction books and a handful of short stories. Critics complained that his best work, *Tortilla Flat*, *Of Mice and Men*, and *The Grapes of Wrath*, was long behind him. And maybe it was. But turning to those pages again, at a time when migrant workers continue to struggle, when their children are rounded up and put in cages, away from their parents, the stories don't seem dated at all. They seem sadly, even terribly, prophetic.

Week 70: *A Portrait of the Artist as a Young Man*, by James Joyce (1916)

Pity the poor reviewers when James Joyce burst onto the scene with *A Portrait of the Artist as a Young Man*. It was 1916, and even his most sympathetic critics, while admitting the book was well-written and the dialogue superb, were confused by the "formless, unrestrained" and "unconventional" nature of the story. Many were put off by its "occasional impropriety", which included the mention of such unspeakable matters as wetting the bed and consorting with prostitutes - two events that, thankfully, take place several years apart.

But even then there were many - T. S Eliot, Virginia Woolf, Samuel Beckett - who admired *Portrait* and even hailed it as a work of genius. Ezra Pound, who had published it in installments in *The Egoist*, predicted that the book would "remain a permanent part of English literature".

He was right, of course. While *Ulysses,* which began to appear in serial form two years later, revolutionized our approach to modern literature, Joyce laid the groundwork with this tale of a youthful Dubliner growing into adulthood at the turn of the last century. His use of interior monologue and free indirect speech, which influenced Woolf's *Mrs Dalloway*, Beckett's *Molloy*, and William Faulkener's *The Sound and the Fury*, became a convention of modern literature employed by such disparate writers as Sylvia Plath (*The Bell Jar*) and Irivine Welsh (*Trainspotting*).

Portrait begins with a little boy listening to his father tell him a story:

"Once upon a time and a very good time it was there was a moocow coming down along the road and this moocow that was coming down along the road met a nicens little boy named baby tuckoo . . ."

The moocow comes down the road where Betty Byrne lives - she sells lemon platt - the little boy wets the bed - his mother changes the sheet. From the very beginning we are seeing the world from the perspective of the child and as the child matures so will the language. The little boy is sent to school, and the bigger boys tease him and there are some boys you can trust and others you cannot. A priest beats him for breaking his glasses. He works up the courage to go to the rector about it and garners a promise that it won't happen again. The boy is learning that he has agency.

The boy is Stephen Dedalus, Joyce's alter ego. Heavily influenced by the religion of his mother and the politics of his father, as was Joyce, Stephen accepts everything at first, as children do. By the time he reaches adolescence he has begun to question the constraints of his church, his family, and his country. It's a time when thousands are doing just that. Home rule for Ireland, the authority of the Catholic church, the mystery of transubstantiation - all of these are fodder for discussion and fierce argument. Charles Steward Parnell is his father's hero, but Parnell, the great Irish hope of the nationalist movement, is discovered to be an adulterer. He dies amid scandal and disgrace, brought down, many feel, by the harsh, inflexible dictates of the Catholic church. And

Stephen's father, although passionately sentimental about the past, cannot deal with the present. Unable to manage his financial affairs, he becomes debt-ridden and loses the family home. The priests, on the whole, get off lightly, it seems to me. Perhaps if Joyce had been aware of the abuses perpetrated by so many of the clergy, he might have dealt with them more harshly.

Having won a cash prize for his performance at school, Stephen goes on a bit of a bender, you might say. He begins to frequent prostitutes, indulging his sensual nature while struggling with the knowledge that he is endangering his soul. He and his classmates are taken on a religious retreat, during which a priest subjects them, and the reader, to a harrowing diatribe on the nature of Hell. It rattles Stephen to the bone - to be fair, it rattled me; raised a Baptist as a child I sat through a few of those sermons myself and suffered all the terrors of damnation and the eternal fire. Stephen repents and mends his ways, to the extent that he's considered a good prospect for the priesthood. (I repented, too, but nobody ever suggested I should become a pastor.)

Stephen, as written by Joyce, sees the most important question as, what is the relationship of the artist to his culture, to his race? The answer to that question is exile - the artist must leave his home, his countrymen, his culture. "Ireland is the old sow that eats her own farrow," he tells his friend Davin. "No honourable and sincere man . . . has given up to you his life and his youth and his affections from the days of Tone to those of Parnell but you sold him to the enemy or failed him in need or reviled him and left him for another. And you invite me to be one of you. I'd see you damned first".

So Stephen leaves Ireland, as did Joyce. In 1904 he and Nora Barnacle left for Zurich. After 1912 he never set foot in Ireland again, dying in 1942 a month short of his 59th birthday.

I wouldn't call myself a Joycean. I warm to him when he shows Stephen at school at Clongowes, the Jesuit-run college where the shy, intellectually gifted young boy attempts to learn the schoolboy code. Later, as a student at University College, Dublin, his interactions with his classmates, especially Cranly and Lynch, have the authenticity of being drawn from life. As does the scene over Christmas dinner when Dante, his governess, is so offended by his father's praise of Parnell she walks out in a fury. And I love the language: "his small fatencircled eyes", a "plump woollengloved hand", a "lavishlimbed" young woman.

Overall, though, Joyce puts me off, somehow. He overwrites. I agree with Roddy Doyle, who said he could do with a good editor. And this is *A Portrait of the Artist* we're talking about. Heaven knows how I'd get through *Ulysses*.

Week 71: *The God of Small Things*, by Arundhati Roy (1997)

There is a particular kind of person I cannot stand. It's not the one who shouts into his cell phone on a crowded train - he may be hard of hearing, rather than simply rude. It's not even the one who pushes in front of me in a queue, or even, God help us, the misguided fool who propels an overloaded shopping cart into the no-more-than-15-items express line at the grocery store.

The person I really loathe is the one who condescends to inform me - and they always do it with condescension: "Oh, I never read fiction."

The subtext of this sentence is twofold: a) "I'm too busy reading important books to waste my time reading about people who don't exist" and b) "Actually, I don't read. Period."

At this point I usually excuse myself to get another glass of wine and find reasons not to return to that part of the room for the rest of the evening.

Camus said fiction is the lie through which we tell the truth. Emerson put it this way: "Fiction reveals truth that reality obscures". Earlier this year, Arundhati Roy, who writes powerful nonfiction championing human rights and environmental activism, was asked what it is that the novel makes possible for us that no other form of writing does.

"Only a novel," she said, "can tell you how caste, communalisation, sexism, love, music, poetry, the rise of the right all combine in a society. And the depths in which they combine. We have been trained to 'silo-ise': our brains specialise in one thing. But the radical understanding is if you can understand it all, and I think only a novel can."

There, buddy. Put *that* in your pipe and smoke it.

Roy's first novel, *The God of Small Things,* which won the Man Booker Prize in 1997, is simply extraordinary. Without ever appearing to proselytize, she tackles a myriad of issues, some of them centuries old: Indian politics, the caste system, the oppression of women, the consequences of breaking the rules of "who should be loved, and how. And how much". The characters are drawn so skilfully that if they were to walk into your living room, unannounced, you would know them in a minute.

The story is set in the village of Ayemenem, which is now part of the Kottayam district of Kerala, India. Fraternal twins Rahel and Esthappen are seven years old in 1969 when the tragedy occurs that will define their future. The narrative shifts back and forth between that time and the period, 24 years later, when they are reunited. While Rahel is the main protagonist, both as a child and a young woman, we are also told the story from the perspective of five other characters: Estha, her brother; Ammu, their mother; Chacko, their uncle; Baby Kochamma, their malicious great-aunt, and Velutha, the kind young man who works for the family and is also a Paravan - an Untouchable.

In a series of flashbacks and flashforwards, we learn the family's history, beginning with Pappachi

(Grandfather) who worked as an Imperial Entomologist. Pappachi is an angry, abusive old man; he's never gotten over the fact that he was not given credit for his discovery of a new species of moth. He drinks heavily and beats his wife. His son, Chacko, attends Oxford as a Rhodes scholar and marries an English woman named Margaret. Together they have a daughter, Sophie, but the marriage doesn't last. While pregnant, Margaret meets and falls in love with another man, and once the baby, Sophie, is born she demands a divorce. Broken-hearted, Chacko comes back to India, leaving Sophie to be raised by Margaret and her new husband, Joe.

Chacko's sister, Ammu, is as intelligent as he but because she's a girl there's no thought of sending her to university. Longing to get out of the house, she ends up married to an alcoholic who physically abuses her. The final straw, for Ammu, is when he tries to get her to sleep with his boss. She takes their children, Rahel and Estha, and moves back home. By this time her father, Pappachi, is dead and her mother is running a successful pickle business.

Baby Kochamma is a kind of honorary title given to Pappachi's sister, Navomi Ipe. When she was young, she fell in love with a handsome Irish priest named Father Mulligan. In order to get close to him, she converted to Catholicism and joined a convent. When she realized being a nun would bring her no closer to her priest, she left the convent and went to America to study ornamental gardening at the University of Rochester. Now she lives with her brother's family, nurturing her unrequited love for Father Mulligan and despising Ammu for being a divorcée.

When the novel opens, the family is preparing to welcome a couple of guests: Margaret's husband, Joe, has died in a car accident and Chacko invites her to bring Sophie to spend Christmas with them. The excitement over their arrival causes Rahel a great deal of anxiety: will her mother love her less, once Sophie Mol arrives? Will she, Rahel, be replaced?

On the way to the airport their car is stopped by protestors who surround the car and force Baby Kochamma to wave a red flag and chant a Communist slogan. Rahel recognizes Velutha, the family servant, among them; excited, she calls out to him but he disappears into the crowd. The others say it can't be him - surely Velutha isn't a Communist - but the seeds of doubt have been planted. Baby Kochamma, in particular, begins to harbour a deep dislike of the young man.

They have planned to attend a screening of *The Sound of Music* but by the time they get there the movie has already started. Estha, who loves the film, can't stop singing along. Ammu tells him to go wait in the lobby if he can't keep quiet. While he's standing there alone, the man selling orange and lemon drinks molests him, leaving Estha with a haunting anxiety that plays into the final denouement.

The family spend the night in a hotel and then meet Margaret and Sophie at the airport the following day. The twins, especially Rahel, are prepared to dislike Sophie, given the fuss that is made over her. Baby Kochamma in particular makes sure they understand that Sophie, being half English with light-coloured skin and hair, is the star of the drama - Rahel and Estha are only bit players.

Traumatized by the incident at the movie theatre, Estha is worried that the "Orangedrink Lemondrink Man" will track him down in Ayemenem. *Anything can happen to Anyone,* he thinks. *It's best to be prepared.* He starts stocking up on the necessities of life - food, his favourite toys - in preparation for running away.

Shortly after Margaret and Sophie Mol arrive, Ammu and Velutha become lovers. They meet at night in the abandoned house across the river, and make love under cover of darkness. When their affair is discovered, Ammu is locked in her room. The children stand outside her door, asking her to tell them why she's crying and Ammu, beside herself with grief, screams to them that it's all their fault. Everything that's wrong in her life is because of them.

The children decide to run away. They will use the small boat Velutha mended for them and row across the river to the abandoned house. Sophie begs to go with them, and the twins reluctantly agree. Unfortunately, it's dark and raining heavily. The boat capsizes; while the twins manage to swim to shore, Sophie Mol is drowned.

Baby Kochamma seizes her opportunity. She goes to the police and swears that Velutha, an Untouchable, has raped her niece, kidnapped the twins, and most likely murdered little Sophie. The police go looking for Velutha and find him curled up asleep in the abandoned house, where he has gone to wait for Ammu. They beat him senseless, cracking his skull, his nose, his cheekbones, his ribs. They rupture his intestine and damage his spine, then handcuff him and carry him out. All of which is witnessed by the twins.

"The twins were too young to know that these were only history's henchmen. Sent to square the books and collect the dues from those who broke its laws. Impelled by feelings that were primal yet paradoxically wholly impersonal. Feelings of contempt born of inchoate, unacknowledged fear - civilization's fear of nature, men's fear of women, power's fear of powerlessness".

Later, the Inspector tells Baby Kochamma she has no case. The twins say they went away on their own, Ammu insists she hasn't been raped. If what Baby Kochamma has said is a lie, she will be charged with filing a false statement. Baby Kochamma then turns on the children. Asking to be alone with them for a moment, she tells them it's their fault that Sophie Mol is dead. They will be sent to jail, and their mother will be sent to jail, too. They will never see her again for a very, very long time. Who do they want to save, Velutha or their mother? The Inspector, she tells them, will ask them a question. All they have to do is answer, "Yes".

The twins, as might be expected, choose their mother. The Inspector takes Estha into the lockup and switches on the light, revealing the dead, battered body of Velutha, his friend: "The Inspector asked his question. Estha's mouth said Yes. Childhood tiptoed out. Silence slid in like a bolt. Someone switched off the light and Velutha disappeared".

Shortly afterwards, the children are separated. Baby Kochamma convinces Chacko to send Ammu away, and Estha is returned to his father. Rahel is sent away to school and goes on to study architecture in Delhi. In 1993, learning that Estha has returned to Ayemenem, she returns home. Having been separated for so many years, the twins are finally reunited - in guilt for the part they played in the tragedy and in the knowledge that they, too, will break the rules of "who should be loved, and how".

Fiction. The beautiful lie through which we tell the truth.

Week 72: *The Hours*, by Michael Cunningham (1998)

I'm not sure it's possible to find any kind of weakness in Michael Cunningham's Pulitzer Prize-winning novel. As a work of fiction, it's as perfect in its way as anything I've ever read. And it proves, if it needed proving, that a book does not have to take up a huge amount of shelf space to be considered "great". In just over 200 pages Cunningham explores questions of sexuality, sanity and insanity, the inner conflict created by societal pressures to be "normal". It may have begun life as a homage to Virginia Woolf's *Mrs. Dalloway*, but as a work of art it is unique and unforgettable.

Everything in *The Hours* takes place in the space of a day - four different days involving three different women. In alternate chapters we meet Clarissa Vaughan (Cunningham's Mrs. Dalloway), Laura Brown, and Virginia Woolf. One of these women is writing a book, another is reading it, and the third may be living it. The book begins with a prologue, set on the day in 1941 when Woolf, facing another recurrence of manic depression, decides to take her own life. She leaves the house in East Sussex where she lives with Leonard, her husband, and makes her way down to the river where, having selected a large stone and placed it in her pocket, she walks into the water and drowns.

Fifty years later, on a morning in June, Clarissa, an upper-class housewife like Woolf's heroine, heads out of her New York apartment to buy flowers. She is giving a party for her longtime friend, and sometime lover, Richard Brown. Richard is a poet who has written a huge, difficult novel, and he's just been awarded the Carrouthers, an esteemed poetry prize awarded for a life's work. Richard is also dying of AIDS. As she walks along the pavement, Clarissa is buoyed by the energy of the city - "its intricacy; its endless life". She loves the world for being rude and indestructible and feels privileged to be alive. Along the way she bumps into an acquaintance, Walter Hardy, a successful romance writer, and impulsively invites him to the party. Richard, she knows, will be furious to hear he's been invited, but it seems the right thing to do.

The next chapter takes us back to a morning in 1923 when Virginia Woolf and Leonard are living in Richmond, where he has brought her to get her away from the noise and confusion of London. She's prone to terrible, debilitating headaches that herald the onset of madness. If she can keep them at bay a little longer, the rest cure will be pronounced a success; Leonard will agree to move back to the city. In the meantime, she will begin work on her novel. She picks up her pen and writes, "Mrs. Dalloway said she would buy the flowers herself".

Laura Brown's morning begins in Los Angeles in 1949, on the day of her husband's birthday. Her son, Richie, is downstairs having breakfast with his father and Laura, who is pregnant with their second child, can't summon the energy to join them. She lies in bed reading *Mrs. Dalloway*, wishing she could simply stay there, reading. Never having to get up, never having to play the role of good wife and mother, as much as she loves her family. Eventually, she gets out of bed and goes downstairs, forcing herself to act like a "normal" housewife. She waves her husband off to work, pours herself a cup of coffee, and tells her son they're going to bake a special cake for his father: "She will not go upstairs and return to her book. She will remain. She will do all that's required, and more."

Over the course of these three days, the women are faced with their fears and yearnings, their need to make sense of their lives. Clarissa Vaughan seems the happiest; she is, like her namesake, "destined to charm, to prosper". She has a partner, Sally, she has a daughter, she has money and a nice apartment. But the man who meant the most to her, and still does, is dying. And she can't know if there might have been something she might have done, long ago when they were young, that would have changed the course of events. They were lovers for a time, and then she walked away.

Laura Brown, who wishes to disappear, drives to a hotel, where she takes a room for a couple of hours, and reads. And then, because she must, she returns, a ghost in her own home. She will leave again, eventually, but not today. And she won't commit suicide.

Virginia Woolf, as we know, will give up the struggle. She'll leave a note for her sister, and one for Leonard: "I don't think two people could have been happier than we have been," she will write. And then she will kill herself. But not today.

Cunningham has admitted it was "enormously daunting" to attempt to write a novel that presumed to enter the mind of Virginia Woolf. It's something even the hardiest feminist might balk at, and Cunningham is, of course, a man. But, as he put it, "Well, why would you want to write a novel you know you can write? Why not just go down in big, green flames?"

It's not till near the end that you understand how the three stories, the three women, are linked, and I'm not going to go into that here. But I will say that there are common themes that run through each woman's narrative. It's about the joy that can be found in being alive, and the tragedy of not being able to continue . . . not being able to face the next hour, and the next, and the next. And it's about the understanding that love has its limits, that there are things it cannot do; it cannot save a life if, for whatever reason, that life is not meant to be saved. I found that especially true and especially sad. There's a moment near the end that sums up the terrible, bittersweet nature of the human condition. It brought me to tears and seems, to me at least, to warrant being quoted in full:

"We live our lives, do whatever we do, and then we sleep - it's as simple and ordinary as that. A few jump out of windows or drown themselves or take pills; more die by accident; and most of us, the vast majority, are slowly devoured by some disease or, if we're very fortunate, by time itself. There's just this for consolation: an hour here or there when our lives seem, against all odds and expectations, to burst open and give us everything we've ever imagined, though everyone but children (and perhaps even they) knows these hours will inevitably be followed by others, far darker and more difficult. Still, we cherish the city, the morning; we hope, more than anything, for more".

Week 73: *White Teeth*, by Zadie Smith (2000)

Back in December 2000, a few months after Zadie Smith's first novel was published, winning the Whitbread award, nominated for the Orange prize, thrusting her into the media spotlight, *The Guardian*'s Simon Hattenstone interviewed her at the ICA (Institute of Contemporary Arts) where she was writer-in-residence. Hattenstone began by informing us that Smith, who "looked lovely on the cover of *White Teeth*", was now "all long straight hair and lip gloss"; she looked, he wrote, "like any number of drained All Saints waltzing around clubland".

Pardon my French, but give me a fucking break. What male writer can you think of would be introduced to readers first and foremost by his physical appearance? This is the price you pay, I suppose, when you're a media darling: young (she was 24 when *White Teeth* came out), attractive, talented, and black. And, oh yes, female.

Now that two decades have passed, and Smith has established herself as a pre-eminent fiction writer and essayist, you hear a lot less about her looks. Thank God. She will always, of course, be referred to as "the black female writer Zadie Smith", when no one would ever talk about "the white male writer Martin Amis". Would they? I don't think so.

Anyway, shelving that in the department of Things That Will Likely Never Change, let's talk about *White Teeth*. When I first read it, what struck me was the feeling that it was the first modern novel I'd read about

London. Modern in the way that *Trainspotting* was about a certain section of Edinburgh.

That, however, is where the comparison stops. Smith is not writing about a criminal underclass freaking out on heroin. *White Teeth* is a multigenerational saga of two working-class families, the Bangladeshi Iqbals and the English Joneses, living in Willesden, North London. Samad Iqbal is a waiter in a curry restaurant, Archie Jones holds down a dead-end job in a printing company. The two men were comrades in the Second World War and they've stayed friends over the years, getting together nightly at O'Connell's, a men-only pub, to share memories of the war and commiserate with each other on the trials and tribulations of family life.

Archie is a character whose very existence epitomizes mediocrity. He's so boring his wife walks out on him, and now, at 47, he lives alone in a one-bedroom flat above a chip shop. When, on New Year's Day 1975, he decides to commit suicide, his life flashes before him: "It turned out to be a short, unedifying experience, low on entertainment value, the metaphysical equivalent of the Queen's Speech". A butcher's assistant finds him parked in the shop's loading zone, trying to gas himself in his car, and he's told to move on. As Mo, the shop owner, says, "No one gasses himself on my property. We're not licensed for that."

And so Archie, having realized he's not meant to die after all, chooses to live. He wanders into the aftermath of a New Year's party where he meets a much younger Jamaican woman, Clara Bowden, whose mother,

Hortense, is a devout - even fanatical - Jehovah's Witness. Clara is looking for a way to escape the clutches of Ryan Topps, a former boyfriend who's become involved with the Witnesses. When Archie proposes marriage, she agrees, and shortly afterwards they have a daughter, Irie Jones, who grows up to be overweight, intelligent, and insecure.

Samad, too, is married to a younger woman: Alsana is feisty and opinionated and when it comes to arguing with her husband, which she does constantly, she gives as good as she gets. While Samad works nights at the curry restaurant, Alsana takes in sewing to help make ends meet. Their twin boys, Magid and Millat, are the same age as Irie. Millat is handsome, athletic, and popular; Magid is intellectually gifted. When the boys are 10, Samad, tormented by guilt over a brief affair with his sons' music teacher, decides he must make reparations. He sends Magid to Bangladesh to be properly instructed in the teachings of Islam and Magid effectively disappears from the story for the next 8 years. Millat, who harbours a devotion to Hollywood gangster flicks like *Goodfellas* and *The Godfather*, develops his skills as a womaniser and drinker, and eventually becomes involved with a militant Muslim organization known as Keepers of the Eternal and Victorious Islamic Nation (KEVIN).

Halfway through the book we're introduced to another, very different family: the Chalfens. Joyce and Marcus Chalfen have what they consider the perfect marriage. Marcus is a scientific genius working on a prototype of a genetically modified mouse, and Joyce is a writer and horticulturist. Together they have produced four articulate, amusing sons; their smug belief in their own rightness - their Chalfenism - knows no bounds. Their eldest son, Joshua, who's a bit of a nerd, attends school with Irie and Millat; he has a crush on her and is jealous of Millat, partly because of his social standing but mainly because Irie is in love with him. When the three of them get into trouble at school, the principal decides that Irie and Millat shall spend some time at Joshua's house, working on their schoolwork. There they find a safe haven - Irie is captivated by her introduction to a family so very different from her own, and Joyce is captivated by Millat. Gradually, Joyce's sympathies focus increasingly on Millat, who seems bent on destruction - his own and that of the non-Muslim world. Her concern for the boy comes at the expense of her own son, Josh. Angry and alienated, Josh leaves home to join an animal rights group called FATE - Fighting Animal Torture and Exploitation.

In the meantime, Magid returns from Bangladesh, not, as his father had hoped, a sterling example of Muslim manhood but, as put by Mickey, the pub owner, more English than the English. He's impeccably dressed, well-spoken, and rational, and aspires to be a lawyer. After being introduced to the Chalfens, he begins to work with Marcus on his FutureMouse© project.

There are stories and sub-stories within *White Teeth*; you need a spreadsheet to keep them all straight. I won't go into the history of Samad's great-grandfather, hero of the 1857 Indian rebellion, or how Irie ends up pregnant by one of the twins (she's not sure which one), or why Josh is determined to stay involved with FATE as much as he hates Crispin, its leader. I will say, though, as the time draws closer for Marcus's FutureMouse© to be put on display, the disparate strands of narrative begin to come together. KEVIN decides that Marcus's mouse is an abomination in the eyes of the Creator; they attend the launch of FutureMouse© in order to a) make a speech or b) shoot somebody. The Jehovah's Witnesses, as represented by Clara's mother, Hortense, and Ryan Topps, are in attendance for the same reason, although under the aegis of a different god. The members of FATE go in order to set the mouse free, and Archie, Clara, Samad and Alsana are there to show their support for Magid.

The denouement is as turbulent as you might expect. In the end, the mouse escapes, Irie and Josh go to Jamaica to live with her grandmother, and Mickey finally opens up O'Connell's to women. Considering the bleak state of the place, we can hardly consider this a step forward.

As for the meaning of the title, it's possible that white teeth represent those elements in society that are fake . . . unnatural. Both Irie and Clara have buck teeth; perfectly white, straightened teeth belong to "suntanned white-toothed airline representatives". Maybe Smith is making the point that our fake society demands perfect, fake smiles.

Or maybe it was just a good title.

Week 74: *Mother's Milk*, by Edward St. Aubyn (2006)

Patrick Melrose is a well-born, 40-something London barrister who, having burned through his inheritance, is now reduced to having to work for a living. Married with two young sons, Melrose is what is commonly called a "survivor", although his actual survival is frequently in doubt.

As a young child he was beaten and raped by his father; his neurotic, self-obsessed mother kept her distance, both emotionally and, finally, literally, leaving him to his father's poisonous care in order to go searching for ways to do good for other people. By the time we meet him in *Mother's Milk*, he's a former heroin addict and an off-and-on recovering alcoholic, tempted to jump from high windows and sedating himself with Temazepam to still the voices that torment him.

Patrick is, in other words, a mess. But he is also funny, smart, and hilariously acerbic - much like the author, I suspect. It's that caustic wit, aimed towards himself as often as the members of his atrociously dysfunctional family, that keeps you turning the pages.

The story takes place during four consecutive Augusts, from 2000 to 2003. In the first part, Patrick's son Robert is a precociously observant child who increasingly resembles his father at that age. He's a loner and a scathing mimic, and there's not much about his parent's marriage that escapes him. If I was going to find any fault in St. Aubyn's characters, it would be my skepticism about Robert's command of the English language. There may be three-year-olds who talk like philosophers and remember the trauma of being born ("awake for days, banging his head again and again against a closed cervix"), but I've yet to meet one.

Patrick's wife, Mary, has her own maternal issues. Raised by a cold, withholding mother, she's determined to be everything her mother was not. To Patrick's chagrin, she devotes herself entirely to the care and feeding of her sons, in particular the youngest, Thomas, virtually banishing her husband from the marital bed. And while this angers Patrick, giving him an excuse, if he needed one, to indulge in an affair, it also undermines her sense of herself. By nature a solitary person, she's beginning to feel lost in her roles as mother, wife, and family caregiver - something most women with children feel at one time or another. Unless they're the kind of mothers generally portrayed in *Mother's Milk*: nasty, upperclass women eager to be rid of their offspring.

To be honest, mothers come off poorly in this book. Eleanor, Patrick's mother, is not quite as cold-blooded or aloof as some of them, but she deliberately closes her eyes to her young son's suffering, choosing to save her own life over her child's. She, it turns out, was disinherited by her own mother, who "caved in to the lies and bullying of her second husband" and left him the lion's share of the family fortune. Over and over again the allegiances shift, leaving children and partners bewildered and resentful. As Patrick notes, the poison flows from one generation to the next. Now that Eleanor is old and sick, unable to walk, almost incapable of speech, she comes under the influence of an opportunistic new-age guru named Seamus. She signs over the family estate in Provence to his charitable foundation, choosing once again to be kind to anyone other than her own son. As Patrick says, "In a beauty contest between her family and a complete stranger, my mother chose the stranger".

While this is regrettable, let's remember that Patrick and his family are not by any means rendered homeless. It's not as though they're going to have to apply to the county council for a subsidized flat in Hackney. They're simply less rich than they were, or than they might have been. Which makes Patrick's self-pitying monologues a little tedious.

But this is natural. As Patrick says, "People never remember happiness with the care that they lavish on preserving every detail of their suffering."

Having signed away the family estate, Eleanor lets her son know she wishes to die. She asks him to kill her, and Patrick is torn between his loathing of his mother and his reluctance to commit a crime. She persists, and so he arranges to fly with her to Switzerland in order to have an assisted suicide. At the last minute, in the airport, Eleanor changes her mind.

The weakest point of this book is the beginning, the part narrated by three-year-old Robert. It's too precious, too precocious. I don't believe it and I will tell you right now that if I was to meet that child in person I would banish him to his room to write out 100 times, "I will not be a Royal Pain in the Ass". The strongest scenes are those like the following, in which Patrick reflects - astutely, considering how drunk he is - on his relationship with his wife:

"He had taken Mary, a good woman, and made her into an instrument of torture, a weird echo of Eleanor forty years ago: never available, always exhausted by her dedication to an altruistic project which didn't include him. He had achieved this by the ironic device of rejecting the sort of woman who would have made a bad mother, like Eleanor, and choosing one who was such a good mother that she was incapable of letting one drop of her love escape from her children."

Like *Vile Bodies, Black Mischief,* and *A Handful of Dust, Mother's Milk* is satirical view of English upper class society written from an insider's point of view. The difference being, of course, that Evelyn Waugh was not born an insider while St. Aubyn has a pedigree that goes back to the Norman Conquest. Like Waugh, he aims to portray the speech, manners, and (often loathsome) behaviour of the upper crust, and in doing so he can make you laugh out loud. These are people who would cut you dead if you met them at a party, but you can't help loving them in print.

Mother's Milk, which was short-listed for the Man Booker Prize, is the fourth in a series of semi-autobiographical novels: *Never Mind, Bad News,* and *Some Hope.* Together with the fifth book, *At Last,* they've been made into a five-part television series, starring Benedict Cumberbatch. It was worth getting a subscription to Crave TV just to watch it, but you may be lucky enough to find it in your library.

Ernest Hemingway once said that the best early training for a writer was an unhappy childhood. If he was right, then perhaps St. Aubyn should be grateful to his evil, poisonous father and his faithless, incompetent mother for providing the inspiration for a brilliant literary career.

Then again, perhaps not.

Week 75: *Get Shorty*, by Elmore Leonard (1990)

Elmore Leonard, who died at the age of 87, was one of the most visual writers America has produced. It's no wonder that 26 of his novels and short stories have been adapted for the screen. He had a deceptively simple style that brought his characters to life without a lot of "hooptedoodle", John Steinbeck's word for the parts in a story that you can safely skip and still follow the plot.

In a 2001 article in the New York Times, Leonard shared his "10 Rules of Writing", in which he advised writers to leave out the part that readers tend to skip. "If it sounds like writing," he said, "I rewrite it."

That's Rule #10, but the other nine make just as much sense. I think they're essential reading for any writer, keeping in mind that rules are made to be broken. Leonard himself gave examples of writers who successfully broke several of his rules. Take prologues, for instance: "There is a prologue in John Steinbeck's Sweet Thursday, but it's OK because a character in the book makes the point of what my rules are all about. He says: 'I like a lot of talk in a book and I don't like to have nobody tell me what the guy that's talking looks like. I want to figure out what he looks like from the way he talks.'"

Get Shorty, published in 1990, was made into a movie in 1995, starring John Travolta, Rene Russo, Gene Hackman and Danny DeVito. In 2017 it was adapted into a TV series of the same name. It's about a mobster in love with the movies; besides being the most successful of all his adaptations, *Get Shorty* is a great example of Leonard's rules and the ways in which they can, occasionally, be broken.

Ernesto "Chili" Palmer is a Miami loan shark - a "shylock" - who's decided to get out of the business. Before he can do that, though, Chili has to collect a debt owed to a thug named Ray Barboni, otherwise knows as Ray Bones. Chili and Bones have a backstory: twelve years earlier Ray walked off with Chili's jacket. Chili went after him, punched him in the face and got his jacket back. Later on, during another encounter, Chili grazed Ray's skull with a bullet. Ray, who has never forgiven him, or got over being pissed, is owed $10,000 by a drycleaner named Leo Devoe who supposedly died in a plane crash. When Chili tries to get the money from the drycleaner's widow, Faye, she tells him Devoe faked his death - he was never on the plane and he scammed $300,000 in insurance money from the airline. He was supposed to split the money with Faye but instead he headed to Las Vegas where he's living the high life at the gambling casinos. Faye and Chili make a deal: he'll head west, find Devoe, get the money (if there's any left) and then split it between them.

The trip to Vegas turns out to be only partly successful: Chili does find Devoe and gets the money, but then gambles and loses most of it. While there, he picks up another job, collecting money from a B-movie producer named Harry Zimm who owes money to the casino. Chili heads to Hollywood and tracks down Zimm at the house of Karen Flores, his former girlfriend. Karen's an actress who once starred in Zimm's low-budget horror flicks but hasn't appeared in anything for several years. Zimm, it turns out, has a screenplay for a "proper" movie, if he can only raise the money. He wants Michael Weir, the "Shorty" of the title, to star in it, and is hoping that Karen, who once lived with Weir, will put in a good word for him.

By now Chili has his own idea for a movie: the drycleaner who fakes his death, scams the airline, and flees to Vegas, one step ahead of a shylock. Harry likes the idea, but it's Karen who catches on that this isn't fiction - the story is true and Chili Palmer is the shylock.

There are enough twists and subplots in *Get Shorty* to fuel half a dozen movies, so I'll just say that in the end the good guys, Chili, Karen, and Faye, come out on top, and the worst bad guy, a well-dressed thug named Bo Catlett, gets what he deserves.

Elmore Leonard's 10 Rules of Writing, applied to *Get Shorty*

1. Never open a book with weather:

If it's only to create atmosphere, and not a character's reaction to the weather, you don't want to go on too long. The reader is apt to leaf ahead looking for people.

Here's how *Get Shorty* begins:

"When Chili first came to Miami Beach twelve years ago they were having one of their off-and-on cold winters: thirty-four degrees the day he met Tommy Carlo for lunch at Vesuvio's on South Collins and had his leather jacket ripped off. One his wife had given him for Christmas a year ago, before they moved down here".

2. Avoid prologues:

They can be annoying, especially a prologue following an introduction that comes after a foreword.

Yep, no prologue.

3. Never use a verb other than "said" to carry dialogue:

The line of dialogue belongs to the character; the verb is the writer sticking his nose in. But "said" is far less intrusive than "grumbled", "gasped", "cautioned", "lied". I once noticed Mary McCarthy ending a line of dialogue with "she asseverated" and had to stop reading and go to the dictionary.

Whether his characters are angry, sad, frustrated or bored, Leonard never uses a verb other than "said". And it works.

4. Never use an adverb to modify the verb "said":

. . . he admonished gravely. To use an adverb this way (or almost any way) is a mortal sin. The writer is now exposing himself in earnest, using a word that distracts and can interrupt the rhythm of the exchange. I have a character in one of my books tell how she used to write historical romances "full of rape and adverbs".

Love it. And yes, no adverbs in *Get Shorty*.

5. Keep your exclamation points under control:

You are allowed no more than two or three per 100,000 words of prose.

But here's the exception: *If you have the knack of playing with exclaimers the way Tom Wolfe does, you can throw them in by the handful.*

I couldn't find a single exclamation point in *Get Shorty*. Take this scene early on where Chili tracks down Ray Bones, the one who walked off with his jacket:

"He put on his black leather gloves going up the stairs to the third floor, knocked on the door three times, waited, pulling the right-hand glove on tight, and when Ray Bones opened the door Chili nailed him. One punch, not seeing any need to throw the left. He got his coat from a chair in the sitting room, looked at Ray Bones bent over holding his nose and mouth, blood all over his hands, his shirt, and walked out. Didn't say one word to him".

Does the scene have drama? Yes. Does the scene (pardon the pun) have punch? Yes. Does it use exclamation marks to do so? Nope. No exclamation marks. None needed.

6. Never use the words "suddenly" or "all hell broke loose":

This rule doesn't require an explanation. I have noticed that writers who use "suddenly" tend to exercise less control in the application of exclamation points.

7. Use regional dialect, patois, sparingly:

Once you start spelling words in dialogue phonetically and loading the page with apostrophes, you won't be able to stop.

Once again, I agree. When I first started writing *Harrow Road* I used a lot of 19th century cockney dialect and found it got in the way. The exception is if you're Frank McCourt and you're writing *Angela's Ashes*. I'm not and I wasn't.

8. Avoid detailed descriptions of characters:

In Ernest Hemingway's "Hills Like White Elephants" what do the "American and the girl with him" look like? "She had taken off her hat and put it on the table." That's the only reference to a physical description in the story, and yet we see the couple and know them by their tones of voice, with not one adverb in sight.

When it comes to description, Leonard, of necessity, breaks his own rule. Chili Palmer has short black hair and dark eyes, is well-built and good looking. Michael Weir is surprisingly short, Harry Zimm is fat, and when it comes to Bo Catlett we get him described right down to his socks:

"Seated now in the Delta terminal . . . Catlett had on his dove-gray double-breasted Armani with the nice long roll lapel. He had on a light-blue shirt with a pearl-gray necktie and pearl cufflinks. He had on light-blue hose and dark-brown Cole-Haan loafers, spit-shined. The loafers matched the attache case next to him on the row of seats".

This is a gangster who, like Chili, wants to be a Hollywood producer. And he dresses for the part.

9. Don't go into great detail describing places and things:

You don't want descriptions that bring the action, the flow of the story, to a standstill.

This doesn't mean don't use description, just don't let it interfere with the story. Here's how Chili views Karen Flores, the first time he sees her: "He liked her hair, the way it was now, thick and dark, hanging down close to one eye. He noticed how thin her neck was and took a few more pounds off, got her down to around ninety-five. He figured she was now up in her thirties, but hadn't lost any of her looks to speak of".

10. Try to leave out the part that readers tend to skip.

My most important rule is one that sums up the 10: **If it sounds like writing, I rewrite it.**

Week 76: *The Secret History*, by Donna Tartt (1992)

If every new writer's career had as auspicious a start as that of Donna Tartt, we would all be writers. And we would all, I think, be rich.

In the early 1980s, while a student at Bennington College, Tartt began working on a novel. As she wrote she shared it with her friend-and-maybe-boyfriend Brett Easton Ellis, who was working on *his* first novel, the controversial bestseller *Less Than Zero*. Ellis thought Tartt's novel had the makings of a huge commercial success; in 1989 he introduced her to his agent, Amanda Urban of ICM. To say Urban liked the book is an understatement: she took Tartt on as a client and began to whip up enthusiasm for the 866-page manuscript. The bidding war that ensued resulted in Knopf paying $450,000 for the book - a sum which they made back almost immediately, by the way, and then again in foreign sales. Eagerly anticipated - the book sold out even before it hit the stores - *The Secret History* was an instant bestseller.

While some critics described it as leaden and pretentious, *The Independent* called it "the book of a lifetime", *The Guardian* raved about it, and *The New York Times* said it was "powerful . . . enthralling . . . A ferociously well-paced entertainment". Tartt went on to win the Pulitzer Prize for fiction (in 2014, for *The Goldfinch*), and is one of the few American writers to make Vanity Fair's International Best-Dressed List.

It helps that Donna Tartt is something of a bookseller's dream. She's ridiculously smart, good-looking in a sassy, grown-up-pixie sort of way, and dresses distinctively. And while she's willing to discuss all aspects of her work and quotes reams of poetry at the drop of a hat, she's famously reserved about her private life. Think J. D. Salinger meets Harper Lee. Although, as Ellis has said, "You can't be Salinger and be represented by ICM." None of this would make a whit of difference if the book didn't live up to its hype. It's a good, enjoyable read, with just enough genre-specific elements (stately old homes, ancient rituals, and a couple of murders) to make you keep turning the pages. And, unlike many page-turners, it's very well-written. In close to 500 pages I had only a couple of "moments" - those times when you stop and say to yourself, "Erm, what?" More on those in a minute.

The Secret History is a story of six young people attending a small, ultra-liberal college in Vermont, not unlike Bennington. They study Greek and Latin under a charismatic but eccentric professor of classics, Julian Morrow, who begins his tutorials by saying, "I hope we're all ready to leave the phenomenal world, and enter into the sublime?" His students do more, however, than simply study these ancient languages - they strive to mimic the way the Greeks and Romans thought. This desire to "live" in that other, classical world drives them to enact a Dionysian bacchanal, during which they encounter a local farmer and (accidentally, we think) kill him. This in turn leads to the death of one of their members, Edmund "Bunny" Corcoran, whose murder is described right at the beginning, in the prologue: "The snow in the mountain was melting and Bunny had been dead for several weeks before we came to understand the gravity of our situation". There you have it, folks, one of the all-time great opening lines. Do we want to read on? Absolutely. Who wouldn't?

Besides the unfortunate Bunny, the members of this select cadre are Henry Winter, a tall, wealthy, bespectacled genius; Francis Abernathy, an elegant, angular aesthete who dresses like Lord Alfred Douglas; Charles and Camilla Macauley, blonde, attractive, and incestuous twins, and Richard Papen, the narrator of the story. Richard is the outsider. While the other are from wealthy families - or, in the case of Bunny, are pretending to be - Richard is a scholarship student from a fictional small town in California. He admires the others, and pretty much worships Henry, leading him to go along with keeping some dark and destructive secrets, not to mention taking part in a murder. And it's Richard, more than the others, who comes to understand just what he sacrificed by persuading Julian to allow him to join "the group". Taking classes only with the other five, never being part of the rest of the college community, Richard has become as isolated as if he'd joined a cult and drunk the Kool-Aid.

The Secret History is a *why*dunit, rather than a *who*dunit. We learn right off the bat what's been done, and by whom; the point of the story is learning why it happened. Tartt herself, in an interview with Vanity Fair, says the book is a novel about repressed sexuality: "There's sex all in the book, but it's really pressed down. And that's basically the plot—it's like a water pipe with weak spots, and it'll kind of *explode* in different places. But it's very *controlled.*"

As are the characters. To the point that they often seem lacking in what can only be called "human-ness". They commit murder - twice - and don't seem bothered about it until they realize they may be found out. They care for each other, to some extent, but there are little signs of real affection. Even Richard, the most fully developed character, is mainly a kind of archetype: abused son from a working-class family strives to fit in with his "betters".

As for those occasional "moments' I mentioned: I do think the author makes some odd choices. When referring to a movie obviously meant to be *Platoon*, she calls it *Fields of Shame*. I mean, why bother? It's not like the film's producers are going to holler about being mentioned in a best-selling novel. And then there's Julian's back story: we learn that he worked for a time for the "Isrami" government, an obvious but confusing reference to Iran.

Then, further on, she tells us that George Orwell met Julian Morrow and had this to say of him: "Upon meeting Julian Morrow, one has the impression that he is a man of extraordinary sympathy and warmth. But what you call his 'Asiatic Serenity' is, I think, a mask for great coldness. The face one shows him he invariably reflects back at one, creating the illusion of warmth and depth when in fact he is brittle and shallow as a mirror. Acton" - this apparently, Harold Acton, who was also in Paris then and a friend to both Orwell and Julian - "disagrees. But I think he is not a man to be trusted". This quote was written so authoritatively I had to go to Google just to see if there is, or was, a Julian Morrow who knew Orwell and Acton. There isn't, and maybe that's the point. A little joke on the part of the author. But then why get coy when it comes to Iran and Platoon?

Still. This is a writer who can take the mysteries of an ancient Roman festival and make them live for readers in the 21st century. As Charles describes the bacchanal to Richard, who missed it, you wish, on some level, you were there:

"It was heart-shaking. Glorious. Torches, dizziness, singing. Wolves howling around us and a bull bellowing in the dark. The river ran white . . . It was like a film in fast motion, the moon waxing and waning, clouds rushing across the sky. Vines grew from the ground so fast they twined up the trees like snakes; seasons passing in the wink of an eye".

Now that, my friends, is some damn fine writing.

Week 77: *Fear and Loathing in Las Vegas*, by Hunter S. Thompson (1971)

"We were somewhere around Barstow on the edge of the desert when the drugs began to take hold. I remember saying something like 'I feel a bit lightheaded; maybe you should drive. . . .' And suddenly there was a terrible roar all around us and the sky was full with what looked like huge bats, all swooping and screeching and diving around the car, which was going about a hundred miles an hour with the top down to Las Vegas. And a voice was screaming: 'Holy Jesus! What are these goddamn animals?'"

As an opening paragraph, this says it all. Welcome to the frenzied, hyper neurotic, ridiculously funny world of America's premier gonzo journalist, Hunter S. Thompson.

"Gonzo" was Thompson's word (although someone else coined it) for his style of reporting. Throwing yourself head first into the story, becoming part of the story - even *becoming* the story. Tossing caution to the wind, along with any semblance of objectivity, fortified with a good supply of recreational drugs and the occasional handgun. He'd been practicing this particular type of journalism since writing an article called *The Kentucky Derby is Decadent and Depraved* for a now defunct magazine called *Scanlan's*. But it wasn't until *Fear and Loathing in Las Vegas: A Savage Journey to the Heart of the American Dream* that he first used the word "gonzo" in print. "Free Enterprise," he wrote. "The American Dream. Horatio Alger gone mad on drugs in Las Vegas. Do it *now*: pure Gonzo journalism."

Fear and Loathing began as an assignment from *Sports Illustrated*. What they wanted was a 250-word piece on the Mint 400, an annual off-road race being held in the Las Vegas desert. At the time, Thompson was heavily involved with Oscar "Zeta" Acosta, a Mexican-American lawyer and activist who was a source for an exposé Thompson was writing on the death of TV journalist Rubén Salazar. The two of them, Thompson and Acosta, decided the Mint 400 assignment would be an opportunity to get out of the racially charged atmosphere of Los Angeles and have a chance to talk. What originally began as a photo caption grew into a serialized feature for *Rolling Stone*. A few weeks later Thompson and Acosta went back to Las Vegas, this time for *Rolling Stone*, to cover the National District Attorneys Association's Conference on Narcotics and Dangerous Drugs. That trip was incorporated into the novel as Part Two.

What we have to remember about Thompson is that he was, among other things, a satirist. *Fear and Loathing* is not a documentary but a *roman à clef*, a novel about real people overlaid with a façade of fiction. It's possible that Thompson, a.k.a. Raoul Duke, and his companion, Acosta, whom he calls Dr. Gonzo and refers to throughout as his attorney, may have ingested as much cocaine, amphetamines, ether, alcohol, mescaline, cannabis, and LSD as reported; then again, maybe they didn't. The line between what happens and what is only imagined by the protagonists is frequently blurred, since so much of the story is driven by their drug-fuelled hallucinations.

The plot, such as it is, centres around their expedition into the heart of America - or at least that section of America's heart known as Las Vegas. Where the tourists look like "caricatures of used car dealers from Dallas and, sweet Jesus, there were a hell of a lot of them at 4:30 on a Sunday morning, still humping the American dream, that vision of the big winner somehow emerging from the last minute pre-dawn chaos of a stale Vegas casino".

Like America itself, Vegas is a weird mixture of hyper-conservatism and extreme oddball wackiness. When he and Dr. Gonzo attempt to check into their hotel, tripping out on acid and a variety of other stimulants, Duke is justifiably paranoid that their behaviour will attract undue attention. It doesn't. As Thompson explains, "In a town full of bedrock crazies, nobody even *notices* an acid freak".

The point of the trip is to cover the Mint 400 but, as you might expect, this never happens. Instead, the two take a truckload of drugs, wreck several hotel rooms, abuse waitresses and hotel staff and in general behave like jerks. While making some excellent points on the coarseness of mainstream America and the sheer weirdness of Vegas itself ("The Circus-Circus is what the whole hep world would be doing on Saturday night if the Nazis had won the war"), *Fear and Loathing* ends up being a kind of adolescent prank taken to illogical extremes. It *is* funny, but it's exhausting.

By the end of his life, Raoul Duke had displaced his creator. In the mind of the public Thompson *was* Duke and vice versa; his legendary appetite for living with one foot over the edge hampered Thompson from being a participant in the stories he created. Duke was larger than life - he couldn't pass through a crowd unnoticed any more than Elton John could walk into your local bar and order a beer.

Then again, the parallels between Thompson and his alter ego are significant. Consider this: Before setting off for Las Vegas, Duke and his attorney stock up on drugs:

"We had two bags of grass, seventy-five pellets of mescaline, five sheets of high powered blotter acid, a salt shaker half full of cocaine, and a whole galaxy of multi-colored uppers, downers, screamers, laughers . . . and also a quart of tequila, a quart of rum, a case of Budweiser, a pint of raw ether and two dozen amyls . . . The only thing that really worried me was the ether".

And here, from E. Jean Carroll's biography, we have a picture of Thompson's workday, which started at 3:00 in the afternoon:

"While writing he consumed: Chivas Regal, Dunhills, cocaine, orange juice, marijuana, Heineken, huge helpings of food, LSD, Chartreuse, clove cigarettes, gin and pornographic movies. He then spent some time in the hot tub with champagne and Dove Bars."

On February 20 2005, in failing health and more than a little depressed, Hunter Thompson put a gun to his head and pulled the trigger, after leaving a note for his wife:

"No More Games. No More Bombs. No More Walking. No More Fun. No More Swimming. 67. That is 17 years past 50. 17 more than I needed or wanted. Boring. I am always bitchy. No Fun – for anybody. 67. You are getting Greedy. Act your old age. Relax – This won't hurt."

It's a pity he didn't stick around a few more years. He hated Richard Nixon and wrote a vitriolic obituary for *Rolling Stone* when Nixon died: "I beat him like a mad dog with mange every time I got a chance, and I am proud of it. He was scum."

What, oh *what* would he have said about Trump?

Week 78: *The Color Purple*, by Alice Walker (1962)

"He never had a kine word to say to me. Just say You gonna do what your mammy wouldn't. First he put his thing up gainst my hip and sort of wiggle it around. Then he grab hold my titties."

This is what Alice Walker calls "folk speech", the language of the oppressed - in particular, the oppressed African-Americans of rural Georgia. Much of *The Color Purple* is written in this particular dialect. It's strong, effective, and at times quite beautiful. It is the voice of Celie, who narrates the story through her letters to God, letters she begins writing when she's 14 and pregnant:

"Dear God," she writes, "I have always been a good girl. Maybe you can give me a sign letting me know what is happening to me."

What is happening is that she is pregnant, once again, thanks to her father, Alfonso. After raping her he warns her to keep it a secret. "You better not never tell nobody but God," he says. "It'd kill your mammy."

She gives birth to a son and a daughter, both of whom are taken away and, presumably, killed. Her ailing mother blames her for the pregnancies; she dies, cursing her on her deathbed. Alfonso then forces her into a loveless marriage to a widower looking for someone to take care of his children. Albert, whom Celie refers to as Mister, is still in love with his old sweetheart, Shug Avery, a sexy lounge singer. Shug and Albert were lovers once, but when he refused to marry her because of her dubious reputation, she left him. Not being in love with her husband, Celie bears no ill will toward Shug and, in fact, having seen her photograph, she feels a strong connection with this woman she's never met.

Albert treats Celie as every other man in her life has treated her: he beats her, uses her for sex when he has to, makes her life a misery. As does his son, Harpo. When Celie's pretty younger sister, Nettie, runs away from home she takes refuge with Celie and her husband. While there, she urges Celie to fight, to stand up for herself. But, "I don't know how to fight," Celie says. "All I know how to do is stay alive."

In order to protect Nettie from Albert's amorous advances, Celie arranges for her to be taken in by Samuel and Corinne, a local missionary couple. They leave for Africa taking Nettie with them, unaware that their adopted son and daughter are actually Celie's children. In time, Nettie works this out, but the letters she writes to Celie are hidden from her and she eventually believes her sister may be dead.

Celie's life slowly begins to change for the better when Shug Avery comes back to town to sing at a local bar. A sensuous, larger-than-life figure, Shug is pretty much the polar opposite of Celie. Where Celie is plain, submissive, and compliant, Shug is glamorous, assertive and outspoken. When she falls ill, Albert takes her into his house and Celie becomes her nurse. Although Albert and Shug are still in love, she and Celie become friends, then lovers. Through Shug, Celie learns to feel real sexual pleasure, and Shug becomes a strongly nurturing mentor to the younger woman. She encourages Celie to use her sewing skills to start a successful business, and intercedes with Albert to treat Celie more kindly. With Shug as her role model, Celie begins to assert her independence.

Shug Avery isn't the only strong female character in the story: Albert's son, Harpo, marries a feisty young woman named Sofia who will never back down from a fight. When she gets into a physical fight with the Mayor, she's beaten by the police, leaving her with broken ribs, a cracked skull, and blind in one eye. She is sentenced to 12 years in jail where the conditions are so harsh she almost dies. Eventually, she's allowed to serve the rest of her sentence as the Mayor's servant, doing all the housework and caring for the children. Her own children, meanwhile, are raised by Harpo's new woman, Mary Agnes, whom he calls Squeak.

It's Shug who discovers the cache of letters written to Celie by Nettie over the years. The women steam the letters open and read them, and Nettie's letters dominate the second half of the book. Although the information in these letters is interesting for its historical and social detail, we miss the strength and cadence of Celie's voice. Nettie and the missionaries are living in a small village somewhere in Liberia with a tribe of Africans called the Olinkas. Before you waste time searching for the Olinkas on the internet, you should know the name is fictitious; Walker has used the Olinkas to shed light on customs and traditions prevalent in Africa at the time, and to compare and contrast them with life in the States. The Olinkas don't believe girls should be educated, and are shocked that the missionary group includes women. While they generally treat their children with love and respect, girls are expected to stay home and help with the housework, and are subject to ritual scarification and genital mutilation.

None of this is surprising, and to my mind it lessens the impact of the book. It was a mistake, I think, to abandon Celie halfway through the narrative. Although Walker comes back to her and wraps things up in a satisfactory manner at the end, Nettie's letters are, in the words of another reviewer, "lackluster and intrusive".

When Walker began writing *The Color Purple*, she was working at *Ms. Magazine* as an editor. She had published several books of poetry and two collections of short stories, but in this book she wanted to write about her immediate ancestors: her parents, grandparents, and great-grandparents. Born in a rural farming town in Georgia, she was the daughter of poor sharecroppers, themselves the children and grandchildren of slaves. She wanted to tell their stories:

"In most literature, the lives of people I knew did not exist. My mother, for instance, was nowhere in the literature, and she was all over my heart, so why shouldn't she be in the literature? . . . If you deny people a voice, their own voice, there's no way you'll ever find out who they were. And so they are erased."

The Color Purple won the Pulitzer Prize for fiction, the first for a black woman; it has sold 5 million copies, been translated into 25 languages and was made into a movie that grossed almost $150 million. For Walker, the rewards have been mixed: she's been accused of betraying her race, and of feeding stereotypical images of violent black men. The book was kept off school reading lists not just because of the violence but also because of the sexual relationship between Shug and Celie, and several black writers have criticised the "overemphasis" on black male brutality.

In a video posted on the *Huffington Post* website, Alice Walker revealed what she hopes readers will take away from the book:

"What I would like people to understand when they read *The Color Purple* is that there are all these terrible things that can actually happen to us and yet life is so incredibly magical and abundant and present that we can still be very happy".

In this, I feel, Walker has been successful. You come away from *The Color Purple* feeling uplifted, if not, in my case, wholly satisfied.

Week 79: *The Reader*, by Bernhard Schlink (1995, in German; 1997, in English)

The Germans have a word for the struggle of those born after the Second World War to overcome the negatives of the past: V*ergangenheitsbewältigung* can be defined as the public debate that continues to this day to deal with the embarrassment and remorse for the atrocities carried out in the name of National Socialism.

Culturally, the term is associated with the post-war literature that tries to come to terms with the Holocaust. I use the phrase "come to terms with" deliberately; it can never, I think, be fully understood. It is simply beyond comprehension. Günter Grass's novel *The Tin Drum* was an early entry in this particular canon; *The Reader*, by Bernhard Schlink, is another. While *The Tin Drum* has been said to define the 20th century, that definition is not complete without *The Reader*, which explores the ways in which the next generation judged their parents and grandparents, demonizing them at least partly to achieve a certain distance from the horror of the Holocaust.

The Reader asks if such distance is ever possible? To what extent do we all, even those of us who weren't born at the time, share culpability with those who've gone before?

One afternoon in October, 1958, 15-year-old Michael Berg falls ill. He leans against the wall of a building and vomits. A woman pulls him into the courtyard of the building, washes his hands and face, cleans away the vomit, and walks him home. The doctor diagnoses hepatitis, keeping Michael out of school for three months. When he's finally able to get out and about again, he goes to visit the woman who helped him, ostensibly to thank her but really because he can't get her out of his mind. Her name is Hanna Schmitz and she's a 36-year-old train conductor who lives alone. Embarrassed to find himself attracted to her, Michael leaves, but returns a few days later and helps her bring coal up from the cellar. Afterwards, covered in coal dust, he allows Hanna to bathe and then seduce him.

This is the beginning of an intense, short-lived affair that follows a pattern: she bathes him, then asks him to read to her before they have sex. The affair gives Michael new confidence, not just with women but with the boys at his school, and he finds himself torn between wanting to be with Hanna and needing to socialize with his peers. When, after a few months, Hanna suddenly leaves without a trace, Michael is devastated. But he's young; he finds girls his own age to love and the pain of Hanna's departure fades. Still, he cannot escape her. From now on all of his relationships will be tarnished by his memories of Hanna.

The next time he sees her is six years later, in a courtroom. Michael's a law student now, and he and his fellow students have been assigned to follow and report on the Nazi war trials. He's stunned to see Hanna among the defendants, a group of women who were guards at the concentration camp in Krakow. They're charged with allowing a bombed church to burn to the ground with 300 Jewish women trapped inside. Why, the prosecutors ask, did the guards not unlock the doors of the church and save the prisoners?

Why did you choose to let them burn to death? When questioned, Hanna seems confused. "What should I have done?" she wonders. She asks the judge, "What would you have done?"

It comes out that while she was a guard she would take the most frail, the most vulnerable young prisoners under her wing and have them read to her, before sending them back to the gas chambers at Auschwitz. The implication in court is that she was ruthlessly exploiting them, possibly sexually, and then getting rid of them when she was tired of them.

The most damning evidence comes from a woman who wrote a book about the bombing of the church. She and her mother survived the fire, and she is the prosecution's main witness. Day after day, as he watches the proceedings, Michael finds himself in an emotional turmoil over having loved a woman who could do the things Hanna is charged with. He's also bewildered by her refusal to do or say anything to defend herself. When the other women turn on her and blame her for writing the report of the fire, she at first denies it and then, when the court asks for a sample of her handwriting, she panics and says yes, she wrote it. Michael realizes that Hanna is desperate to conceal something she considers more shameful than being tried for murder: she cannot read or write.

Knowing this, he wants to go to the judge and tell him Hanna could not have been the group's leader, as she's been painted in court. But he also knows she would rather go to prison than be branded as an illiterate. While the other defendants are given minor jail sentences, Hanna is the one who's sentenced to prison for life.

After the trial, Michael struggles to come to grips with the situation. Hanna was guilty of a horrendous crime. He knows that. But he had loved her.

"Not only had I loved her, I had chosen her. I tried to tell myself that I had known nothing of what she had done when I chose her. I tried to talk myself into the state of innocence in which children love their parents. But love of our parents is the only love for which we are not responsible". And was it possible that the love his friends and colleagues had for their parents made them somehow complicit in their crimes?

Several years later, Michael begins sending her cassettes of him reading out loud, just as he used to do when they were together. On her own, listening to his tapes while following along with the books she's borrowed from the prison library, Hanna teaches herself to read. She writes to thank him but he doesn't respond. Finally, after 18 years, Hanna is about to be let out of prison. Pressured by the warden, Michael reluctantly goes to visit her in jail and agrees to help find her a place to live, and a job. The day she's to be released, Hanna hangs herself at daybreak. According to the warden, Hanna read all the important post-Holocaust writers, such as Elie Weisel, Primo Levi, Tadeusz Borowski, as well as stories of the camps. We are never told but it seems likely that it's her reading that leads Hanna to her death when she finally, fully comprehends the part she played in this terrible history.

The warden says Hanna has left a request for Michael: she wants him to give all her money to the survivors of the church fire. He travels to New York to see the woman who wrote the book about the fire. When he hands her Hanna's money, contained in an old tea caddy, she refuses to take it, refuses to "grant Frau Schmitz her absolution". The tin reminds her of one she had as a girl, that was stolen from her when she was sent to the camp. She suggests he give the money to a Jewish literacy group, but says she'll keep the tin.

As an exploration of guilt, of public shame and culpability, *The Reader* asks more questions than it answers. Which is as it should be. Another writer would choose an easier route . . . would cast Hanna as a cold-hearted, two-dimensional villain. Schlink's elegant prose never allows moral outrage to overwhelm the narrative. He leaves that to the reader.

Week 80: *Tess of the D'Urbervilles*, by Thomas Hardy (1891-1892)

There's something about the start of a new year that makes me want to look back - in this case, quite a ways back, to England during what was known as the Long Depression of the 1870s. A financial crisis linked to a dramatic fall in grain prices triggered two decades of stagnation that resulted in "bankruptcies, escalating unemployment, a halt in public works, and a major trade slump that lasted until 1897".* British society, especially in rural areas, was transformed almost overnight. Men and women who had lived and worked their little plots of land for generations were displaced, forced into nomads who traveled from farm to farm, getting work where they could. As Thomas Hardy puts it in his penultimate novel, "The landlord does not know by sight, if even by name, half the men who preserve his acres from the curse of Eden. They come and go yearly, like birds of passage, nobody thinks whence or whither".

Tess of the D'Urbervilles is set in the fictional Wessex County, an area of rural southwest England comprising Dorset, Somerset, Hampshire, and Wiltshire. Like Faulkner's Yoknapatawpha County and Munro's Jubilee, Wessex stands in for a part of the world where the author grew up. He knew it well, and he loved it. More than anything else he ever wrote, *Tess* is a portrayal of the new, unsettling mobility of the agricultural class and the unfairness disguised as modernism that governs its members.

The story begins with the shiftless, impoverished peddler, John Durbeyfield, meeting up with the local parson on his way home from a day at the market. The parson, as a bit of a joke, refers to him as "Sir John", and then explains that Durbeyfield is in fact descended from the D'Urbervilles, an ancient noble family whose members once held positions of importance in this part of the world. The line has gone extinct, the parson says; their stately homes were sold and abandoned long ago, their fortunes have melted away, and their bodies now lie forgotten in the cold stone vaults of various churches scattered throughout the county.

This astounding news puts Durbeyfield into a kind of ecstasy. As he puts it, "There's not a man in the country o' South-Wessex that's got grander and nobler skillentons in his family than I."

In the meantime, John's beautiful eldest daughter, Tess, is taking part in the annual May Dance rituals on the edge of the village. Three young men of a "superior" class, in the middle of a walking tour, stop to watch. These are the Clare brothers, sons of a respectable provincial minister; one of them, Angel, stays to ask some of the girls to dance. Angel is the only son who has not followed his father into the Church. A self-proclaimed secularist and freethinker, he has decided to set himself up as a farmer. It is only after Angel has danced with several girls, and is preparing to leave, that he notices Tess, and wishes he'd seen her earlier.

An unforeseen accident brings Tess into contact with the so-called "real" D'Urbervilles, a wealthy family who've adopted the ancient name to give themselves a pedigree. Alec D'Urberville, the handsome, amoral scion of the family, lives with his mother on a large estate in the village of Tantridge. Believing them to be kin, Tess reluctantly agrees to approach them and ask for assistance after the family's only horse is killed. Alec, greatly attracted to Tess, offers her work tending the chickens, an offer she accepts against her better judgment.

As we might expect, Alec, being an out-and-out villain, wastes no time in seducing this innocent country girl. Tess finally rejects him and returns home, ashamed and pregnant. She gives birth to a son who dies in infancy, after which she leaves home to work at a dairy some distance away. There she becomes friends with three other milkmaids, Izz, Rhetty, and Marian, and meets Angel Clare, the gentleman from the May Day dance, who is working at the dairy in order to learn as much as he can about agriculture.

All the girls are in love with Angel, but he falls in love with Tess. When he proposes marriage she refuses to consider it. In her mind, as in the mind of all virtuous Victorians, Tess is damaged goods. If she agrees to marry him without telling him about Alec and the baby, she will be deceiving him. If, however, she confesses her past she has no doubt he will hate her.

Not knowing anything of her previous experiences, Angel looks upon Tess as a pure, unsullied daughter of nature. His parents, he knows, will be disappointed if he marries a farm girl, but he believes they'll change their minds when they meet her. Who, after all, couldn't love Tess? But Tess is more complicated than he knows: she's been educated, to a point, she is deeply sensitive, and she has a broader view of the world than her parents. In many ways she symbolizes the changing nature of agricultural society in the late 19th century: machines are replacing workers, and rural inhabitants, deprived of their traditional employment, are fleeing to the cities in search of work. An angry god has stacked the cards - the poor cannot compete against the forces of change any more than Tess, whose deep moral sense works against her, can escape her tragic destiny.

Finally persuaded that Angel loves her enough to forgive her anything, Tess agrees to marry him. The night of their wedding, Angel confesses that he had an affair with an older woman in London. Tess is thrilled to hear it as it means he can't possibly be angry with her for a similar moral lapse. She tells him about Alec and the baby; to her dismay he is horrified: this cannot possibly be the woman he loves, the woman he saw as the archetype of purity and goodness. He begs her to take it back, to say it was a lie, but she steadfastly holds to the truth. The freethinking Angel is revealed as a Victorian prig. Unable to forgive her, he gives her some money and boards a ship for Brazil, promising to send for her if he can ever bring himself to love her again.

Things go from bad to worse. Half of the money Angel gives Tess is given to her parents to rebuild their roof, and she is too proud to approach his parents for more. Unable to find work as a dairymaid, she joins her friend Marian at a starve-acre farm called Flintcombe-Ash. Hardy's depiction of the unrelenting, back-breaking work involved here is painted from life - we know he witnessed men and women involved in the most difficult jobs agriculture had to offer. He may have performed them himself. His description of the new-fangled threshing machine, accompanied by its smoking black engine, is nothing short of hellish. The machine's insatiable appetite is a dystopian vision of the future.

There is no happy ending in *Tess of the D'Urbervilles*; there can't be - the characters are doomed. Angel forgives Tess too late - she finally stands up for herself and in so doing condemns herself to death. Hardy, ever the realist, understands that Tess must be punished, and so he allows "justice" to take its course. Tess blames herself for her fate; Hardy, along with the reader, never does.

* The quote in the first paragraph is taken from W. B Sutch, *The long depression, 1865–1895* (1957).

Week 81: *Ethan Frome*, by Edith Wharton (1911)

"I had the story, bit by bit, from various people, and, as generally happens in such cases, each time it was a different story".

The story, as we will learn, is the strange, sad case of the reclusive Ethan Frome, a New England farmer who, decades earlier, suffered a terrible accident. The "smash-up" has left him with a vivid red gash across his forehead and shortened and warped his right side so that "it cost him a visible effort to take the few steps from his buggy to the post-office window". Tall, gaunt, and grizzled, Ethan is the most striking figure in the town of Starkfield, Massachusetts, and the narrator, who's spending the winter there on business, is driven to learn his story.

By questioning his landlady and various townspeople he learns that Ethan was studying to be an engineer but had to leave college when his father became ill, and was never able to return. Apart from that, the people who know Ethan are unwilling to say any more.

The narrator (who is never named) needs to get to the train station each morning in order to travel to his job at Corbury Junction. When the horses in the livery stable fall ill, someone suggests he hire Ethan to drive him to the station, implying that Ethan could use the money. Coming back from one of their journeys, the two of them are caught in a blizzard; Ethan offers to shelter the narrator for the night:

"It was that night that I found the clue to Ethan Frome, and began to put together this vision of his story".

The rest of the story is told in flashbacks. As a young man, Ethan is recalled to his parents' farm when his father is ill; after he dies Ethan must stay and work the farm. When his mother, too, becomes ill, a distant cousin, Zenobia (Zeena) Pierce arrives to act as her nurse. After several yers his mother dies and Ethan, suddenly afraid to be alone, asks Zeena to marry him. She, who was as healthy as a horse when she was caring for his mother, turns sickly and demanding. They invite Mattie Silver, a young cousin of Zeena's, to board with them and help out around the house. Mattie was left destitute when her parents died and has no prospects or means of living on her own. Although Ethan resents the idea at first, from the moment he picks Mattie up from the station he's smitten. She's sweet-natured and lovely with a naturally outgoing disposition - pretty much the direct opposite of Zeena - and Ethan falls in love with her. Passing the graveyard, it occurs to him that, "We'll always go on living here together, and some day she'll lie there beside me."

Zeena, who's nobody's fool, sees the growing attachment between Mattie and her husband and, quite naturally, resents it. She hints that Mattie, who is not adept at housework or nursing, will have to leave one day; Ethan cannot bear the idea and tries not to think about it. The more he cares for Mattie, the more he realizes the regrets the impulse that led him to marry a difficult, nagging shrew.

Zeena leaves for an overnight visit to consult with a specialist; on her return she informs Ethan that's she's much sicker than he knows. She has "complications", and Ethan knows immediately what that signifies:

"Almost everybody in the neighbourhood had 'troubles', frankly localized and specified; but only the chosen had 'complications'. To have them was in itself a distinction, though it was also, in most cases, a death-warrant. People struggled on for years with 'troubles', but they almost always succumbed to 'complications'".

According to Zeena, the doctor has told her she's too sick to do anything at all around the house. She must have a properly trained hired girl live with them and to that end, Mattie will have to leave. This is terrible news for Mattie, who has nowhere else to go and no way to support herself. Nothing Ethan can say will change Zeena's mind. Distraught, he fantasizes about running away with Mattie, but knows his finances, or lack of them, make it impossible.

On the day Mattie is to leave, Ethan drives her to the station; they both know they will never see each other again. They stop at a hill and, on a whim, they borrow a sled and coast down to the bottom. In her despair, Mattie begs him to take her down again and this time run the sled into a tree so that they'll be killed and never have to part. He refuses at first but finally, seeing no way to go on living without her, he agrees.

They crash headlong into a large elm tree, but, unfortunately, they survive. I say "unfortunately" because the ending is worse than if they had died. Mattie is left paralyzed, and becomes a sour, embittered woman, old before her time. Zeena, who had insisted she was close to death, miraculously revives. She brings Mattie back to live with them and becomes her lifelong caregiver. Day after day, hidden away from the rest of the community, the three of them live a lonely, isolated existence. Zeena does the housework and nursing, Mattie sits in her chair and complain, and Ethan does his best to keep a roof over their heads.

"I think it's *him* that suffers most," the narrator's landlady says. "Anyhow, it ain't Zeena, because she ain't got the time."

She goes on to say there was one day, about a week after the accident, when everyone thought Mattie couldn't live.

"Well I say it's a pity she *did*. . . . And I say if she'd ha' died, Ethan might ha' lived; and the way they are now, I don't see's there's much difference between the Fromes up at the farm and Fromes down in the graveyard; 'cept that down there they're all quiet, and the women have to hold their tongues".

Edith Newbold Jones, who used her married name of Wharton when writing, was descended from wealthy English and Dutch American merchants. Her family took summer vacations in Europe and owned a large house in the fashionable seaside resort of Newport, Massachusetts. It's said that her father's family was the inspiration for the phrase "keeping up with the Joneses". For much of her career, Wharton's writing concerned the manners and mores of American high society, in particular the monied elite of old New York. It was a world she knew well; some critics, in fact, disputed her ability to write about anything else, especially the isolated backwaters of rural New England.

Those critics, of course, were wrong. *Ethan Frome* is the best-loved of all Wharton's books, and has been compared to a kind of fairy tale, in terms of its moral concepts. In Mattie Silver she created a character fully representative of the plight of women living in isolation and dependence: the young woman's naturally affectionate, easygoing nature is crippled by the harsh New England winters, and the brutality of the culture at the time. Zeena, married to an impoverished farmer, has only two courses available to her for achieving status: she can be known and pitied for her 'troubles' or celebrated for her nursing. As for Ethan, having had to decide between doing his duty and following his heart, he chooses to do his duty, and is punished for it.

A starkly beautiful, harrowing tale that will stay with you long after you read it.

Week 82: *Tropic of Cancer*, by Henry Miller (1934)

Reading Henry Miller is like being cornered by a loud, overbearing drunk at a party who leans over you breathing whisky in your face while he insists on telling you every detail of his love life. You smile and squirm and desperately try to get away, knowing that any moment now he's going to try to grab your ass or your breasts or, at the very least, offer to show you his "etchings". As he drones on about all the girls he's fucked, you finally say, "Really? Are you trying to convince me or yourself?" And then you go looking for the restroom.

Set in Paris in the early 1930s, *Tropic of Cancer* is part biography, part fiction, and part stream-of-conscious meditation on the human condition. And by human, we should read "male". For someone who spent a lot of time bedding women, he didn't like them very much. Kate Millet (*Sexual Politics*), while believing Miller to be an important and gifted writer, argued that he hated, even feared, women; certainly his descriptions of them leave something to be desired. In Miller's world - and here you may stop reading if certain words offend you as much as they do me - men are men and women are "cunts". Prostitutes are cunts, girlfriends are cunts, young women who come to Paris to study art are "rich American cunts with paint boxes slung over their shoulders".

God forbid, though, that any of these "cunts" have a brain. Miller compares Germaine, a prostitute who knows her business, loves it, and doesn't pretend to be anything but a whore, to Claude, who is more delicate:

"Claude had a soul and a conscience; she had refinement, too, which is bad - in a whore . . . while it's all very nice to know that a woman has a mind, literature coming from the cold corpse of a whore is the last thing to be served in bed".

He makes love to a young woman named Elsa who has a gift for playing the piano. Afterwards he asks her to play for him, which she does, and begins weeping about her recent abortion. "Somehow," he writes, "I feel sorry as hell for her and yet I don't give a damn. A cunt who can play as she does ought to have better sense than to be tripped up by every guy with a big putz who happens to come along".

Enough said. You get the point. Miller, the narrator, has no love, no real empathy, for anyone. Not for the women he fucks, the Jews he mocks, the friends and acquaintances he sponges off. He despises homosexuals, looks down on those poor slobs who work for a living, and resents those who refuse to part with their cash. "If there's anything worse than being a fairy," he tells us, "it's being a miser".

For a revolutionary thinker, which he was, Miller has some pretty primitive concepts of gender. He craves masculinity in all its aggressive, achievement-oriented forms, and believes the whole world conspires against this:

"If there were a man who dared to say all he thought of this world there would not be left him a square foot of ground to stand on. When a man appears the world bears down on him and breaks his back . . . If at intervals of centuries there does appear a man with a desperate, hungry look in his eye, a man who would turn the world upside down in order to create a new race, the love that he brings to the world is turned to bile and he becomes a scourge". And so forth.

If Miller were not the writer he is (or was, having died in 1980), it would be easy to write off his works as pornography. Certainly that's what *Tropic of Cancer* was considered when it was first published in 1934 by the Obelisk Press in Paris. It was banned almost everywhere else until 1961 when Grove Press had the courage to publish it in the States. This led to a series of obscenity trials culminating with the 1964 ruling by the US Supreme Court that the book was not obscene. It then went on to take its rightful place in the literary canon.

I say "rightful" because, like James Joyce, William Faulkner, Simone de Beauvoir and others, he broke new ground. Two-thirds of the way through the book, Miller says he wants to "get off the gold standard of writing". *Tropic*, however, set a brand new gold standard for explicit, merciless, and, at times, intoxicating writing. The Paris of *Tropic* is so far removed from *The Sun Also Rises* it might be set in another country. If you were to rely on Hemingway's version you'd imagine a city of expats and socialites lounging about in cafés all day, drinking champagne and tossing off novels in their spare time. Miller gives us the expats and the champagne but he also portrays the filth, the bedbugs, the misery, and the downright poverty experienced by those who came to Paris to live the life of a Bohemian. Hemingway's Paris is more attractive but Miller's, I think, is closer to the truth.

Henry Miller was a gifted writer, an accomplished artist, and an amateur pianist. He wrote several important books and influenced a long list of writers, including one of my favourites, Erica Jong. I still wouldn't want to get stuck next to him at a party.

Week 83: The Forsyte Saga: The Man of Property, by John Galsworthy (1906)

If you're old enough to remember it airing on PBS in 1969, the *Masterpiece Theatre* series is probably what comes to your mind when you think of *The Forsyte Saga*. That is, if you think of it at all, which is unlikely. John Galsworthy's multi-generational chronicle of an upper middle-class family, similar to his own, is a bit of a chestnut these days. While many, like me, still read the Brontës and Thomas Hardy continues to resonate, Galsworthy, who was awarded the Nobel Prize in Literature in 1932, has been relegated to the dusty back shelves of used book stores and thrift shops.

Well, time moves on. The England he was writing about, the England of the late Victorian period, leading up to the First World War, was deeply stratified . . . class conscious and diverse only in dialect. Divorce was fodder for scandal, and to have predecessors who made their money from "trade" mattered enough to be a source of embarrassment, even shame.

Even when the BBC first dramatized it 50 years ago the main appeal of the series, besides the fact that it was very well done, was nostalgia. Like modern-day Brexiters who long for a return to "this other Eden, demi-paradise", viewers embraced the "leisurely evocations of a vanished world", as one reviewer has put it. England shut down on Sunday nights: worshippers stayed home from church so as not to miss an episode; pubs closed early; streets were deserted. In all, when the program was broadcast worldwide, 100,000,000 viewers in 26 countries watched *The Forsyte Saga,* most of whom never read the books.

But Galsworthy was not a complacent, jingoistic Englander. On the contrary, he was a skilled and perceptive satirist who wrote about these smug, "purse-proud" characters as only a true insider can. And he was a feminist. *The Man of Property*, the first novel in the saga and arguably the best, has been compared to *A Doll's House* and there are certainly similarities between Irene Forsyte, Galsworthy's beautiful, unhappy heroine, and Ibsen's Nora Helmer. Nora, however, gets away in the end - Irene does not.

The "man of property" in this novel is Soames Forsyte, a grim, humorless lawyer whose most valuable property, in his own mind and that of his peers, is his wife. Irene is an acknowledged beauty who initially refuses his proposals many times before suddenly, in a moment of weakness, agreeing to marry him. She makes him promise, though, that if ever she wants to leave the relationship, he will let her go. In marrying her, Soames, for once, follows his heart rather than his head as Irene has very little money of her own. For her part, Irene is physically repelled by Soames and grows increasingly unhappy and restless in his company.

Irene has befriended young June Forsyte, who is engaged to Philip Bosinney, a talented but penniless architect. June is the granddaughter of the family patriarch, old Jolyon, and has lived with him since she was three, when her parents separated, creating a scandal that still reverberates all these years later. Her father, young Jolyon, ran off with the family's governess and later married her after June's mother died. Because of this, old Jolyon hasn't spoken with his son for fourteen years.

But he has a weak spot for his granddaughter; he loves her very much and finds himself unable to say "no" to her, which is why he's agreed to the engagement with Bosinney. All goes as planned until Soames hires Bosinney to build him a house - a stately country home befitting his status as a wealthy, up-and-coming man of property. This throws Bosinney and Irene together; they fall in love and Irene asks Soames to release her from the marriage, as he promised. He refuses - she is, after all, his property. Instead he makes arrangements to move her into the new house, once it's completed, and get her out of London and away from all the "influences" that are making her unhappy.

As Galsworthy writes it, the Forsytes are more than a family. They are representatives of an entire class of property-owners and, as young Jolyon explains to Bosinney, there are hundreds of them on the streets of London; you meet them wherever you go:

"'And how do you tell them, may I ask?' said Bosinney.

'By their sense of property. A Forsyte takes a practical - one might say a common-sense - view of things, and a practical view of things is based fundamentally on a sense of property . . . what I call a "Forsyte" is a man that is decidedly more than less a slave of property. He knows a good thing, he knows a safe thing, and his grip on property - it doesn't matter whether it be wives, horses, money, or reputation - is his hall-mark.'"

Soames is so sure of his sense of property that he determines to restore marital relations with his wife whether she wants to or not. In a horrifying climax to the story, he rapes her, leaving her devastated and destroyed. The reader is meant to be shocked, as was Galsworthy, who did not ascribe to the almost universal belief that a man could not be declared criminal for having nonconsensual sex with his wife. (It would be another hundred years before a landmark court judgement put that notion to rest, in England, anyway.)

In the meantime, a dispute has arisen between Soames and Bosinney over the cost of decorating the finished house. Soames decides to sue the architect, knowing if he wins it will force him into bankruptcy. June, who still loves Bosinney in spite of his defection to Irene, approaches her grandfather, and begs him to buy the house and relieve Bosinney of his debt. Old Jolyon agrees to consider it, knowing he'll comply with her wishes because, as we know, he can't refuse her anything. The day of the court case, Irene, who has left Soames, meets with Bosinney and tells him that her husband forced herself on her. Greatly upset, Bosinney goes wandering through the night fog and is accidentally run over and killed. The suspicion arises that it may have been a suicide. Irene returns to Soames, having nowhere else to go.

One final note: John Galsworthy, whose career spanned the first third of the 20th Century, was a popular and prolific writer. In 1929 the readers of *The Manchester Guardian* were asked to name the authors they believed would still be widely read in 2029: Galsworthy led the list. *Sic transit Gloria mundi.*

Week 84: *Thank You, Jeeves*, by P. G. Wodehouse (1934)

So here's the thing: you either love Jeeves and Wooster or you don't. Or, poor thing, you've never read them (by "them" I refer to the 15, by my count, novels and short story collections about Bertie Wooster and the world's most perfect manservant). If that's the case, all I can say is, get started. There's only so much reading time allotted to us in this life; you don't want to go to your grave without having read at least one book by the man who could write, "It was one of those still evenings you get in the summer, when you can hear a snail clear its throat a mile away."

I've been a Wodehouse fan for a long time, so you will understand right off that this is not going to be a cool, collected, unbiased kind of review. It will be, for the most part, a fan letter. I say for the most part because there are parts of *Thank You, Jeeves*, written as it was in the early 30s, which are dated and unfortunate. I'll get to those in a minute.

First, the author: Sir Pelham Grenville Wodehouse, who died on Valentine's Day, 1975, at the age of 93, was one of the most popular and prolific humorists of the 20th century. He hated his name, by the way, and was known to family and friends as Plum, a shortening of Pelham, making him sound like a character in one of his books. It may have been as a form of comic revenge that he gave a similar name to his most popular fictional hero: Bertram Wilberforce Wooster, commonly known as Bertie. In fact, all the characters in the Wodehouse canon, especially the young men, have stupendously silly names. Longtime readers will be familiar with, among others, Gussie Fink-Nottle, "Catsmeat" Potter-Pirbright, "Barmy" Fotheringay-Phipps, and Reginald "Pongo" Twistleton, to name a few.

While some of these bright sparks do have jobs, Bertie is first and foremost a gentleman of leisure. We understand that he inherited a large sum of money when his parents died and was raised by his aunts. When he's not lounging about his club - aptly named the Drones - he spends much of his time avoiding marriage, being what you might call a "confirmed bachelor".

Bertie is a well-meaning, even generous sort, but is not thought to be particularly intelligent. His own valet has remarked that while he has a heart of gold, he is "mentally somewhat negligible". It's the valet who's the brains of the outfit. Jeeves, who's perhaps 10 years older than Bertie, is loyal, erudite, dignified, and respectful. The closest he comes to expressing an emotion is the occasional lifting of an eyebrow or, when amused, a slight twitching of the mouth. As Bertie describes it, Jeeves most commonly wears "that expression of quiet intelligence combined with a feudal desire to oblige".

The Jeeves and Wooster stories are generally set in England, in stately homes and castles peopled by wealthy eccentrics and occasional badly-behaved young boys. You get the impression that Plum didn't like children very much; he had none of his own although when he married his beloved Ethel he adopted her daughter, Leonora, whom he adored.

Thank You, Jeeves begins with a contretemps (sorry - reading Wodehouse gets you into using all kind of $10 words) between our two heroes. Bertie has lately taken up playing the banjo, an instrument Jeeves loathes. When his neighbours threaten him with eviction if he doesn't stop playing, Bertie chooses to move out of his apartment and retire to a cottage in the country. This is the last straw for Jeeves, who reluctantly gives his notice. Bertie, just as reluctantly, accepts it, and the two part company.

Bertie takes a cottage on the estate of his friend, Lord "Chuffy" Chuffnell, who has now become Jeeves's new employer. I suppose you'd say Chuffy is "house poor"; he owns this vast estate and the whole village of Chuffnell Regis but, as he tells Bertie, the rents he receives barely cover the cost of keeping up the estate. What Chuffy is pinning his hopes on is selling Chuffnell Hall to an old foe of Bertie's, a rich American nerve specialist (or "loony doctor", as Bertie calls him) named J. Washburn Stoker. Bertie was recently engaged - briefly - to Stoker's daughter, Pauline, before her father broke off the engagement. Now that she and Chuffy have met and fallen in love, they hope to marry. But Chuffy won't propose to her until the sale of the Hall goes through; he's feels it would be wrong to put her in the position of marrying a poor man.

Bertie comes up with a plan to kiss Pauline in order to make Chuffy jealous and push him to propose. Unfortunately, it's her father, not Chuffy, who sees the kiss, leading him to assume that Bertie and his daughter are still in love. He takes Pauline back to his yacht and keeps her there, to keep her away from Bertie. Chuffy writes a love letter to Pauline and gets Jeeves to smuggle it on board and give it to her. With assistance from Jeeves, she manages to escape and swim to shore, arriving at Bertie's cottage unannounced in the middle of the night, planning to visit Chuffnell Hall in the morning and throw herself into Chuffy's arms.

In the meantime, Bertie needs a place to sleep. After trying the garden shed and being discovered by the local police constable, Bertie heads to the garage to sleep in his car. Once again he's spotted by the officer who alerts Chuffy. Thinking his friend has had one too many, Chuffy drags Bertie back to the cottage. There he sees Pauline in bed in Bertie's pyjamas; they argue and go their separate ways, vowing never to see each other again.

The next day Pauline's father, having learned of her visit to Bertie, lures him to the yacht on the pretext of celebrating his son Dwight's birthday. Once there, Stoker locks Bertie in a stateroom, determined to keep him there until he marries his daughter. Again, Jeeves comes to the rescue. Stoker has hired a minstrel troupe to entertain his son, white musicians in blackface posing as black performers. Jeeves suggests Bertie cover his face and hands with shoe polish, and pose as one of the minstrels, in order to get away. The ruse works, although once he's back on land Bertie finds that soap and water won't remove the polish. Deciding that butter is needed, he returns to his cottage, only to be met by his new valet, the highly excitable Brinkley, who's drunk, armed with a carving knife, and believes that Bertie in blackface is the devil. Bertie barely escapes with his life while Brinkley inadvertently sets the cottage on fire, destroying everything in it, including the banjo.

Bertie then goes to the back door of Chuffnell Hall to see if Jeeves can rustle up some butter for him. He's met by Mary, the scullery maid, who screams at the sight of him and goes into fits, leading Bertie to ponder the effect his darkened appearance is having on people:

"I mean to say, Bertram Wooster with merely a pretty tan calling at the back door of Chuffnell Hall would have been received with respect and deference . . . But purely and simply because there happened to be a little boot polish on my face, here was this female tying herself in knots on the doormat and throwing fits up and down the passage."

It's unfortunate that blackface takes up so much of the rest of the plot. As far as I can tell, it doesn't appear in any of his other books, and I've never read anything else by Plum that I would call racist. Still . . .

P. G. Wodehouse's reputation suffered a severe blow in the early days of World War Two, but it had nothing to do with race. In 1940 he was living in northern France and was captured by the Germans. In an ill-considered move, he agreed to record a series of comic broadcasts which were aired in the US via German radio. These provoked a severe backlash in Britain; politicians and journalists accused him of treason, he was "reviled . . . as a traitor, collaborator, Nazi propagandist, and a coward". Although it later came out that he had been manipulated by the Nazi propaganda machine, he was deeply confused and embarrassed by the scandal. He removed himself to the US and became an American citizen in 1955. Shortly before his death he was awarded a knighthood but he never returned to his homeland.

Whatever we may think about his politics or his racial views, his stories remain a (somewhat) guilty pleasure. As other reviewers have said, the Jeeves and Wooster plots are almost indistinguishable from one another: Bertie is almost trapped into marrying some strong-minded, assertive young woman, and manages to escape with the help of the inimitable Jeeves. In the case of *Thank You, Jeeves*, I can assure you of two things: Jeeves returns to his employ and Bertie's bachelorhood remains secure.

It's all you really need to know.

Week 85: *The Little Prince*, by Antoine de Saint-Exupéry (1943)

I've always maintained that you shouldn't read a story looking for clues to the author's life - the story should stand apart, having its own life, its own universe, if you will. But this particular story has so many parallels with the writer's own narrative it simply begs to be discussed. And it has been: several biographers have argued that *The Little Prince*, a children's tale written for adults, is an allegory of the writer's own life.

Antoine Marie Jean-Baptiste Roger, comte de Saint-Exupéry, like the pilot in this book, was an aviator who survived several crashes, including one that landed him in the desert. Born into an aristocratic but impoverished family in southern France, he was deeply affected by the death of his older brother, François, later writing that François ". . . remained motionless for an instant. He did not cry out. He fell as gently as a [young] tree falls".

After failing to complete a degree in architecture, Saint-Exupéry worked at odd jobs until 1921 when he began his military service in Strasbourg. There he took private flying lessons and eventually became one of the pioneers of international postal flight, flying between Toulouse and Dakar. At the same time he began writing short stories, many of them inspired by his experiences as a pilot. In 1931, *Vol de Nuit* (*Night Flight*) won the *Prix Femina* and established him as a literary star. But it's *The Little Prince*, published in 1943, a year before his death, for which he is most remembered. And loved.

The story goes like this: An aviator crash lands somewhere in the Sahara Desert. He awakens at daybreak to find a golden-haired child standing over him, gently asking him, "Please, will you draw me a little lamb!" The child is alone, there's no sign of an adult or any means of transport, just this well-dressed little boy asking for a drawing of a lamb.

The pilot takes out a pen and paper and sketches something resembling a lamb. The boy isn't satisfied: "That one looks very sickly," he says. "Draw another one."

The second lamb is dismissed because it has horns, and the third one is too old.

"I want a lamb that will live for a long time," the boy says.

So the pilot, running out of patience and wanting to get back to working on his plane, draws a box with air holes.

"That's the crate. The lamb you want is inside," he says.

Delighted, the child accepts the drawing and falls asleep.

Bit by bit, the pilot puts together the story of how the little boy, who is the prince of a tiny planet, came to leave home. We learn that this planet, named by a Turkish astronomer in 1909, is so small the prince can watch the sun set simply by turning his chair around. "One day," he tells the pilot, "I watched forty-four sunsets!"

There are good plants and bad plants on this planet, and the worst ones are the baobabs. If allowed to grow they will take over the planet and destroy it, so they have to be pulled up the minute they begin to sprout. "It's something you have to do every day," the little prince explains. "It's a very boring job but it's very easy."

There are also three tiny volcanoes on his planet. Two are active, which is handy for cooking breakfast in the morning, and one is extinct. But, as the prince says, you never know. So he sweeps all three of them every day.

There is also a flower on his planet, a solitary rose who complains about the cold and demands a screen to protect her from the elements. She's lovely, and the prince is eager to please her, but she can be very unkind and hurtful. She has thorns, after all, so he learns to be wary.

At the time he wrote this, Saint-Exupéry was living in exile in North America, enjoying (and frequently enduring) a tempestuous relationship with his wife, the diminutive Consuelo Suncin, a Salvadoran writer and artist who was both his muse and the source of much of his malaise. He would leave her many times, and have numerous affairs, but she was most certainly the rose.

"I should have judged her by her acts and not by her words," says the prince. "She wrapped herself around me and enlightened me. I should never have fled. I should have guessed at the tenderness behind her poor ruses. Flowers are so contradictory but I was too young to know how to love her."

Having decided to visit other parts of the world, the little prince says goodbye to his flower, latches on to a flock of migrating birds and is lifted out into space. Finding himself in the region of a group of asteroids, he decides to pay each of them a visit. The first asteroid is home to a king who lives alone with no subjects. When the prince asks him who he rules over, the king says he rules over everything - his planet, the other planets, and the stars. As impressive as this sounds, the little prince sees that even with nothing to command, believing himself to have power is the only thing he lives for. *Grown-ups really are very strange*, the prince thinks as he leaves.

The second planet is inhabited by a show-off, who lives to be admired. The fact that there's no one around to admire him doesn't seem to matter. Again, grown-ups are really strange.

The next planet is inhabited by a drunkard who drinks because he's ashamed. Ashamed of what? Of drinking. The fourth planet belongs to a businessman, who is so busy counting the stars he has no time to look at them. The fifth planet, the smallest of them all, is inhabited by a lamplighter and a lamp. Because the planet spins so swiftly, he must light the lamp and then put it out every minute. The king, the show-off, the businessman, and the drunkard would look down on this man, the prince thinks, but he's the only one who doesn't seem ridiculous. He, at least, is looking after something other than himself.

The sixth planet is the biggest, ten times bigger than the others. An elderly gentleman sits at a desk surrounded by books. As he explains to the prince, he's a geographer; he writes down the facts about mountains, rivers, deserts, oceans, and towns. He has no idea if there are any of these on his own planet, though, because he's not an explorer. He advises the prince to visit the planet Earth: "We have good reports of it," he says.

And so the seventh planet is Earth. Which appears, at first, have no people in it. He meets a snake, who says he'll help him to leave if he ever feels homesick for his planet, and has a brief encounter with a flower. Eventually he finds himself in a garden full of roses in bloom. This makes him think of his flower, back home, which he now realizes was not so special after all. His planet contained three tiny volcanoes and a very ordinary flower; he was not much of a prince. The boy lies down in the grass and begins to cry.

At this point a fox appears, and talks to him of friendship. "To you, I'm a fox who's exactly like a hundred thousand other foxes. But, if you tame me, we will need each other. To me, you'll be absolutely unique, and to you, I'll be absolutely unique". He tames the fox, and they become friends. The fox tells him that the little flower on his home planet is unique after all, because the little prince has tamed her. Before they part, the fox tells him a secret:

"It's very simple," he says. "You only see clearly with your heart. The most important things are invisible to the eyes."

This is just one of the lessons the fox has to impart. There are several others, but this is, perhaps, the most important. You can't, or shouldn't, judge the true worth of a thing, or a person, based on what you see. What is really important can only be felt.

Eventually, the prince prepares to leave Earth. It's the anniversary of the day he came to this planet - it's time for him to go. With the help of the snake, he will abandon the body that's become too heavy to carry. The pilot will look at the stars and know his friend is living on one of them. "It's good to have had a friend," he says, "even if you're going to die".

And then, like Saint-Exupéry's brother, François, "He didn't cry out. He fell softly, the way a tree falls. He didn't even make a thud, because of the sand".

After his American hiatus, Saint-Exupéry joined the Free French Air Force in North Africa, flying reconnaissance missions to collect intelligence on German troop movements. On the 31st of July 1944 he set off from Corsica on his ninth such mission, and never returned. He disappeared over the Mediterranean, and is believed to have died at that time.

Scholars and reviewers alike have devoted much time and many written words to the inspiration for the innocent who fell out of the sky. In 1942, while living with a philosopher friend in Quebec City, Saint-Exupéry met his eight-year-old son, who had blond curly hair. Earlier, during an overnight stay in Long Island, he was introduced to the young, golden-haired son of Charles and Anne Morrow Lindbergh. Another child on a train is referred to, in an essay, as an "adorable . . . little prince".

Personally, I think he was writing to the child he had been, the little boy who earned the family nickname *le Roi-Soleil* ("the Sun King") because of his curly golden hair.

Because, in the end, all our stories are written for ourselves.

Week 86: *The Picture of Dorian Gray*, by Oscar Wilde (1890)

"The road to hell is paved with adverbs."

Stephen King wrote that in *On Writing: A Memoir of the Craft*. He might just as well have been speaking about adjectives. Too many of them can get in the way of telling a story.

Mark Twain would have agreed. He had this to say on the subject, in a letter he wrote to a student:

"When you catch an adjective, kill it. No, I don't mean utterly, but kill most of them—then the rest will be valuable. They weaken when they are close together. They give strength when they are wide apart. An adjective habit, or a wordy, diffuse, flowery habit, once fastened upon a person, is as hard to get rid of as any other vice."

I'm harping on adjectives at the moment because Oscar Wilde never met one he didn't like. Take, for instance, the second sentence of the opening chapter to *The Picture of Dorian Gray*, published in 1890:

"From the corner of the divan of Persian saddlebags on which he was lying, smoking, as was his custom, innumerable cigarettes, Lord Henry Wotton could just catch the gleam of the honey-sweet and honey-coloured blossoms of a laburnum, whose tremulous branches seemed hardly able to bear the burden of a beauty so flame-like as theirs; and now and then the fantastic shadows of birds in flight flitted across the long tussore-silk curtains that were stretched in front of the huge window, producing a kind of momentary Japanese effect, and making him think of those pallid jade-faced painters of Tokio [sic] who, through the medium of an art that is necessarily immobile, seek to convey the sense of swiftness and motion".

Whew.

There's more, but you get the picture. I wouldn't call it purple prose, exactly - Wilde was too good a writer for that - but "florid" certainly comes to mind. He was, after all, creating a work of art; defending himself against a critical review he wrote, "My story is an essay on decorative art".

Which raises the question: can an essay on decorative art also be a novel? Well, yes, it can, although I maintain it would be a better novel without the decoration.

The Picture of Dorian Gray, like *Dr. Jekyll and Mr. Hyde* and *Frankenstein*, is one of those stories most of us know without ever having read the book. An artist paints a picture of a beautiful young man. The young man, gazing at the portrait, makes a fervent wish: if only he could remain this youthful, this attractive, all his life. If only it could be the painting that ages, becomes decrepit and ugly. His wish comes true: as time passes he becomes increasingly corrupt and decadent, but his youthful appearance is unchanged. He remains as outwardly attractive as the day he sat for the painting. His portrait, however, shows the corruption of his soul.

The young man in question is Dorian Gray, who sits for a series of paintings by the artist, Basil Hallward. Hallward, a deeply ethical and serious character, has nevertheless become obsessed with Dorian. He believes the portrait he's recently completed is his masterpiece. When his friend, Lord Henry Wotton, visits Hallward's studio, he agrees.

"It is your best work, Basil," he tells him, "the best thing you have ever done."

He urges Hallward to exhibit the painting next year at the Grosvenor Gallery, but the artist refuses. "I have put too much of myself in it," he says, confessing that Dorian has become everything to him.

"I couldn't be happy if I didn't see him every day," he says. "He is absolutely necessary to me."

In contrast to Hallward, Lord Henry is a dandy and a libertine; he pretends to take nothing seriously and argues that the only true aim of life is self-development through the pursuit of beauty. Upon meeting Basil for the first time, he expounds on his theory of hedonistic gratification:

"I believe that if one man were to live out his life fully and completely, were to give form to every feeling, expression to every thought, reality to every dream – I believe that the world would gain such a fresh impulse of joy that we would forget all the maladies of mediævalism, and return to the Hellenic ideal – to something finer, richer than the Hellenic ideal it may be".

Dorian is immediately impressed by his newfound friend and becomes a willing disciple to his corrupting influence. He begins to explore the darker, less respectable parts of London and, in so doing, falls in love with a beautiful young actress. Sibyl Vane is poor and innocent, but she has a powerful stage presence. Captivated, Dorian soon proposes marriage and follows it up by inviting Hallward and Lord Henry to the theatre to watch her perform. Unfortunately, falling in love with Dorian has turned Sibyl into a bad actress; experiencing the real thing, she feels she can no longer pretend to be in love on stage. She performs poorly that night and Dorian, angry and embarrassed, breaks off the engagement and tells her he never wants to see her again. When he returns home he's shocked to observe that his portrait has altered: there's a hint of cruelty to the mouth that wasn't there before.

In a fit of remorse, Dorian decides to go to Sibyl the next day, beg her forgiveness, and renew the engagement. The next morning, however, he learns that she killed herself the night before. Dorian locks the painting away in an upper room and resigns himself to a life of decadence and debauchery. For the next 18 years he sinks ever deeper into sin and corruption. He becomes the subject of salacious gossip - it's said he's done unspeakable things - and yet no one, looking into his charming, youthful face can believe him guilty of such transgressions. When Basil Hallward turns up one night to confront him about the things people are saying, Dorian shows him the painting, which has become hideous, and then kills him in a fit of rage.

Eventually, Dorian vows to summon the courage to confess his crimes. The painting, however, sneers at him, revealing the hypocrisy of his repentance. In a fury, Dorian picks up the knife he used to kill Basil and slashes the painting to pieces. His servants, hearing a crash, break into the room. The painting, as youthful and fresh as the day it was painted, is hanging on the wall; their master, old, wizened and hideously disfigured, lies on the floor with a knife through his heart.

In this, his first and only novel, Wilde was critiquing two antithetical belief systems: the moral hypocrisy of 19th century society and the so-called "new hedonism". It's obvious, though, that his personal sensibilities were allied with the aesthetes, personified by Lord Henry Wotton. He's the most interesting character in the book, and Wilde gives him all the best lines:

"The only way to get rid of a temptation is to yield to it."

"There is only one thing in the world worse than being talked about, and that is not being talked about."

"I can believe anything, provided that it is quite incredible."

And my favourite: "I can't help detesting my relations. I suppose it comes from the fact that none of us can stand other people having the same faults as ourselves."

Week 87: *Slaughterhouse-Five*, by Kurt Vonnegut, Jr. (1969)

"All this happened, more or less. The war parts, anyway, are pretty much true".

So begins the introduction to *Slaughterhouse-Five*, Kurt Vonnegut's first really successful novel. Vonnegut served in the American army in World War II, was captured by the Germans, and, in February, 1945, survived the Allies' bombing of Dresden by hiding in the basement meat locker of the building where he and the other POWs were quartered.

That event affected him profoundly. For years, whenever he was asked what he was writing, he said he was working on a book about Dresden; *Slaughterhouse-Five,* published in 1969, is that book. It was written as a response to a war that could not be explained, much less justified. "It is short and jumbled and jangled," he writes, "because there is nothing intelligent to say about a massacre". It was the first of his books to become a bestseller, and has been ranked by the Modern Library as one of the 100 best English language novels of the 20th century. Appearing at about the time the US began sending troops to Vietnam, it was hailed as an anti-war manifesto for a new generation: he was invited to speak at rallies and college commencements, received several honorary degrees, and, in 1972, saw his most famous work made into a movie. The book's repetition of "So it goes", said whenever a death occurred, became a catchphrase of the left.

The story is nonlinear in style, switching back and forth in time and told from the perspective of the narrator, who is Vonnegut himself, and the main protagonist, Billy Pilgrim, an optometrist-turned-reluctant-soldier. Billy frequently becomes "unstuck in time", traveling back to a period when he was young, or ahead to the future when he's married with children. Or, more and more often, to the planet of Trafalmadore where he's put on display in a zoo made entirely of glass.

Before we learn any of this, we are told that Billy was born in 1922 in Ilium, New York. He studies optometry, is drafted into the army, and, after the war, finishes his optometry training and becomes engaged to the overweight daughter of the founder of the school. After suffering a nervous collapse, he's given shock therapy and released, marries his fiancée, and goes on to become rich and father two children. In 1968, on a trip to an optometry convention in Montreal, Billy's plane crashes on top of Sugarbush Mountain, in Vermont. Everyone but Billy is killed. While he's recuperating in hospital, his wife dies of carbon monoxide poisoning on her way to see him. Billy then heads to New York City hoping to get on a talk show - he wants to tell people about being kidnapped by a flying saucer in 1967 and how, while there, he was mated with an Earthling movie star named Montana Wildhack.

As Billy explains to his daughter, he first came unstuck in time in 1944, long before his trip to Trafalmadore. He was a chaplain's assistant in the war and got caught up in the Battle of the Bulge. Dazed and disoriented, he joined three other survivors wandering through enemy territory, attempting to avoid Germans. One of these men was an anti-tank gunner named Roland Weary. Obsessed with dreams of grandeur - and pretty stupid to boot - Weary saves Billy's life several times, in spite of Billy not particularly wanting to be saved. Weary eventually dies of gangrene caused by ill-fitting shoes; as he's dying he rants about Billy, blaming him for his death. Another soldier, Paul Lazarro, promises to track Billy down after the war and kill him. Revenge, he says, is life's sweetest pleasure.

The men are captured by Germans and taken to a POW camp containing a lot of dying Russians and a handful of English military officers who've been there almost since the beginning of the war. None of the officers have seen a woman, a flower, or even a bird for four years, and they have little experience of the war as it's now being fought. As one of them confides,"You know, we've had to imagine the war here, and we have imagined that it was being fought by aging men like ourselves. We had forgotten that wars were fought by babies. When I saw those freshly shaved faces, it was a shock. 'My God, my God -' I said to myself, 'It's the Children's Crusade.'"

The newly arrived American prisoners are fed and clothed and then shipped off to Dresden to work as forced labour. They are housed in a former slaughterhouse, and it is while they are interned there that the British and American forces carry out a series of aerial attacks, dropping more than 3,900 tons of high-explosive bombs and incendiary devices on the city, destroying over 1600 acres and killing between 35,000 and 135,000 people, depending on whom you believe. When Billy and the others venture out of the slaughterhouse, they see a landscape that resembles the surface of the moon. Put to work among the ruins, with the task of interring dead bodies, they are warned against looting. When one of their members finds a teapot, he's summarily put on trial and shot.

After receiving an honourable discharge and being sent home, Billy spends some time in hospital being treated for what we now call post traumatic stress disorder. While there, he's introduced to the works of Kilgore Trout, an unsuccessful science fiction writer who Vonnegut based his friend and fellow writer, Theodore Sturgeon. ("Trout", "Sturgeon" - both fish. Get it?) He's also been viewed as Vonnegut's alter ego. Most of Trout's novels "dealt with time warps and extrasensory perceptions and other unexpected things". Vonnegut obviously was fond of the character. He appears in seven of Vonnegut's novels and plays a major role in three of them.*

Billy Pilgrim has seen his birth and his death many times, so he knows exactly how and when he will die. In 1976, he's 54 years old and is giving a speech in Chicago about his alien abduction. He tells the crowd that Paul Lazarro, a man he knew during the war, will either kill him or have him assassinated. And that, apparently, is what happens.

In my view, Kurt Vonnegut is a science fiction writer for those who don't tend to read science fiction. I wouldn't know Kim Stanley Robinson if he sat on my face, and I've often wondered about the difference between science fiction and fantasy. (Although I read recently that Isaac Asimov said that science fiction, with its grounding in science, is possible, while fantasy is not. So that helps.) I love Vonnegut because he created characters I can relate to. He was a humanist, an atheist, and a pacifist. He was also pretty cynical about humanity in general so although he was against war he was resigned to it, believing that wars, like death and taxes, would always be with us.

Vonnegut's last book, in 2005, was a collection of biographical essays, "A Man Without a Country." It concludes with a poem he wrote called "Requiem," which has these closing lines:

"When the last living thing has died on account of us, how poetical it would be if Earth could say, in a voice floating up perhaps from the floor of the Grand Canyon, 'It is done.' People did not like it here."

And so it goes.

*If you're *really* interested in Kilgore Trout you can check out *The Narrative Function of Kilgore Trout and His Fictional Works in Slaughterhouse-Five* by Jesús Lerate de Castro (*Revista Alicantina de Estudios Ingleses* 7, 1994: 115-22)

Week 88: *One Flew Over the Cuckoo's Nest*, by Ken Kesey (1962)

Milos Forman's film of Ken Kesey's best-selling novel made Jack Nicholson a star. And deservedly so. Who can forget his portrayal of Randle Patrick McMurphy, the subversive troublemaker who wages psychological warfare with the Big Nurse, played by Louise Fletcher? The film, released in 1975, put McMurphy front and centre, allowing "Chief" Bromden, the 6' 7" son of a Chief of the Columbia Indians, a very small supporting role, until the very end.

In the book, however, Bromden has a larger presence: he's the narrator of the story, and it's through his eyes that we view the residents and staff of the Oregon psychiatric hospital where he's been a patient for over a decade. Bromden is what you would call an unreliable narrator; his paranoid delusions shape his world-view, and these include the belief that society is controlled by a powerful organization called the Combine. This group hates anyone who doesn't fit the accepted pattern of normality and punishes them for it. Bromden's response to the Combine is to pretend to be deaf and mute. As a result, he's allowed access to places forbidden to the other patients and is privy to the secrets of both patients and staff.

The residents, all men, are divided into two groups: the Acutes, who can be cured, and the Chronics, who can't. The Acutes, with Bromden pushing a broom and looking on, take part in daily Group Meetings, run with mechanical precision by a well-endowed former army nurse. (Her breasts are important: we're meant to understand that Nurse Ratched has an ongoing war with her feminine side, leading McMurphy to identify her as a "ball-cutter".) During these sessions, the nurse encourages the men to confess their private thoughts and past indiscretions, using shame to keep them in submission. When not conducting meetings, she sits behind the glass of the nurse's station overlooking the day room, monitoring their every move. On the rare occasions when a patient steps out of line, or asserts himself in some way that threatens her authoritarian regime, she has them taken down to the "Shock Shop" for electroshock treatments or, in extreme cases, a lobotomy.

When the bumptious R. P. McMurphy is admitted to his ward, Chief Bromden sees at once that the new guy is different, "different from anybody been coming on this ward for the past ten years, different from anybody they ever met outside. He's just as vulnerable, maybe, but the Combine didn't get him". McMurphy comes to the ward fresh from the Pendleton Work Farm, where he was serving a six-month sentence for battery and gambling. He has faked mental illness in order to be transferred to the hospital, assuming life here will be easier than in prison. McMurphy is loud, swaggering, and unpredictable, and his presence disturbs Nurse Ratched's peaceful world from the very beginning. He gets the men involved in gambling for money, enlivens their basketball games, and persuades them to stage a protest in front of the blank TV set when the nurse refuses to let them watch the World Series.

The other men are wary of McMurphy at first. He laughs, loud and often, a sound seldom heard in this place. He freely admits to being a con man and a fighter, teases them about women, goads them to stand up for themselves, and becomes in short order, their *de facto* leader. He is, after all, the only one "man enough" to stand up to Nurse Ratched. His freewheeling defiance suffers a blow when he learns that, having been committed to the hospital, his release date is up to the nurse. The other men are there voluntarily, a fact he finds completely bewildering:

"Jesus, I mean you guys do nothing but complain about how you can't stand it in this place here and then you haven't got the guts just to walk out? What do you think you are for Christ sake, crazy or something? Well, you're not! You're not! You're no crazier than the average asshole out walking around on the streets."

Suddenly fearful of the power the nurse has to keep him confined indefinitely, McMurphy makes an attempt to follow the rules. When one of the men, Charles Cheswick, tries to get the others to take a stand against the nurse, he looks to McMurphy, as usual, for support. McMurphy, however, stays silent; shortly afterward Cheswick drowns in the pool, his death a possible suicide.

Cheswick's death prompts McMurphy to rethink his decision to conform. He organizes a deep-sea fishing trip for ten of the men, accompanied by a female friend of his, Candy Starr, a prostitute from Portland. Billy Bibbit, who stutters and is terribly shy, is attracted to Candy and McMurphy promises to arrange a "date" between them. The chaos that ensues after this trip results in both Bromden and McMurphy being taken to the Disturbed ward and given electroshock treatments.

Once he's back on the ward with the other Acutes, McMurphy makes plans to fulfill his promise to Billy.

He bribes the night aide to sneak Candy and her friend, Sandy, into the hospital, along with a supply of liquor and marijuana. While Candy and Billy enjoy each other privately, the rest of the men party till dawn. The idea is that McMurphy will leave with the women before the day shift arrives and escape to Mexico in Sandy's car. But when the time comes, he's too wasted to move. Nurse Ratched arrives, finds the ward in disarray and discovers Billy and Candy half-naked, in each other's arms. With a newfound confidence born, no doubt, from having had his first sexual encounter, Billy stands up to the nurse, without stuttering. She, in turn, has a response she knows will bring him back into line:

"What worries me, Billy," she says, "is how your poor mother is going to take this . . . You know how she is when she gets disturbed . . . She always spoke so proudly of you".

She gets the reaction she hoped for; Billy is reduced to a trembling, stuttering wreck. Frantic, practically hysterical, he blames the girl. And McMurphy. Once he's completely defeated, she forgives him and leads him to the doctor's office. Left alone there, Billy cuts his throat. The nurse accuses McMurphy of being responsible for Billy's death; McMurphy, in a rage, lunges at her and attempts to strangle her. In so doing he rips her shirt, revealing her naked breasts. He's restrained by the orderlies and taken upstairs to the Disturbed ward, where he's lobotomized. When he's brought back to the ward, silent, motionless and in a vegetative state, Chief Bromden performs an act of mercy: he suffocates his friend with a pillow. He then goes to the room that houses an enormous control panel, weighing some 400 pounds. Using all of his strength, he lifts the panel from its base, throws it through a window, and makes his escape.

At the time he wrote this, Kesey was working as a night aide at the Menlo Park Veterans' Hospital in California. He was also taking part in some highly secretive experiments sponsored by the CIA studying the effects on volunteers of LSD and other psychoactive drugs. It's pretty safe to say that some of Chief Bromden's more outrageous hallucinations were inspired by his experiences taking these drugs. According to Tom Wolfe, author of *The Electric Kool-Aid Acid Test,* the character of Chief Bromden came to Kesey one night on the ward when he was high on peyote. Wolfe said Kesey would "write like mad under the drugs" and then cut out the "junk" when he came down.

One Flew Over the Cuckoo's Nest, published in 1962, was an immediate success with both critics and the public. Almost 60 years later, it holds up in practically every way - the characters are strong, and the story grips you. Only the character of the Big Nurse feels dated. You'd have difficulty these days selling women on the concept of a "ball-cutting" female denying her "femininity" and using her power to emasculate men. Some of us might object.

Week 89: *Catch-22*, by Joseph Heller (1961)

Back in 1977, Joseph Heller wrote the following for a collection of essays about the 1960s: "The concept of the novel came to me as a seizure, a single inspiration. I'd come to the conclusion that I wanted to write a novel, and moving back to New York after two years of teaching college in Pennsylvania sent the ambition coursing again. I had no idea what it would be about, however. Then one night the opening lines of *Catch-22* - all but the character's name, Yossarian - came to me: 'It was love at first sight. The first time he saw the chaplain he fell madly in love with him.'"*

Heller didn't have the hero's name at this point, the chaplain could have been anywhere - he could have been a prison chaplain, for all Heller knew - and he didn't even have the title. For seven years, while the book was being written, edited, and made ready for publication, it was called *Catch-18*. Then, early in 1961, just a few months before Simon and Schuster were preparing to launch the novel, Leon Uris came out with *Mila 18*. Uris was a best-selling author; Heller was practically unknown to the general public. A new title was required. *Catch-11* was promising, but it was too close to Frank Sinatra's hit movie, *Ocean's Eleven,* which had come out the year before. Heller came up with *Catch-14,* which had the same number of syllables, but his editor, Robert Gottlieb, didn't like it.

This time it was Gottlieb who had the late-night flash of inspiration: *Catch-22,* he insisted, was the perfect title. The rest, as they like to say, is history. Catch-22 became a colloquialism "used to describe a paradoxical situation from which an individual cannot escape because of contradictory rules or limitations", to quote Wikipedia.

This is the kind of trivia I love. I can spend entire mornings, especially when I have more important things to do, scrolling through page after page of material only remotely relevant to something I've been reading. Or mean to read. Or once read a very long time ago.

Catch-22 is one of those books. I read it, I think, in high school, although it certainly wasn't on the curriculum. I do remember seeing "YOSSARIAN LIVES" written on the walls of my alma mater so by the time I got to university the book had achieved cult status (which is, I often think, the only status that really matters).

Set on the island of Pianosa off the coast of Italy in the last days of World War II, the novel is a satirical take on the madness and futility of war, based on Heller's wartime experiences. Like Yossarian, Heller was a bombardier with the US Army Corps. He would later say that he personally never had a bad officer, and the anti-war message of the book was influenced more by the Korean War and McCarthyism. Nevertheless, Heller paints a grim picture of military incompetence at the highest levels and you can't help but feel he experienced at least some of that.

The hero - or anti-hero, perhaps - is Captain John Yossarian, a 28-year-old bombardier who is driven by a single, desperate, impulse: he does not want to die. And everybody, he believes, is trying to kill him.

Yossarian has flown more than 50 bombing missions but each time he reaches the quota and hopes to be discharged, the colonels raise the number of missions required in order to be sent home. He sees the war as a personal attack on his person, and the ones he's the most afraid of are his commanding officers.

Colonel Cathcart, for instance, continually volunteers his men for perilous missions in a bid to be promoted to General. Colonel Cargill, employed as an Army troubleshooter, is a former marketing executive who "could be relied on to run the most prosperous enterprise into the ground. He was a self-made man who owed his lack of success to nobody". Major _ _ de Coverley, the head of the squadron, is so revered by his men they're afraid to ask his first name, yet he does nothing all day but play horseshoes and rent apartments for officers in cities the Allies have taken. As for Major Major Major Major,

"Some men are born mediocre, some men achieve mediocrity, and some men have mediocrity thrust upon them. With Major Major Major Major it had been all three. Even among men lacking all distinction he inevitably stood out as a man lacking more distinction than all the rest, and people who met him were always impressed by how unimpressive he was".

Those serving in other positions are not much better. The army medic, Doc Daneeka, is more concerned with his own welfare than that of his patients. The military has dealt him a terrible blow, he says, keeping him away from his lucrative medical practice. The mess officer, Milo Minderbinder, is a sociopathic entrepreneur whose sole loyalty lies with those who pay him. At one point he contracts a fleet of German pilots to bomb his own squadron. And A. T. Tappman, the chaplain, is an Anabaptist who is steadily questioning his faith in a supreme being the longer the war goes on. Who, after all, could blame him?

After a young gunner dies in his arms on a bombing mission over Avignon, Yossarian loses all taste for battle. He decides "to live forever or die in the attempt" and spends a lot of time in hospital, faking illness, in order to get out of combat duty. He pleads with Doc Daneeka to have him declared insane so he can be discharged and sent home. The doctor agrees that Yossarian would be crazy to keep on flying. But if he knows he'd be crazy to fly then he's sane, and so he can't be certified as crazy. Which means Yossarian has to keep on flying. This, the medic says, is Catch-22:

"Catch-22 . . . specified that a concern for one's own safety in the face of dangers that were real and immediate was the process of a rational mind. [A bombardier] was crazy and could be grounded. All he had to do was ask; and as soon as he did, he would no longer be crazy and would have to fly more missions. [A bombardier] would be crazy to fly more missions and sane if he didn't, but if he was sane he had to fly them. If he flew them he was crazy and didn't have to; but if he didn't want to he was sane and had to."

Yossarian says, "That's some catch, that Catch-22".

And the doctor agrees: "It's the best there is".

This is a long, convoluted, and somewhat confusing novel, alternating between nightmare and hilarity. It flashes backward and forward in time, and involves at least 50 characters by my own count, each with their own story and having some connection with Yossarian. There's Lieutenant Nately, the 19-year-old son of a wealthy family, who falls in love with a prostitute, is killed on a mission by a pilot from his own squadron, and whose prostitute, known as "Nately's whore", goes after Yossarian in a bid for revenge. There's Snowdon, the gunner who died in Yossarian's arms during a bombing mission over Avignon; Hungry Joe, the former *Life* photographer who's obsessed with trying to take pictures of naked women; and Orr, the simple-minded bomber pilot who crash lands every plane he flies, escaping unscathed every time. Until, finally, he sets off on a mission and never comes back.

Yossarian takes Nately's death very hard. He decides he's done with war, done with flying yet another mission. He's flown 70 of them by now, and once again the quota's been raised, this time to 80. He absconds to Rome, and spends a nightmarish, hallucinogenic night wandering the streets, before being arrested for being in the city without a pass. He's taken back to Pianosa where he faces a court-martial for refusing to fly. Colonel Cathcart offers him a deal: he'll send Yossarian home with an honourable discharge as long as he promises that when he gets back to the States he'll praise the military for how they're handling things here, and support Cathcart's 80-mission policy. Reluctantly, Yossarian agrees to the deal, but as he's leaving the room he's attacked by Nately's whore and ends up in the hospital.

There, he has a change of heart. He's not going to go along with the colonels: it's an odious deal, that will put other men's lives at risk. The chaplain bursts in with electrifying news: Orr isn't dead, after all. He crash landed his plane deliberately and washed ashore in Sweden. Yossarian realizes Orr must have planned this all along, and if Orr managed to escape, there's hope for them all. He, too, will run away to Sweden, and leave the insanity of the war behind him. He gets dressed and steps outside, where Nately's whore is waiting for him. She tries to stab him, misses, and he runs off into the distance.

The book ends there. We are not to know if Yossarian was successful in his escape, if he eventually got to Sweden or not. I take comfort in the thought that whoever penned that graffiti was right: somehow, somewhere, Yossarian lives.

The Sixties, ed. Lynda Rosen Obst (New York: Random House/Rolling Stone Press, 1977), p. 50.

Week 90: *Brave New World*, by Aldous Huxley (1932)

O wonder!
How many goodly creatures are there here!
How beauteous mankind is! O brave new world,
That has such people in't.

— *William Shakespeare, The Tempest, Act V, Scene I*

Brave New World was not the first dystopian novel of the 20th century; that honour goes, most likely, to Yevgeni Zamyatin's *We*, a satire on life in a collectivist futuristic state located in the middle of a jungle. And although he denied it, it's probably safe to say that Aldous Huxley was at least partly influenced by *We* when he sat down to write his own version of a totalitarian society.

Where *Brave New World* differs from *We*, and from Orwell's *Nineteen Eighty-Four*, is in its concept of a regime that controls its populace not by terror but by genetic engineering. Instead of "a boot stamping on a human face, forever", we have embryonic conditioning and recreational drugs.

In his foreword to the 1947 edition of the book, Huxley wrote the following:

"A really efficient totalitarian state would be one in which the all-powerful executive of political bosses and their army of managers control a population of slaves who do not have to be coerced, because they love their servitude".

Written in 1931 and published the following year, the novel is set in London in the year A.F. (After Ford) 632 (about 500 years from now). Traditional societal norms have been turned on their heads: "mother" is a dirty word, babies are not born but decanted, sexual promiscuity is actively promoted, and the natural aging process is viewed with horror and disgust. The World State operates along the lines of Henry Ford's assembly line - God, in fact, has been replaced by Ford. Citizens celebrate Ford Day and invoke his name when swearing.

The story begins in the Central London Hatchery and Conditioning Centre where human eggs are fertilized and genetically modified in order to be placed into five distinct classes: Alphas and Betas, who are at the top of the social hierarchy, conditioned to be intelligent and capable of performing work that requires a certain level of decision-making; and Gammas, Deltas and Epsilons, genetically engineered to be fit for the most mundane and mindless tasks.

The Director of the Centre is taking a group of students on a tour of the Centre, beginning at the Fertilizing Room, and moving on to the Bottling Room, the Social Predestination Room, and the Decanting Room. Along the way he explains the Bokanovsky Process, whereby fertilized human eggs belonging to the lowest classes are repeatedly cloned. This, he says, is "a major instrument of social stability":

"One egg, one embryo, one adult - normality. But a bokanovskified egg will bud, will proliferate, will divide. From eight to ninety-six buds, and every bud will grow into a perfectly formed embryo, and every embryo into a full-sized adult. Making ninety-six human beings grow where only one grew before. Progress."

The cloned eggs are deprived of oxygen and their blood surrogate is poisoned with alcohol, in order to stunt their growth and reduce their mental capabilities as adults. Once the babies are decanted, they are subjected to years of hypnopaedic conditioning while they sleep, in order to reinforce class consciousness: "Gammas are stupid. They all wear green, and Delta children wear khaki. Oh no, I *don't* want to play with Delta children. And Epsilons are still worse". And so on.

Halfway through the tour we are introduced to one of the main characters, a beautiful young nurse named Lenina Crowne. Huxley refers to Lenina, several times, as "pneumatic", a word that puzzled me when I read the book back in high school. Its literal meaning is "filled with air" but when applied to a woman I believe it's meant to be "curvaceous". Besides being curvy, Lenina is also a "freemartin", one of the 30% of women who haven't been sterilized. Popular and conventional, Lenina enjoys sex with a variety of men and is generally quite happy. On the rare occasions when she feels a little stressed, she treats herself to a "soma holiday", a drug-induced period of relaxation that leaves her with only a very slight hangover.

Lenina has been having a four-month affair with a co-worker, Henry Foster. During that time, she's done something unusual: she's abstained from having sex with anyone else. In a society where "everyone belongs to everyone else", this is distinctly quirky. Her friend,

Fanny, urges Lenina to see other men; after all, Henry certainly has other women:

"Trust Henry Foster," Fanny says, "to be the perfect gentleman - always correct".

Lenina agrees: "He patted me on the behind this afternoon".

"There, you see!" Fanny was triumphant. "That shows what he stands for. The strictest conventionality".

At this point Lenina confesses that she's attracted to another co-worker, Bernard Marx, an Alpha-Plus psychologist who has some very odd notions. For one thing, he likes to spend time alone (horror of horrors) and for another, he hates her sleeping with other men. He's also shorter than most Alpha males, due, rumour has it, to an accidental injection of alcohol into his blood surrogate. Bernard is critical of much of society, and doesn't hesitate to voice his opinions. Nevertheless, when Bernard invites Lenina to accompany him to a remote Savage Reservation in New Mexico, she agrees.

Before they leave, the Director confides to Bernard that he visited the Reservation years ago. The woman he was with went missing during the trip, and he returned to civilization without her. Having confessed his terrible secret, the Director then turns on Bernard and threatens to deport him to Iceland.

For Lenina, the Reservation is a terrible place - dirty, uncomfortable, and full of unattractive, half naked savages. The natives still marry and have children in the old way, and, unlike the citizens of the World State, they practice religion. A non-native woman named Linda comes out to greet them. She's middle-aged, wrinkled and fat. Neither Bernard nor Lenina have ever seen an old person who actually looks old. Where they come from, technology keeps people youthful and fit right up to the moment they die. Unable to bear the hideousness of this terrifying natural world, Lenina takes a large dose of soma and spends the rest of the holiday in a stupor.

Bernard, however, is intrigued. He discovers that Linda is the woman who accompanied the Director 20 years ago. She has stayed on the Reservation because she was pregnant and gave birth to a son, sired by the Director. This shameful event has prevented her from returning home. Reviled for her promiscuity, Linda is an outcast her on the Reservation. She has, however, taught John to read, and he's memorized almost every word of the only book he owns, the complete works of William Shakespeare. Linda's stories of the "civilized world" she left behind make it sound like a kind of paradise, something out of one of Shakespeare's plays.

Bernard seizes the opportunity to have the upper hand; he invites Linda and John to come to London with him, where he achieves a kind of celebrity as a friend of John "the Savage". He introduces Linda to his boss, referring to the Director as John's "father".
Humiliated, the Director leaves, refusing to have anything to do with Linda. As everyone else finds her equally repulsive, Linda takes refuge in soma, lying in bed permanently drugged.

John is confused and then repulsed by the superficiality of this society. Crowds of people flock to see him, as if he's an exhibit in a zoo. He and Lenina are attracted to each other but his idea of courtship doesn't fit her idea of normal behaviour. When Lenina tries to seduce him, he physically attacks her, and then learns that his mother, Linda, is dying. He hurries to the hospital and runs into a group of Delta workers awaiting their daily allowance of soma. The words from *The Tempest* come back to mock him: "O brave new world!" The phrase rings in his ears as a clarion call to action - he must stop the workers from taking this "poison". Bernard and his friend Helmholtz Watson arrive just in time to see the workers turn on John in a fury. The resulting riot ends in John, Bernard and Watson being arrested and taken to face judgment from Mustapha Mond, the Resident World Controller of Western Europe

Mond explains that the World State was created to ensure stability and happiness. In order to do that, it was necessary to eliminate truth. Bernard and Watson are banished to the Falkland Islands, but John will be kept in London so Mond can keep an eye one him. Left alone, Mond and John carry on a debate which is really at the heart of the novel: is it best to be free to live as an individual, risking death, disease, despair, and all the inconveniences that afflict humankind? Or is it better to give it all up for the sake of being happy? In a speech that sounds very much like that of the author, John rejects the comforts of this mechanized, mass-produced life:

"I don't want comfort," he says. "I want God, I want poetry, I want real danger, I want freedom, I want goodness. I want sin."

"In fact," says Mustapha Mond, "you're claiming the right to be unhappy".

"All right then," the Savage says, defiantly, "I'm claiming the right to be unhappy".

The book should end there, but it doesn't. John removes himself to a remote lighthouse where he works in his garden and practices self-flagellation. Word gets out that the Savage is behaving weirdly; dozens of helicopters descend on the property, filled with sightseers. Lenina is among them.

"Strumpet!" he cries, rushing at her like a madman. As he whips her the crowd stampedes towards them: "Pain was a fascinating horror". They begin to strike each other, mimicking his movements, while John continues to beat himself and Lenina in turn. Finally, around midnight, the helicopters leave, and John falls into a soma-induced stupor. The next day it all comes back to him, his own behaviour and that of the others. Overcome with remorse, he hangs himself.

We're left with the feeling that yes, there will always be rebels, but most of us, like the Romans, will opt for bread and circuses.

Week 91: *The Inheritance of Loss*, by Kiran Desai (2006)

Kiran Desai's second novel, which was awarded the Man Booker Prize in 2006, is a multigenerational tale of migration, identity, and the cultural legacy of colonialism. If this sounds a bit too academic for your tastes, let me assure you that *The Inheritance of Loss,* while disturbing and, at heart, pretty cynical, is a perceptive and frequently witty read. Something you can't always say about the books that win the big prizes.

Set in the 1980s, at a time when India's political landscape is being fundamentally transformed, the story begins in Kalimpong, where Sai, an orphaned teenager, lives with her grandfather in a damp and decaying house in the north-eastern Himalayas. The grandfather, Jemubhai Patel, is a former judge who, as a young man, went to Cambridge on a scholarship, full of idealistic notions of the English. He found a cold, class-driven society where, shy and self-conscious, he withdrew into himself, as isolated as if he were invisible: "For entire days nobody spoke to him at all . . . elderly ladies . . . moved over when he sat next to them in the bus, so he knew that whatever they had, they were secure in their conviction that it wasn't even remotely as bad as what he had".

He returned to India ground down and bitter, hating the British for being the cause of his humiliation, and despising all things Indian. This includes his young wife, whom he married just before setting off for England. After repeatedly abusing her, he sends her back to her parents, refusing to see ever see her again, or the daughter she gives birth to a few months later. Keeping himself aloof from his countrymen, he refuses to let himself feel anything but contempt for his neighbours. His education and adopted mannerisms are English but his skin colour is not; as such, Patel lives a reclusive existence as a man effectively without a country. His only companions are his granddaughter, his drunken cook, and his beloved dog, Mutty.

Biju, the son of Patel's cook, is determined to leave the squalor of India behind him. He lands a US visa and arrives in New York full of dreams of success and prosperity. What he finds is what you might expect him to find; he is, after all, an undocumented immigrant without money, skills or connections. Unable to find work that pays him a ling wage, Biju drifts from one menial restaurant job to another, working for next to nothing and living in squalid basement rooms cheek by jowl with other immigrants. The caste system that drove Britain's colonial empire is thriving in America: "Above the restaurant was French, but below in the kitchen, it was Mexican and Indian . . . It was horrible what happened to Indians abroad and nobody knew but other Indians abroad. It was a dirty little rodent secret".

Back home in Kalimpong, Sai has fallen in love with her tutor. Gyan, who is four years older than Sai, is Nepalese and initially as naive as she. For a brief period, their burgeoning love affair not only provides the one note of hope in the story but gives Desai an opportunity to play with the narrative, as she describes the delight they take in each other's appearance: "Her ears she displayed like items taken from under the counter and put before a discerning customer in one of the town's curio shops, but when he tried to test the depth of her eyes with his, her glance proved too slippery to hold; he picked it up and dropped it, retrieved it, dropped it again until it slid away and hid."

All too soon, however, Gyan becomes involved with the Gorkha National Liberation Front, a group of activists demanding a separate state for the Nepalis in India. Under their influence, he comes to view Sai in a different light: "It was a masculine atmosphere and Gyan felt a moment of shame remembering his tea parties with Sai on the veranda, the cheese toast, queen cakes from the baker, and even worse, the small warm space they inhabited together, the nursery talk— It suddenly seemed against the requirements of his adulthood." He breaks off relations with her, much to her despair, and although he later regrets his actions and resolves to win her back, they are still apart at the end of the book. His rejection has completely changed her worldview: "Never again could she think there was but one narrative and that this narrative belonged only to herself, that she might create her own tiny happiness and live safely within it."

The Nepali separatist movement becomes increasingly violent; paramilitary groups roam the countryside, terrorizing the villagers and helping themselves to food and ammunition. When Gyan reveals the fact that Sai's grandfather has some old Army guns in the house, soldiers break in, steal the guns, and humiliate the old man by making him serve them tea. In a harrowing climax to the story, a GNLF demonstration turns violent and bloody, leaving many dead wounded and initiating a dark, troubling period of unrest.

Back in New York, Biju is worried about his father. When he manages to contact him by phone, the connection is poor - neither of them can hear the other and he eventually decides the only way to put his fears to rest is to return to India. Months of living in filth, dealing with poor plumbing, bad food, and exploitive working conditions, have combined to make him forget the wretchedness he left behind. He longs for the comforts of home, forgetting that there aren't any.

"This way of leaving your family for work had condemned them over several generations to have their hearts always in other places, their minds thinking about people elsewhere; they could never be in a single existence at one time".

Against the advice of his friends in the States, Biju buys himself a plane ticket home, via London, Frankfurt, Abu Dhabi, Dubai, Bahrain, Karachi, Delhi, and Calcutta, from where he plans to get a bus to Kalimpong. But when he finally arrives in Calcutta he finds that, with all the upheaval in that part of the world, the buses to Kalimpong are no longer running. He accepts a ride from some soldiers who rob him of his luggage, his savings, and even his clothes. His great American experience has left him with less than he had when he started.

The Inheritance of Loss is a wonderful book to read, but a hard one to love. Desai is such a wonderful writer, especially of comic scenes that have you laughing out loud, that you want to embrace this expansive intergenerational tale of wholeheartedly.

The message, however, is simply too bleak. Where other writers (Zadie Smith comes to mind) would have us believe the world is becoming more diverse and welcoming, Desai paints a grim picture of an international caste system that keeps the immigrant - the poor ones, anyway - firmly at the bottom.

Week 92: *The Talented Mr. Ripley*, by Patricia Highsmith (1955)

The genius of Patricia Highsmith in this, her first Tom Ripley novel, is to create a villain so complex and vulnerable that you can't help rooting for him. He cons his way through life, defrauds and exploits those who trust him, and even commits murder. Twice.

And yet you want him to get away with it. At least, I did. I'll admit that successive Ripley novels (she wrote four more about Tom between 1970 and 1991) haven't affected me in quite the same way. Tom is older and less conflicted about his sociopathic behaviour, more able to justify that what's good for Tom Ripley is good, period.

But the first book in "the Ripliad", published in 1955, presents us with a young man whose working-class background and insecure nature has made him jealous of the rich, self-assured New Yorkers he sees around him. Highly intelligent, with a gift for mimicry and deception, he has a chameleon-like ability to blend in with whatever company he keeps. And Tom very much wants to keep a better sort of company.

When we first meet Tom, he's sharing an apartment in a shabby brownstone building, trying his hand at some small-time forgery and extortion. He loathes his friends, detests the woman who brought him up after his parents died, and is currently without a job. A chance meeting in a hotel bar with the wealthy industrialist, Herbert Greenleaf, turns all that around. Greenleaf's son, Dickie, has been living the good life in the small Italian village of Mongibello, and seems inclined to stay there. His father wants him to come back to New York and join the family business and offers to pay Tom to go to Italy and persuade him. Mr. Greenleaf is under the impression that Dickie and Tom are friends. In fact, they scarcely know each other but Tom knows a good thing when he sees it. He exaggerates his friendship with Dickie, gains the older man's confidence, and departs for Italy.

Once there, Tom manages to "bump into" Dickie and his girlfriend, Marge, and insinuates himself into their company. Sensing that Dickie is growing tired of Marge, whom he cares for but doesn't love, Tom becomes Dickie's new best friend; he moves into the house Dickie's renting and for the next few weeks they spend all their time together, with Marge and without her. She quickly begins to resent the intrusion, and tells Dickie his new friend is sponging off him. She also implies that Tom is gay, which certainly may be the case. If it's true, it's not something Tom can consciously deal with. This is 1955, after all, when homosexual activity was still a crime. All Tom knows is that he's repulsed by Marge and attracted to Dickie, to the point of wanting to *be* him.

Identity, in the hands of a writer as gifted as Highsmith, is a mutable thing. It can be put on and taken off like a suit of clothes. And Tom does just that: one afternoon, when he thinks Dickie is in bed with Marge, Tom goes into Dickie's bedroom and puts on his clothes. He stands in front of the mirror, aping Dickie's mannerisms and gestures. Dickie enters unexpectedly, shocked and then angry. From that moment on his behaviour towards Tom changes. He resents his presence and wants him gone. Tom has to face the painful fact that he and Dickie are not friends. They never have been:

"Tom felt a painful wrench in his breast, and he covered his face with his hands. It was as if Dickie had suddenly been snatched away from him . . . They didn't know each other. It struck Tom like a horrible truth, true for all time, true for the people he had known in the past and for those he would know in the future: each had stood and would stand before him, and he would know time and time again that he would never know them, and the worst was that there would always be the illusion, for a time, that he did know them, and that he and they were completely in harmony and alike".

Mr. Greenleaf writes to say that as Tom hasn't been successful at getting Dickie to agree to come home, their contract is finished. But Tom is nowhere near finished with the luxurious lifestyle he's been enjoying and he's definitely not ready to go back to being poor old Tom Ripley. He convinces Dickie to join him on a short trip to San Remo. They rent a small fishing boat and, once they're out in the water a good distance from land, Tom kills Dickie and throws his body overboard, weighted down with a large anchoring stone. He then scuttles the boat and heads to Rome, where he rents an apartment in Dickie's name and lives off Dickie's trust fund. He writes letters to Marge, forging Dickie's signature, in which he says he needs to be alone for a while, in order to work on his painting.

His idyllic life in Rome is interrupted by a visit from an American friend of Dickie's, Freddie Miles. When Freddie sees Tom in "Dickie's" apartment, dressed in some of Dickie's clothes, he becomes suspicious. Tom insists Dickie is out at the moment and sends Freddie on his way, but, heading back downstairs, Freddie stops to talk to the landlady. Tom can hear the landlady telling Freddie that "Signor Greenleaf" lives alone, and that he's upstairs now. Freddie turns around and comes back up the stairs to confront Tom, who promptly kills him with an ashtray, and then gets him out of the apartment later that night by pretending Freddie's too drunk to walk. He drags him downstairs and into his car, then drives out to a remote section of the cemetery and dumps Freddie's body behind a tombstone.

The next morning, Freddie's body is found and the police come to question "Dickie Greenleaf". Tom says he and Freddie had a few drinks together; Freddie, he says, was definitely not too drunk to drive. The police accept his explanation but ask him to stay in Rome while they pursue their investigations. Shortly afterwards, a possibly bloodstained boat is found near San Remo, and the police begin to speculate that Tom is the one who's been killed. Dickie Greenleaf is now a suspect in two possible murders - Freddie Miles and Tom Ripley.

A less confident, perhaps less deranged, individual would lose his cool at this point, having to speak on the phone to Marge as Tom, and masquerade as Dickie to everyone else. But this is where sociopaths are different from the rest of us; with a breathtaking facility of reinvention, Tom switches back to being "Tom", moves to Venice, and persuades Marge, Dickie's father, and the American detective Mr. Greenleaf has hired, that Dickie, depressed about his painting, has committed suicide.

Tom sails to Greece, wondering if he's going to be arrested when the boat gets to port. The Greenleafs, however, have accepted that Dickie is dead and, even better, have given their blessing to a will, forged by Tom, in which Dickie leaves everything to Tom. Our hero is rich, safe, and no longer under suspicion of murder. He's free - or is he?

As he leaves Athens and prepares to make his way to Crete, he imagines four Cretan policemen waiting for him on the pier. "Was he going to see policemen waiting for him on every pier that he ever approached?"

Tune in to the sequel, *Ripley Underground*, to find out.

Week 93: *Kieron Smith, boy*, by James Kelman (2008)

I have come late to James Kelman and have a lot of catching up to do. While he was winning the Booker Prize (*How Late it Was, How Late,* 1994), and being castigated for it, I was working on my own first novel and reading authors on this side of the Atlantic: Michael Ondaatje (*The English Patient*); Carol Shields (*The Stone Diaries*); Margaret Atwood (*Alias Grace*); Alice Munro (*Open Secrets*). Oh, and *Bird by Bird,* by Anne Lamott, still one of the best books on writing to appear in the last 20 years. (Stephen King's *On Writing* is a close second but, to me, still a second.)

I did read Irvine Welsh and discovered Ian Rankin through the Inspector Rebus series on ITV, but somehow missed the Glasgow novelist who's been compared to James Joyce and Samuel Becket, and whose work divides the critics like a sharp knife through butter. One of the Booker judges denounced *How Late it Was* as unreadable "crap" and said the awarding of the prize to Kelman was "a disgrace". *The Times* called it "literary vandalism"; Kingsley Amis dismissed it as "one of the last and least of the big-fuck novels".

The London Review of Books, however, has praised him as "a radical Modernist writer of exceptional brilliance". And the New Zealand-born Scottish writer Kirsty Gunn has called him "the greatest British writer of our time". It's the profanity, among other things, that gets up the noses of certain people, which may be why Kelman, in *Kieron Smith, boy*, has chosen to use asterisks in place of letters. He sprinkles them throughout the narrative in a kind of thumb-nosing, up-yours manner, giving us c**k and f**k and c**t and f*****g. Some of these, like w*****g and t****r, need a bit of puzzling out, but by the last few chapters Kelman drops the niceties and we get the words in full.

Now there, I've misled you. There are no chapters in *Kieron Smith, boy*. There's no plot, either, to speak of. Just the somewhat incoherent ramblings of a young boy from a rough working-class district of Glasgow. Growing up, I think, in the 1950s, but it could be earlier. There are no dates, and few references to the outside world although we learn that his family moves from their tenement flat to one of the new housing schemes built on the outskirts of the city after the Second World War.

Five years old when the story begins, Kieron is the youngest in a family of four. His father's in the merchant navy, and his older brother, Matt, wants nothing to do with him. Like most younger children, Kieron believes that life isn't fair. His questions go unanswered, his natural curiosity is discouraged. At home, his brother is favoured with a proper desk and the window side of the bedroom while Kieron gets nothing but blame and "doings" from his da (an all-encompassing term for anything from a slap on the bum to a full-on beating). To be fair, Matt pays attention in school and studies hard to get ahead, while Kieron skips out to visit his grannie or take a ferry up the Clyde. His teachers complain that he doesn't concentrate in class, and he's certainly no stranger to the strap. (Side note: the sheer brutality of some of his instructors brought back memories of more than one elementary school teacher who ruled the classroom by humiliating his students. Are you listening, Mr. Dale?)

Kieron's name is a source of angst to some extent. He worries that it's a Catholic name, and he's been brought up to hate "Papes". As a "Proddy" he has to beware of wandering into Catholic territory, an especial problem in that he lives not far from the Rangers football stadium. (In sectarian Glasgow, Rangers F.C. is a Protestant club while Celtic is Catholic.) When Celtic fans come to see their team play, the rivalry is played out on the field and off. Parts of the neighbourhood are either Catholic or Protestant; turning up in the wrong place is asking for trouble.

While Kieron has all the prejudices of his class there is much in him to admire. He loves his grandparents, especially his granddad, who was a champion boxer when he was young and teaches him how to defend himself without stooping to "dirty" fighting. He pals around with Podgie and Mitch, who are relatively bad apples, but he has a strong moral compass. He's not a bully, is kind to animals, and is pretty fearless, standing up for himself against bigger boys, and climbing everything in sight. When neighbouring women get locked out of their apartments, it's Kieron who shinnies up the ronepipe (roof gutter) and gets through the upstairs window.

Language is at the heart of the narrative; Kieron's mother, in particular, has bought into the idea that speaking well means speaking like an English person, not a Scot. Kieron self-censors (hence the asterisks) because he's been brought up to believe that certain words are inherently bad. Speaking like a Glaswegian is bad; he must learn to speak properly, which means using what we used to call "the King's English". His mother demands it; she remonstrates with her husband, who uses mild profanity at every turn, and encourages her sons to speak nicely. The teachers at school reinforce it: "It was say yes and not aye, down and not doon, am not and no um nay, ye were just to speak nice."

Kelman, who considers Scotland to be an occupied nation, has written reams on the cultural oppression, or suppression, of language. At the Booker awards dinner, a black-tie affair which he attended in a business suit and open neck shirt, he gave a spirited defence of his use of the vernacular: "My culture and my language have the right to exist, and no one has the authority to dismiss that . . . A fine line can exist between élitism and racism. On matters concerning language and culture, the distance can sometimes cease to exist altogether."

The characters in *Kieron Smith, boy* are limited - they have limited opportunities, limited futures. But the dreams of a child are not limited; without any of the trappings of fancy phrasing, Kieron's dreams soar beyond the street litter, the dead-end jobs, and the crumbling tenements into the stratosphere of possibility. By the time we leave him, teetering on the verge of adolescence, we hope for the best for this boy, who imagines himself climbing yet another ronepipe, losing his grip, and being rescued by the ghost of his grandfather:

"So yer granda would be there, his spirit would come to yer rescue, maybe a breath of wind or a hard blowing wind, to stop ye hitting the ground heid first, ye would land one foot at a time, nice and soft, or else in a big pile of sacks and just get up and walk away. Oh that was lucky, and it would be, except if it was him, yer granda".

Week 94: *The Unbearable Lightness of Being*, by Milan Kundera (1984, in French and English; 1985, in Czech)

The Prague Spring was a period of mass protests against the Soviet Union, beginning in January, 1968, and continuing until August of that year. For a few months, under the leadership of Alexander Dubček, the citizens of the former Czechoslovakia experienced a liberalization of restrictions on travel, free speech, and the media. On the night of August 20–21, the Kremlin sent in 200,000 Russian, Bulgarian, Polish, and Hungarian troops, along with 2,000 tanks. The reforms were cut back, hard-line Communists reclaimed their positions of power, and Dubček was deposed.

Milan Kundera experienced the invasion first hand. An outspoken advocate of reform communism, he was expelled from the Association of Writers in 1969, his publications were banned, and his books were removed from the bookstores. In 1975 he went into exile in France and became a naturalized French citizen in 1981. He continues to live there and even after the events of the Velvet Revolution of 1989 he has rarely returned to his homeland.

The Unbearable Lightness of Being, published in 1984, is set against the background of the curtailed protest movement, and so in that way it can be considered a political novel. But it's also a meditation on the nature of existence, and the unbearable fact that we live our lives only once and can never know where another path might have taken us. This, then, is the "lightness" of being, as opposed to the Nietzschean concept of eternal recurrence, the idea that the universe and its events have already occurred and will recur *ad infinitum*. And while this lightness is upsetting to some, it is also a source of freedom: if we are here for a short time and then gone forever, life has no meaning and the decisions we make carry no weight.

"The heavier the burden," Kundera writes, "the closer our lives come to the earth, the more real and truthful they become. Conversely, the absolute absence of burden causes man to be lighter than air, to soar into heights, take leave of the earth and his earthly being, and become only half real, his movements as free as they are insignificant. What then shall we choose? Weight or lightness?"

The characters in the book represent the two opposite ends of the spectrum: light and heavy. The main character, Tomáš, is a surgeon, and a womanizing intellectual. Briefly married in the past, he has no wish to communicate with his ex-wife and has nothing to do with their son. He sees his sexual adventures as a way of keeping himself light, and continues to see other women after Tereza, a pretty young waitress and occasional photographer, comes to live with him. Tereza is a gentle soul who believes in the romantic ideal of a life-long commitment to another person. She's devoted to Tomáš in spite of her knowledge of his lechery (sorry, but there's no other word for it) and suffers because of it. To keep her happy he marries her, but the smell of other women permeates his hair and disturbs her sleep. She becomes depressed and has nightmares in which her husband is going to kill her, or humiliate her in front of other women. In one dream she's buried alive; Tomáš comes to visit her and digs out some of the dirt, but she knows that eventually he will stop coming and she'll be left to die.

The one constant element of Tomáš' erotic life is his mistress, Sabina, who embodies lightness, or freedom. Beautiful, talented, and open-hearted, she befriends Tereza and finds her a job as a photographer. When the Soviets invade the city, she, Tomáš, and Tereza flee to Switzerland, but Tereza doesn't stay long. She returns to Czechoslovakia and is followed, a short while later, by Tomáš. Returning to Prague means giving up his freedom - because of a dissident article he once wrote criticizing the communist regime, they will not be allowed to leave again.

Back home, he's subjected to pressure by both underground dissidents (in the form of his estranged son) and the authorities, and regards each side as a form of heaviness. Offered the chance to redeem himself by signing a denunciation of his article, he chooses not to sign it, and loses his position as a surgeon as a result. Tereza convinces him to move to the country with her. There, away from Prague, his erotic adventures come to an end. And so, later on, does his life. Driving through the hills one night, their pickup truck hurtles down a steep incline, instantly killing both Tereza and Tomáš.

As for Sabina, who has stayed behind in Geneva, she falls in love with Franz, a university professor. Franz is married and tortured by the thought that he must betray his wife in order to be with Sabina. When he finally leaves his wife in order to be with Sabina, she flees, first to Paris and then to America:

"She had left a man because she felt like leaving him. Had he persecuted her? Had he tried to take revenge on her? No. Her drama was a drama not of heaviness but of lightness. What fell to her lot was not the burden, but the unbearable lightness of being."

I should state right here that my favourite character is not any of these deeply flawed human beings but a dog. Karenin is Tereza and Tomáš' pet, although she bonds more closely with Tereza, keeping her company when Tomáš is off having adventures. Like her owners, she finds peace and contentment in the countryside, making friends with Mephisto, a pig. Unlike the humans in the story, Karenin is capable of steadfast loyalty and unconditional love. Her death from cancer is to me the one truly poignant note in a book I found cerebral and austere.

Week 95: *The Poisonwood Bible*, by Barbara Kingsolver (1998)

There is something refreshingly old-fashioned about this, Barbara Kingsolver's best-selling tale of an evangelical minister who takes his family to the Republic of Congo in 1959, just as the country is on the verge of putting an end to colonial rule. The story is told in a series of interior monologues, a style pioneered by Wilkie Collins in the 19th century and later employed by William Faulkner (*As I Lay Dying*) and Virginia Woolf (*To the Lighthouse, Mrs. Dalloway, The Waves*). There are five speakers in *The Poisonwood Bible*, each with a strong, unique manner of speaking and looking at the world. We have the minister's wife, Orleanna, and their four daughters: Rachel, Leah, Adah and Ruth May. The minister himself never speaks directly to the reader but his voice is heard - loud, clear, and fanatical - throughout the book.

Nathan Price is a former soldier whose World War Two experiences have left him with a deep sense of guilt and a fiery determination to be an instrument of the Lord, whatever the cost. He takes his family from their home in Georgia to Kilanga, a remote village in the Congo, where he plans to "save the heathens" (my quotes) by baptizing them in the Kwilu River. His blinkered view, both of Christianity and of the citizens of Africa, prevents him from ever learning anything important about people he's trying to save. While he's pushing baptism, we learn that the villagers' refusal to take part in this watery ritual is because the river is home to crocodiles; one young girl fell in and was killed. The people believe the minister plans to sacrifice them all.

The book is divided into seven sections; the first five begin with a monologue by Orleanna from her home on Sanderling Island, Georgia, where she has settled after leaving her husband and most of her family in Africa. Orleanna has tried, in her way, to be a good wife and mother. Being a good wife, however, has meant sacrificing herself and her children to the grim willfulness of a man who could probably never love her: "It would have trespassed on his devotion to all mankind".

Rachel, the oldest daughter, is 16 when the book opens. Blonde, pretty, and exasperatingly shallow, she hates everything about Africa and learns nothing from the Congolese. Given to malapropisms, she says she misses deodorant and flush toilets and "other simple things in life I have took for granite". Of all the characters in this book, Rachel is the one who doesn't change. By the end of the novel, having married and divorced several times, Rachel remains as self-centred and shallow as the day she set foot in the jungle. So what does it say about me that I found her monologues some of the most engaging pieces in the book? Whatever else you can say about Rachel, she's not trying to convert anybody. And she probably comes closest to representing the white population of Africa at the time, or a certain segment of it, at any rate.

Fourteen-year-old Lean and Adah, the twins, are next in line. Leah is as idealistic as her father and tries desperately to win him over by following in his footsteps. She helps him plant a garden with seeds brought from home, against the advice of their housekeeper, Mama Tataba, who warns them that the seeds will be washed away the next time it rains. She also tells him not to touch the roots of the poisonwood tree, as it will hurt him. Nathan ignores her advice, and wakes up the next morning with a painful rash on his hands, arm, and eye. When the heavy rains wash out his garden, he replants it in the manner Mama Tataba originally suggested; this time the seeds sprout but fail to flourish. The insects needed to pollinate those plants don't exist in this part of the world.

Gradually, over time, Leah's faith in her father and his God begins to falter, especially once she comes to know and love Anatole Ngemba, the schoolteacher who acts as an interpreter for her father's sermons. Through Anatole, Leah is given a glimpse into the real lives of the Congolese, and learns about the move towards independence. The following year the people hold an election and Patrice Lumumba, a former postal worker, becomes the first democratically-elected Prime Minister of the Republic of Congo. Nathan takes Leah with him to Léopoldville to attend the independence ceremonies where they're joined by the Underdowns, the couple who run the Mission League that pays Nathan a small salary. The Underdowns are planning to leave the Congo and are shocked that Nathan is insisting on staying on. They try to explain to him that staying will not only be dangerous but will mean doing without the monthly stipend they've been receiving. Nathan, however, is adamant: he and his family are not about to run away like cowards. There are still many souls that need saving.

Adah, the other twin, is as intelligent as her sister but unable to express it. She was damaged while still in the womb and is unable - or unwilling - to speak. She also walks with a limp, dragging her right foot. Her unique situation in the family has supplied her with a cynical outlook, and a gift for seeing the world in unusual ways. When she finishes reading a book front to back, she then reads it back to front. "It is a different book, back to front, and you can learn new things from it". She delights in palindromes: *Evil, all its sin is still alive!* Her own name, as she thinks of it, is Ecirp Nelle Hada. She and her mother are the only two members of the Price family who make it back to the States. There, inspired by what she experienced in Africa, she devotes herself to the study of viruses. She submits to a colleague's research project and learns to walk and speak like others. And she stays close to her mother.

At five, Ruth May is the baby of the family. She's also fearless, which leads her to fall out of a tree and break her arm at one point. She recovers, but falls ill with malaria when she refuses to swallow the quinine pills her mother dishes out. Eventually, she's bitten by a green mamba snake left in the chicken house by the village medicine man. The child dies instantly, leaving her mother to grieve and berate herself for not following the Underdowns out of Africa.

While Kingsolver claims she never writes autobiography, The Poisonwood Bible has its seeds in something she personally experienced when she was a child. Her father was a doctor and when she was seven she accompanied her parents to Léopoldville, now Kinshasa, Zaire. As she says in her introduction, "I was the fortunate chid of medical and public health workers, whose compassion and curiosity led them to the Congo". There they lived as villagers, without electricity, running water, or automobiles, while her parents offered their services "in support of a newly independent African democracy". It was years later that she, and the rest of the world, learned of the sinister forces that worked undercover to snatch independence from the people of the Congo. Thanks to the CIA, with the support of several Western governments, Lumumba was deposed and the puppet tyrant, Colonel Mobutu, put in his place. For 30 years, Mobutu oversaw a corrupt, totalitarian regime that bilked the country of billions of dollars and gave birth to the term *kleptocracy*.

It's given to Ruth May to grasp, through her death, the essence of the Congolese term *muntu*, which makes "no special difference between living people, dead people, children not yet born, and gods". It's simply the life force, eternal and unbreakable. I forgive you, she tells her mother in the final chapter of the book. Forgive yourself. Move on. Walk forward into the light. Yes.

Week 96: *The Cider House Rules*, by John Irving (1985)

John Irving has said that he always starts with the last sentence, then works his way backwards through the plot, to the beginning of the story. It's a technique that has served him well; he's written 14 novels and nine of them have been bestsellers. *The Cider House Rules* was his sixth; published in 1985, it ends like this:

"To Nurse Edna, who was in love, and to Nurse Angela, who wasn't (but who had in her wisdom named both Homer Wells and Fuzzy Stone), there was no fault to be found in the hearts of either Dr. Stone or Dr. Larch, who were - if there ever were - Princes of Maine, Kings of New England".

Set in rural Maine in the first half of the 20th century, *The Cider House Rules* tells the story of Dr. Wilbur Larch, the director of an orphanage in the town of St. Cloud's, and his favourite, beloved orphan, Homer Wells. Parallels have been drawn between this book and *Oliver Twist*, but I can assure you that Charles Dickens never wrote a character like Dr. Larch, whose story is told in flashbacks. An obstetrician, an abortionist, and a saint, the doctor contracted gonorrhea from a prostitute while he was in medical school and takes ether to relieve the pain. Later, while working as an intern at Boston's Lying-In Hospital, he's called to deliver a dead baby and recognizes the woman as Mrs. Eames, the prostitute. Her uterus is so terribly disintegrated he has no choice but to remove it. She survives the operation but dies a few days later when her abdomen fills with blood. The next day her daughter comes to see him, and shows him a bottle of something that's supposed to induce a miscarriage. Her mother drank so much of this liquid her intestines lost the ability to absorb Vitamin C, and she died of scurvy.

The woman's daughter is also pregnant, although not as far along as her mother. She wants Larch to give her an abortion. The risks, for both doctor and patient, are significant. At the time (near the end of the 19th century) performing an abortion was punishable by a year in jail or a thousand-dollar fine, or both, and you could lose your license to practice. When Larch refuses, she leaves, after telling him to "shit or get off the pot". A few days later she's brought into the hospital with a dead fetus imprisoned in her womb, the result of a failed abortion. Her panties are pinned to one shoulder of her dress; to the other is a note that says, "Shit or get off the pot". Before Larch can operate on her, the young woman dies.

This death weighs heavily on his conscience, and will do so for the rest of his life. His guilt is compounded by the discovery of an old photograph of that same young woman posing with a pony's penis in her mouth. Larch wonders if she agreed to pose in order to pay for the abortion. He resolves that he will never again turn away any woman who comes to him with such a request. As long as abortion is illegal, he will be of use to these women. Under his directorship, the orphanage becomes a place of sanctuary, where women can come to deliver their babies or receive a safe abortion - free.

It's a tough subject, abortion, and it takes up much of the narrative. It's definitely not easy reading, no matter what you think about abortion rights. While one doctor calls it the work of the Devil, Larch argues that what he's doing is actually the Lord's work. And he's disgusted with those who condemn the women who choose that route:

"These same people who tell us we must defend the lives of the unborn - they are the same people who seem not so interested in defending anyone but themselves after the accident of birth is complete! These same people who profess their love of the unborn's soul - they don't care to make much of a contribution to the poor, they don't care to offer much assistance to the unwanted or the oppressed! How do they justify such a concern for the fetus and such a lack of concern for unwanted and abused children?"

In this endeavour, Larch is assisted by his two nurses, Nurse Edna and Nurse Angela, and by the one orphan who never finds a home. Larch cares for all the orphans, calling them "princes of Maine, kings of New England", but he grows to love Homer Wells like a son. When Homer's adoptions fail to work out, Larch accepts that Homer belongs to the orphanage and begins to train him as an obstetrician. Although Homer assists in these procedures, even delivering a child when the doctor's unavailable, he refuses to perform abortions. The "products of conception" are human; he believes they have a soul.

Larch hopes Homer will attend medical school; by the time he's a teenager he's already adept in many surgical procedures and would make an excellent doctor if he can find a patron to put him through school. But Homer is ambivalent, not sure what he wants to do, and when a handsome young couple come to St. Cloud's for an abortion, he ends up leaving with them. He and the young man, Wally, become best friends, working together in the family apple orchard, Ocean View. He secretly falls in love with Candy but is careful not to reveal it to Wally, as he and Candy plan to be married. When the Second World War breaks out, Wally joins up and is trained as a pilot. His plane is shot down over Burma and he's presumed dead. Homer stays working at the orchard; Dr. Larch has falsified Homer's records, stating that he has a heart condition, making him unfit to fight. Believing Wally to be dead, he and Candy finally give in to their mutual passion and make love. When Candy gets pregnant, they return to St. Cloud's so she can have the baby. They name him Angel and bring him back to Ocean View as an orphan whom Homer decided to adopt. Angel grows up believing Homer to be his adopted father and Candy a loving mother figure who isn't really his mother. When Wally eventually returns to Maine, having lost the use of his legs but survived, he and Candy marry, and the four of them - Homer, Angel, Wally, and Candy - live together in the big house on the orchard estate.

It's a long book, with a few too many characters and several subplots. One concerns Melony, another orphan who was never adopted. A tough, angry young woman, she initiates Homer into sex and makes him promise he'll never leave the orphanage without her. When he leaves with Wally and Candy, Melony devotes her life to looking for him, but when she does eventually find him she immediately recognizes Angel as the spitting image of Homer when he was young. She also sees traces of Candy in the boy and is devastated that Homer, whom she considered a hero, would do something so terrible: have sex with the wife of a man in a wheelchair. In the end, she forgives him and when she dies, she has her body sent back to St. Cloud's so it can be used for anatomical research.

As for Homer, he ends up doing what he refused to do for years. A young woman named Rose is impregnated by her father, the head picker on the orchard estate. His son, Angel, is in love with Rose and comes to his father for advice about procuring an abortion. Homer calls the orphanage asking to speak to Dr. Larch only to learn that the doctor has died, having succumbed to an accidental overdose of ether. It's up to Homer to be "of use". He gives Rose a safe abortion and then heads back to St. Cloud's to succeed Wilbur Larch as the director of the orphanage. He retains his distaste for abortions but decides that as long as they're illegal, he'll honour the wishes of the women who come to him.

The cider house rules, by the way, are a list of rules posted every year for migrant workers to follow. The rules are consistently ignored, because the workers can't read. Like the antiquated laws against abortion, some rules are made to be broken.

Week 97: *Love in the Time of Cholera*, by Gabriel García Márquez (1985, in Spanish; 1988, in English)

Gabriel José de la Concordia García Márquez, who died in 2014 at the age of 87, has been called the greatest Colombian who ever lived. Affectionately known throughout Latin America as Gabo, or Gabito, he was awarded the 1972 Neustadt International Prize for Literature and the Nobel Prize in Literature ten years later. Although he did not personally invent the concept of magic realism, he's so closely identified with the genre that it's impossible to say his name without calling it to mind.

Having said that, *Love in the Time of Cholera* is set more firmly in the real world than the magical. It begins with the death of Jeremiah Saint-Amour, longtime friend and chess competitor of Dr. Juvenal Urbino, who kills himself at the age of 60 so that he will not grow old. After being called in to examine the body, Dr. Urbino returns home to discover that his pet parrot has escaped from its cage and is perched on a top branch of a mango tree. Attempting to retrieve the bird, Dr. Urbino falls to his death, leaving his wife, Fermina Daza, a widow.

The good doctor's body is scarcely cold when the hero of our story, Florentino Ariza, turns up on her doorstep, hoping to pick up where they left off, 51 years, nine months, and four days ago. He has loved her all that time, despite the fact that she has never once, since breaking off their youthful courtship, given him a single encouragement to do so. Appalled that he's had the temerity to approach her like this,

Fermina sends him packing. Florentino, however, is not one to be deterred. He has, after all, nurtured his love for this woman for half a century - there has not been a day, scarcely even a minute, when she's not been in his thoughts.

He is, in fact, sick with love, a condition comparable to cholera, which was rampant in Latin America in the 19th century. Like cholera, love causes physical and emotional pain and in Florentino's case it plagues him relentlessly for half a century; there is no cure.

We are then taken back to the time, all those years ago, when the disease of love infected him. A shy, forlorn young man, Florentino dresses unfashionably, writes unremarkable poetry, and works as a telegraph operator. In spite of his demeanour, the young women of the town are fascinated by him, and hold lotteries to decide who will date him. Florentino goes along with all this, but keeps himself apart, determined to maintain his innocence until the right woman comes along. One day, while delivering a telegram to Lorenzo Daza, he catches sight of Daza's beautiful daughter, Fermina, who studies at the Academy of the Presentation of the Blessed Virgin and is escorted there and back by her Aunt Escolástica. Florentino begins to stalk her as she walks to school and eventually he manages to recruit her aunt's assistance, and the two young people begin to exchange letters. Her father, however, is against the marriage: Florentino is poor, after all, and even worse, he was born out of wedlock. Her father sends her off to stay with her cousin. When she eventually returns, she realizes she doesn't love him after all, breaks off the engagement, and marries someone else. Someone more suitable, in the person of Dr. Juvenal Urbino, a wealthy and accomplished national hero.

On the face of it, she's made the right decision. She has wealth, financial security, and an adoring partner. They seem in every way to be the ideal married couple. The author's point, I think, is that they are: any two people who live, love and argue together for 50 years have a right to call theirs a successful marriage; most of us don't get anything close to it.

Love in the Time of Cholera is set in a city on the banks of the Magdalena River, at the turn of the 20th century. The city is never named, but it's likely based on Cartagena, whose walled city and fortress was designated a UNESCO World Heritage Site in 1984. Cartagena is where García Márquez went to university, studying law, and where he began his career in journalism. He evokes the richness of the city in all its perverse beauty with lyrical descriptions of the old colonial mansions with their whitewashed balconies draped in bougainvillea, the former monasteries and convents, the horse-drawn carriages, the crowded markets teeming with traders, the filthy, sewage-covered streets. And, of course, the brothels. It reminded me intensely of Savannah, Georgia, as depicted in John Berendt's *Midnight in the Garden of Good and Evil:* a city populated by eccentric characters and ancient ghosts, some of whom continue to wield power amongst the living.

Florentino is disappointed when Fermina rejects him, but he's not finished by a long shot. He's nurtured this passion, this illness, for so long, he would be lost without it. And so, ever so gently, he renews his courtship, writing her daily in the hope that one day she will write back - assuming, of course, that she reads his letters before tossing them in the fire. He knows he can't win her with fire and passion; he's too old for that - they both are. But he's the master of slow, steady persistence, and he believes in his cause. He's waited all these years for Dr. Urbino to die; now, the only thing standing in the way of perfect happiness is Fermina herself.

García Márquez was in his late 50s when he wrote this book, and I think that's significant. It's not a youthful love story but rather one of middle age. It's a story of endurance, of a love - even a passion - that lasts for half a century, but is fraught with irritations, disagreements, and with the petty annoyances that creep up on us as we age. As a romantic hero, Florentino is deeply flawed. He's selfish, promiscuous, and chronically constipated. He claims to have had sex (not always consensual) with more than 600 women, one of whom has just turned 14 (when he was over 70). And while Florentino himself would have you believe he has stayed single because he's saving himself for Fermina, the real reason may be less chivalric: as a married man he would have less opportunity to go out stalking women day and night, and taking them to bed. As he admits to himself in a moment of anger: "My heart has more rooms than a whorehouse".

So no, I didn't like Florentino very much, but I found myself rooting for him in the end. I wanted Fermina to soften, to accept him as a companion, if not a lover, if only because that kind of dogged determination deserves some kind of reward. I was pleased when she came to the conclusion that appearances be damned: if she wanted to spend time with Florentino she would.

As she tells her daughter-in-law, "They can all go to hell . . . If we widows have any advantage, it is that there is no one left to give us orders."

Amen to that, sister.

And I was pleased when she agrees to accompany him on a journey up the river, and finally admits - to herself and to him - that she loves him. When they reach La Dorada, everyone but Florentino and Fermina disembarks and the boat prepares to take on passengers for the return journey. Fermina frets that some of them may recognize her and Florentino persuades the captain to fly the yellow flag of cholera, preventing anyone else from coming on board. It's as if, by doing so, all three characters, the captain included, are accepting that true love is indeed an illness - a plague, even - and those who suffer for it should receive special dispensation. Back in their home port, however, the captain is told that because of the cholera flag they can't leave the boat until the authorities have investigated the situation. When the truth comes out it will be devastating for the captain - he could very well lose his licence. Florentino's solution is to turn the boat around and head back to La Dorada. The captain looks at the two old people: "he was overwhelmed by the belated suspicion that it is life, more than death, that has no limits."

"And how long do you think we can keep up this goddamn coming and going?" he asked.

Florentino had kept his answer ready for fifty-three years, seven months, and eleven days and nights.

"Forever," he said.

Love in the Time of Cholera is written, I think, as a fable, although I'd be hard pressed to find the moral. Perhaps it's simply this: that if you live long enough, and try hard enough, you might eventually get what you want, after all.

Week 98: *The White Tiger*, by Aravind Adiga (2008)

Balram Halwai's fate was decided before he was born. The son of a rickshaw puller, he was meant to be a sweet-maker, according to his name and caste. But Balram has the heart - and cunning - of an entrepreneur, and he uses them to transcend his lowly state in life and pull himself out of the Darkness (the name given to the impoverished rural villages of India) and into the Light of the big cities: Delhi, Mumbai, and Bangalore. How he goes about it and what he sacrifices along the way make for one of the most engaging works of fiction I've ever read. It's also one of the angriest books I've read, and one of the funniest.

Published in 2008, *The White Tiger* made Aravind Adiga the second-youngest author ever to win the Man Booker Prize. It begins with the news that the Premier of China, Wen Jabao, is due to make an official visit to India. Balram Halwai, a successful entrepreneur in Bangalore, decides to write to the Premier, and fill him in on the "real" India, the one his Indian handlers are unlikely to show him. Over a period of seven nights, Balram writes a long letter to the Premier, narrating the story of his life. And, in doing so, the story of his country.

Balram's India is a messy, complicated, colourful place, where the wealthy flaunt their luxurious lifestyles while the poor slip further into the mud. One of Balram's earliest memories is attending his mother's cremation on the banks of the Ganges River. As her body is enveloped by flames, he has a moment of epiphany:

"Soon she would become part of the black mound... And then I understood: this was the real god of Benaras—this black mud of the Ganga into which everything died, and decomposed, and was reborn from, and died into again. The same would happen to me when I died and they brought me here. Nothing would get liberated here".

"Here" is the Darkness - in particular, the village of Laxmangarh, where Balram is born. The region is controlled by four landlords, known locally as the Wild Boar, the Stork, the Buffalo, and the Raven. These men, by means of corruption and extortion, have their fingers in every conceivable pie; nothing that happens here is beyond the range of their control. By taxing fishermen and farmers, goatherds and shopkeepers, they ensure that the "Rooster Coop" keeps the people trapped, unable to escape their fates.

Balram lives with his parents, his brother, Kishan, and his formidable grandmother, Kusum, as sly and controlling as any matriarch who ever lived. His brother is taken out of school to work in a tea shop but Balram, being exceptionally quick and intelligent, does well at school and his father pins his hopes on him. The school itself is wretched, the teacher is drunk, but somehow Balram learns to read and write. When a school inspector drops in for a visit, he sees the potential in the boy, describing him as that rarest of creatures, a white tiger. Tigers, especially white ones, symbolize power, freedom, and individuality, and Balram is more than happy to see himself in that light. Eventually, though, a female cousin gets married and Balram is taken out of school and sent to work with Kishan, in order to pay for her dowry. At the tea shop Balram spends more time eavesdropping on the customers than doing any real work. By his own admission he's a bad servant but a good listener.

When their father dies of tuberculosis, Kishan gets married and he and Balram move to the city of Dhanbad to look for work. There, Balram learns that drivers earn better money than other servants, so he pays someone to teach him how to drive and lands a job as a driver for Mr. Ashok, the son of the Stork. Ashok is kinder than his father - he's spent time in America and is appalled at the corruption he sees all around him. He trusts Balram and defends him to his wife, Pinky. But he's weak, and in his own way he's as trapped as Balram by society's expectations. He professes to care for Balram but when his wife kills a child with the family car, Ashok goes along with the plan to have Balram sign a confession, saying he was the one driving, not Pinky.

It never occurs to Ashok that Balram might rebel. He takes it for granted that his driver, who earns a pittance, will deliver large amounts of cash for him without touching a single rupee. The master is, after all, the master, and in India servants are resigned to their fate.

Balram experiences another epiphany when he visits the city zoo. Standing in front of the cage of the white tiger, watching the trapped animal pace back and forth, he faints, just as he did at his mother's funeral. When he comes to, he realizes that life is not worth living if you live it in servitude. He murders his employer, steals a bag of money, and flees with his young cousin to Bangalore, where he uses his ill-gotten gains to build a successful business. Knowing full well that his description on the "Wanted" poster would fit half the men in India, he has no fear of getting caught, and only a little guilt. His entire extended family will be murdered by the Stork's henchmen; any not killed will be shunned by the rest of the community and driven out of the village. Unlike Balram, they were content to remain slaves. He wasn't.

In Balram's view, this is what it took for him to become a man and control his own destiny. The sacrifice is the price of freedom.

In an interview after the book came out Adiga was asked why so many poor people remain honest and faithful to their masters:

"It is, like, basically you follow your dharma or code of life because who you are depends on the economic well-being of your family and the name your family has. You cannot take the money and run because that will put your entire family in peril or in disgrace."

The White Tiger is an attempt to answer the question: What kind of man would be prepared to break with tradition, to put his family's reputations, even their lives, at risk, in order to rise out of the mud? The answer, it appears, is only a man who is, at heart, essentially ruthless. As Balram himself says, "Only a man who is prepared to see his family destroyed ... can break out of the coop".

Adiga believes the centuries-old social structure is beginning to break apart. So *The White Tiger*, besides being hugely entertaining, should possibly serve as a warning.

Week 99: *Death in Venice*, by Thomas Mann (1912, in German; 1925, in English)

In 2003 Germaine Greer ignited a furor (as is her wont) with the publication of a book devoted to the youthful male face and form. *The Beautiful Boy*, which one critic described as a combination of art history and coffee-table erotica, was full of pictures of, in her words, "'ravishing' pre-adult boys with hairless chests, wide-apart legs and slim waists". On a British talk show she argued that admiring beautiful young people, both male and female, is part of the joy of life:

"What is important to me about the Boy is that once upon a time his beauty was understood and celebrated by people of both sexes. A boy was allowed to dress in very bright colours, he was allowed to show himself off in the street, he dyed his hair, he wore make-up, he wore a little cap tipped over his eye with a big feather in, he wore tight pants and cropped jackets and so on. And the girls looked down from behind their jalousie and talked about the best-looking boys."

I mention this because the photo she chose for the cover of her book is of Bjorn Andresen, the adolescent star of Luchino Visconti's adaptation of Thomas Mann's *Death in Venice*. Neither Greer nor her publisher asked Andreson for permission to use the photo and he was furious when the book came out. "I have a feeling of being utilised," he said, "that is close to distasteful."

Since appearing in the film almost 50 years ago, Andreson has been dogged with the tag of "the most beautiful boy in the world". He dislikes the fact that his younger self was preyed upon, visually at least, by men old enough to be his father.

"Adult love for adolescents is something that I am against in principle," he says. "Emotionally perhaps, and intellectually, I am disturbed by it - because I have some insight into what this kind of love is about."

It was that kind of creepiness, I think, that bothered me when I watched the film back in the day. (It was showing at my university campus, on a double-bill with *Performance*, starring Mick Jagger - definitely not mainstream fare.) Visconti's images, gorgeous as they were, of the half-naked form of a young boy being leered at by the 50-year-old Dirk Bogarde didn't sit well, to be honest. (I had a similar reaction a few years later to Louis Malle's *Pretty Baby*, with Brooke Shields playing a 12-year-old prostitute.) It was my dislike of the film that kept me from reading the book until now, and I'm sorry for that. Because Mann's novella is a classic, and not just because it may be the first time that a gay character made it into mainstream fiction.

The story begins outside a cemetery in Munich. Gustav von Aschenbach, a famous writer who has dedicated his life to his art and lives alone, his wife having died years ago, stops to stare at an odd-looking foreigner. The foreigner, obviously a tourist, catches his eye and stares back at him with some belligerence. This brief encounter leads von Aschenbach to think about traveling, and he experiences a sudden craving to get away from home - perhaps leave the city for his house in the mountains. Instead, he heads for a resort town in Croatia, but before he gets there he changes his mind and makes his way to Venice. On the boat, he witnesses an older man in makeup trying to ingratiate himself with a group of young men. His attempts to appear younger disgust the writer, and he does his best to avoid him.

Once in Venice, von Aschenbach checks into a luxury hotel on the Lido - the same hotel, as it happens, where Mann and his wife stayed in 1911 and where the author saw the young boy who inspired him to write the novella. At dinner that first night, he observes a wealthy Polish family, three sisters and their brother, accompanied by their governess. The sisters are dressed very plainly, almost like nuns, but the boy is shockingly beautiful:

"His face recalled the noblest moment of Greek sculpture - pale, with a sweet reserve, with clustering honey-coloured ringlets, the brow and nose descending in one line, the winning mouth, the expression of pure and godlike serenity".

This observation is important, as von Aschenbach has dedicated himself to Apollo, the god of restraint, form, and the intellect, according to Nietzsche, denying the power of Dionysus, the god of passion and impulse. His scrutiny of the young boy is a hint that Dionysus, long repressed, is about to rise to the surface.

Von Aschenbach becomes obsessed with the boy, whose name is Tadeusz and is nicknamed Tadzio. He never speaks to him, but goes out of his way to be on the beach when he knows Tadzio will be there. Eventually, he starts following the boy and his sisters, trying to keep out of sight. At one point, sharing an elevator with Tadzio and his family, he's close enough to see that the boy looks rather sickly, and he guesses he won't live very long. This, the fact that his beauty is fleeting, makes him all the more precious.

Still, it's weeks before the older man admits to himself that he's in love. As an intellectual, he needs to justify his passion for the boy; he needs to convince himself that his feelings are more than pure lust. To this end he imagines himself as Socrates discussing erotic love with Phaedrus: beauty, he argues, is the only spiritual form that can be perceived by the senses. So the pursuit of one who embodies beauty is a noble, uplifting endeavour.

Unfortunately, von Ashenbach's obsession with Tadzio only degrades him. He becomes dissatisfied with his appearance - his wrinkled cheeks, grey hair and so on. In an ill-advised visit to a barber, he allows the man to dye his hair and apply makeup in a misguided attempt to make him look younger. What he looks like, of course, is the old man he saw on the boat, flirting with the youngsters. He continues to follow Tadzio around Venice, and becomes aware that the boy knows it. Tadzio does nothing to discourage his silent suitor, but his mother, with a parent's eye for these things, calls him away when she sees von Aschenbach in the vicinity.

Von Ashenbach starts noticing that the hotel's clientele is shrinking. People are leaving Venice, and there's a distinct, unpleasant smell of disinfectant everywhere. All the Germans leave, as their newspapers are printing stories of a growing cholera epidemic. But the authorities continue to deny there's anything wrong. Whatever is happening is a dirty secret, similar to the one von Ashenbach carries within his heart. A British travel agent finally confirms it: a fatal cholera strain, starting in India, has worked its way east and north, showing up in Venice a few months ago. The authorities, fearful of losing the tourist business, are keeping it a secret.

Now it becomes clear that he should leave; moreover, he should tell the Polish family to leave as well. But his desire to keep the boy in his vicinity as long as possible prevents him from warning them. He will stay, he thinks, as long as they stay. He has disturbing, nightmarish dreams that signify his descent into moral degeneracy; his love for Tadzio has made him ill, both physically and spiritually. One morning he comes down to the lobby to find the Polish family's luggage stacked in the lobby - they are leaving after lunch. He wanders out to the beach and watches Tadzio playing with his friends. One of them grapples Tadzio and wrestles him to the ground. When he finally releases the boy, Tadzio gets up and walks away, then turns around and looks directly at von Ashenbach, as if inviting him to follow. The older man is about to do so, when he suddenly slumps back in his chair. A few minutes later, people rush to his aid: "And before nightfall a shocked and respectful world received the news of his decease".

Death in Venice fascinates on so many levels. It's a story of what it means to be an artist, and the nature of art. It's about love and lust, morality and mortality, the pitfalls associated with idolizing beauty, the dangers of self-repression. It's about so much more than a pretty boy and a middle-aged man. I wish I'd read the book decades ago. If you haven't, I strongly suggest you do.

Week 100: *Of Human Bondage*, by Somerset Maugham (1915)

"The summer came upon the country like a conqueror".

It's not the first line of Somerset Maugham's masterpiece, but it's one of many I wish I'd written. I first read this book many, many years ago (don't like to say just how many) and loved it. I was swept away by the characters, especially the protagonist, a young man with a club foot who is, as you might guess, inordinately sensitive about it. It's not an understatement to say it profoundly shapes his outlook on life, given that he's ridiculed by classmates and colleagues, who resort to calling him a "cripple" when they really want to wound.

Of all the novels Maugham wrote, *Of Human Bondage* is the closest to autobiography. His parents died when he was a child, and he was sent to England to live with his uncle, the Vicar of Whitstable. His uncle was cold and emotionally distant, and school was a difficult experience. As he put it later in *The Summing Up*, he had much going against him:

"I was small; I had endurance but little physical strength; I stammered; I was shy; I had poor health. I had no facility for games, which play so great a part in the normal life of Englishmen; and I had, whether for any of these reasons or from nature I do not know, an instinctive shrinking from my fellow men that has made it difficult for me to enter into any familiarity with them."

If you substitute the stammer for a club foot, that passage is an apt description of Philip Carey, Maugham's fictional protagonist. Philip also loses his parents at an early age and is sent to live with an uncle, the Vicar of Blackstable. His aunt, who's never had children of her own, cares for him, but for the most part it's a loveless childhood, relieved only by his uncle's vast collection of old books. As lonely children have always done and will likely continue to do, Philip finds solace in reading: *The Thousand Nights and a Night*, Butler's *Lives of the Saints*, and *The Admirable Crichton*, to name a few.

Sent off to boarding school in Tercanbury, Philip's experiences closely mirror those of the author. He is shy, has difficulty making friends, and is mocked because of his disability. Left on his own to study, he does well academically and has every chance of winning a scholarship to Oxford. His uncle hopes he will go into the Church but Philip, who has at times been very religious, is sick of school and makes up his mind to go to Germany. There he comes under the influence of an idealistic Englishman named Hayward who reads Browning and Shelley, dabbles in art history, and enjoys spouting poetry - his own and that of others.

Under Hayward's guidance, Philip's taste in art and literature matures, and for a long time he's blind to his friend's pretentions. When Weeks, an American friend, dismisses Hayward as "a pretty fair speciment of a waster", Philip defends him: Hayward, of course, is a poet while Weeks, a theology scholar, is merely a pedant.

Philip's guardians persuade him to return to England, and he takes a job in London as a shop assistant. He hates the work, and is terribly lonely, but a business trip to Paris inspires him to move there and study art. Paris proves to be much more agreeable. He loves the city, makes friends among the other art students, and develops an understanding of art far deeper than the airy pronouncements Hayward is given to. Through his friend Lawson, Philip is introduced to Cronshaw, an eccentric poet who's regarded with a certain amount of awe.

"He knows everyone worth knowing," Lawson explains. "He knew Pater and Oscar Wilde, and he knows Mallarme and all those fellows."

It's Cronshaw who comes closest to giving Philip the answer he wants; if there is no God - and Philip has decided there probably isn't, then what is the meaning of life?

"Have you ever been to the Cluny, the museum?" Cronshaw asks. "There you will see Persian carpets of the most exquisite hue and of a pattern the beautiful intricacy of which delights and amazes the eye. In them you will see the mystery and the sensual beauty of the East, the roses of Hafiz and the wine-cup of Omar; but presently you will see more. You were asking just now what was the meaning of life. Go and look at those Persian carpets, and one of these days the answer will come to you."

It is later, much later in the book, that Philip comes to understand what Cronshaw was saying. Life, he realizes, is a tapestry of experiences, some comic, some tragic. There are "tears and laughter, happiness and woe; it was tedious and interesting and indifferent; it was as you saw it: it was tumultuous and passionate; it was grave; it was sad and comic; it was trivial; it was simple and complex; . . . There was neither good nor bad there. There were just facts. It was life."

While in Paris, a fellow art student, Fanny Price, befriends him, almost against his will. Fanny is rude, sullen, and disliked by almost everyone; she goes out of her way to be unpleasant, and seems to hate the world. She is also completely without talent, but believes herself to be a genius. When Fanny eventually hangs herself, having run out of money and reached the point of starvation, Philip is deeply shaken, knowing that she was in love with him and wondering if he could have done more to help her.

Unlike Fanny, Philip eventually accepts that he'll never be a great artist. He returns to England and, like Maugham, trains to be a doctor. (Maugham studied medicine for five years but gave it up to write full-time after the success of his first novel, *Liza of Lambeth*.) It's at this stage of the narrative that we finally meet Mildred Rogers, as unpleasant a piece of work as you might ever hope to meet. Or not. For reasons that remain inexplicable to me, Philip falls passionately in love with her, after encountering her in the coffee shop where she works. She's boring, vapid, unpleasant, and rude, and not even all that good-looking, but Philip is obsessed with her. It would take another page to describe all the ways she uses him - suffice to say she's a bad apple and when she finally disappears from the story, suffering, we think, from syphilis, the reader can only breathe a thankful sigh of relief.

As much as I dislike Mildred, I accept that she plays a hugely important role: she's a living, breathing personification of the impulses that keep men and women in bondage. Maugham borrowed his title from Part IV of Spinoza's *Ethics*, wherein he states that our inability to control our emotions constitutes a form of servitude. Philip is unable to control his passion for Mildred and she, in turn, is a victim of her own impulsive behaviour.

So while Mildred is nasty, she's necessary.

While I think of it, if you want a laugh, check out Bette Davis' portrayal of Mildred in the 1934 movie version. Her interpretation of a Cockney waitress is almost as awful as Dick Van Dyke's chimney sweep 30 years later. Leslie Howard as Philip is quite wonderful but nothing will ever compare with the book. Not even close.

Week 101: *Fugitive Pieces*, by Anne Michaels (1996)

There was so much hype about this book when it came out that I put off reading it for several years. More than 20, in fact. This was partly because I was in the throes of finishing my own first novel (which came out the following year to no hype whatsoever), and partly because the reviews were so overwhelmingly fulsome I could only assume I'd be disappointed when I read it.

Having finally got around to reading Anne Michaels' debut novel, I find that to be only partly true. As a novel, it's disappointing, but as a kind of extended poem it's nothing less than magical.

The book is divided into two parts: Part One tells the story of Jakob Beer, a renowned poet who, just before his death, has begun writing his memoirs. A child during the Nazi invasion of Poland, he survives the destruction of his village and is found, days later, practically buried in mud, by a Greek geologist named Athos Roussos. Athos takes the boy to Greece and hides him until the end of the war. Haunted by memories of his family - especially his older sister, Bella - Jakob still learns to appreciate the beauty of the natural world, thanks to Athos' teaching.

When the war ends, Athos and Jakob emigrate to Toronto where Athos teaches and Jakob studies to be a translator. He meets a spirited young woman and marries her, but his obsession with the past eventually comes between them. He leaves his wife and, years later, marries Michaela, a much younger woman. Together, they move to Greece. There, in the old

Roussos family home on the island of Idhra, Jakob is able to write, and to finally let go of the past.

Part Two offers up a new protagonist - Ben, a Canadian professor whose parents survived the Holocaust. He has met Jakob, admires his poetry, and is impelled, after Jakob's death, to travel to Greece to retrieve the poet's journals. While Jakob was obsessed by dark, terrifying memories of the war, Ben, who wasn't born at the time, has been raised by parents so deeply damaged by their experiences they cannot offer him any emotional security. As immigrants with a terrifying past, they can never let themselves feel completely safe; their sense of home can be taken from them at any random moment. Ben inherits their insecurity; tragedy, like genetics, is passed from generation to generation.

I said earlier that, for me, the novel is a disappointment. When it comes to fiction, I crave, above all else, a good story. I need characters I can believe in, even if I don't particularly like them. I want dialogue that's written the way people speak, even if they're saying horrible things. And please, please give me action. The action in *Fugitive Pieces* takes place, for the most part, in the past. It is remembered rather than lived, told to us through the tormented dreams and memory fragments of its protagonist. Much of it is told so obliquely and wrapped in so many layers of metaphor it's often difficult to know just what is happening.

Critics have described the writing as "lyrical", "magical" and "incandescent"; they're right. In fact, the text is saturated with beautiful sentences that could only come from the pen of a poet. Often, however, on reflection, those sentences leave the reader confused:

"If one needs proof of the soul it's easily found. The spirit is most evident at the point of extreme humiliation." Really? Or this: "Just as the earth invisibly prepares its cataclysms, so history is the gradual instant".

The language of metaphor carries on into the dialogue of the characters: "Some stones are so heavy only silence helps you carry them". And again: "Koumbaros, we are lightning rods for time". It would be lovely if people spoke like this. For the most part, they don't. But every character in *Fugitive Pieces* speaks like a poet - or rather, like the poems in Anne Michaels' head.

I found myself wishing for a cleaner narrative arc. The problem with the book, although it was heresy to say it when it came out, and may still raise hackles in certain quarters, it doesn't really work as a novel. As a poem, yes . . . a lyrical meditation on loss and the legacy of war, absolutely. It is, as has been said, "gorgeously written"and "exquisitely fabricated". The prose, however, gets in the way of the story.

Fugitive Pieces simply doesn't have the platform, the framework on which to build a story. I kept being reminded of Gertrude Stein's description of Los Angeles: "There's no there there". The narrative structure, such as it is, is puzzling, in that it's designed to continually deflect the reader from the main characters, the ones you should care about. Always a fan of a good digression, I find it confusing to be taken, suddenly and without warning, to Scott's ill-fated Antarctic expedition or, out of nowhere, a passage on the Catalan Atlas, which seems to have nothing to do with the story. And the shift, two-thirds of the way through the novel, to the story of Ben, doesn't really work.

Michaels' writing is never less than powerful. And much of it is beautiful. I kept making notes of sentence fragments that moved me:

". . . history only goes into remission, while it continues to grow in you until you're silted up and can't move. And you disappear into a piece of music, a chest of drawers, perhaps a hospital record or two, and you slip away, forsaken even by those who claimed to love you the most".

Beautiful, right? Although, like so much of the book, I don't honestly understand it.

TITLE INDEX

A Bend in the River 164
Absalom, Absalom 255
A Confederacy of Dunces 131
A Farewell to Arms 214
A Fine Balance 25
Alias Grace 17
American Rust 287
A Pale View of Hills 66
A Portrait of the Artist as a Young Man 328
A Severed Head 159
Atonement 190
Brave New World 432
Catch-22 426
Death in Venice 478
Decline and Fall 185
Ethan Frome 385
Eugene Onegin 240
Fall on Your Knees 210
Fanny Hill 91
Fear and Loathing in Las Vegas 365
Fifth Business 45
Franny and Zooey 314
Fugitive Pieces 488
Get Shorty 353
Great Expectations 122
Howards End 200
Infinite Jest 179
Keep the Aspidistra Flying 261
Kieron Smith, Boy 449
Les Liaisons Dangereuses 95
Life of Pi 34
Little Women 117
Lives of Girls and Women 31
Lolita 320
Lord of the Flies 136
Love in a Cold Climate 126
Love in the Time of Cholera 468
Madame Bovary 195

Moll Flanders 86
Mother's Milk 348
Neuromancer 49
Of Human Bondage 483
Of Mice and Men 325
One Flew Over the Cuckoo's Nest 421
Portnoy's Complaint 225
Quartet in Autumn 76
Rebecca 81
Sense and Sensibility 111
Slaughterhouse-Five 416
Sons and Lovers 244
Tess of the D'Urbervilles 380
Thank You, Jeeves 398
The Accidental 70
The Beggar Maid 37
The Bell Jar 141
The Children's Book 174
The Cider House Rules 463
The Color Purple 370
The Diviners 19
The Electric Kool-Aid Acid Test 219
The Elegance of the Hedgehog 229
The English Patient 41
The Fall of the House of Usher; The Pit and the Pendulum 234
The First Garden 53
The Forsyte Saga: The Man of Property 394
The Gathering 169
The God of Small Things 332
The Great Gatsby 205
The Hours 339
The Inheritance of Loss 439
The Line of Beauty 309
The Little Prince 404
The Maltese Falcon 154
The Master 293
The Namesake 303
The Picture of Dorian Gray 411
The Poisonwood Bible 458
The Portrait of a Lady 298

The Postman Always Rings Twice 146
The Reader 375
The Scarlet Letter 106
The Secret History 360
The Shining 249
The Shipping News 266
The Stone Diaries 28
The Tale of the Bamboo Cutter 12
The Talented Mr. Rigby 444
The Thirty-Nine Steps 150
The Tin Flute 22
The Unbearable Lightness of Being 454
The Vicar of Wakefield 272
The Virgin Suicides 282
The Wars 58
The White Tiger 474
The Woman in White 10
Through the Looking-Glass and What Alice Found There 13
To Kill a Mockingbird 62
Tropic of Cancer 390
Veronika Decides to Die 277
White Teeth 343
Wuthering Heights 100

Printed in Dunstable, United Kingdom